County Almshouse

Kitsman

J. Crawford

GETTYSBURG

Stevens Run

Stevens Institute

Stevens Run

W

Penn College

Brick Kiln

H.L. Baugher

Gasometer

York Pike

Wm Culp

420,7

County Fair Grounds

Spring

struggle for a vast future

Struggle for a vast future

Editor
Aaron Sheehan-Dean

First published in Great Britain in 2006 by Osprey Publishing,
Midland House, West Way, Botley, Oxford OX2 0PH, United Kingdom.
Email: info@ospreypublishing.com

A CIP catalogue record for this book is available from the British Library

ISBN 1 84603 011 0

The authors, Aaron Sheehan-Dean, James M. McPherson, William A. Blair,
Richard Carwardine, Robert K. Krick, Gerald J. Prokopowicz, Mark Grimsley,
Craig L. Symonds, Jeffery S. Prushankin, Michael Vorenberg, William B. Feis, Victoria E. Bynum, and
Hugh Dubrulle, have asserted their rights under the Copyright, Designs and Patents Act, 1988, to
be identified as the Authors of this Work.

Every attempt has been made by the Publishers to secure the appropriate permissions for
materials reproduced in this book. If there has been any oversight we will be happy to rectify the
situation and written submission should be made to the Publishers.

Design: Ken Vail Graphic Design, Cambridge UK (kvgd.com)
Index by Alison Worthington
Maps by The Map Studio
Originated by United Graphics, Singapore, UK
Printed and bound in China through Worldprint

06 07 08 09 10   10 9 8 7 6 5 4 3 2 1

FOR A CATALOGUE OF ALL BOOKS PUBLISHED BY OSPREY MILITARY AND AVIATION PLEASE CONTACT:

NORTH AMERICA
Osprey Direct, c/o Random House Distribution Center, 400 Hahn Road, Westminster, MD 21157
Email: info@ospreydirect.com

ALL OTHER REGIONS
Osprey Direct UK, P.O. Box 140 Wellingborough, Northants, NN8 2FA, UK
E-mail: info@ospreydirect.co.uk

www.ospreypublishing.com

Acknowledgments

I would like to take this opportunity to thank all the contributors. Their willingness to dive in
quickly, their skill at producing fine essays, and their attention to deadlines made this a
remarkably easy project to manage. Gary Gallagher, Steve Engle, Susanna Lee, and Megan
Sheehan-Dean provided assistance at various stages and their help is sincerely appreciated.
James McPherson generously agreed to write the foreword. Having his experienced eye on
the manuscript strengthened it considerably. Last, and most important, I would like to thank
Jo de Vries for inviting me to participate in this project. She has been a model editor
throughout and done more than her share of the heavy lifting. It has been a pleasure to work
with her.

From the first taking of our national census to the last
are seventy years; and we find our population at the end
of the period eight times as great as it was at the beginning.
The increase of those other things which men deem desirable
has been even greater. We thus have at one view, what the popular
principle applied to government, through the machinery
of the States and the Union, has produced in a given time;
and also what, if firmly maintained, it promises for the future.
There are already among us those, who, if the Union be preserved,
will live to see it contain two hundred and fifty millions.
The struggle of today, is not altogether for today – it is
for a vast future also. With a reliance on Providence,
all the more firm and earnest, let us proceed in the great
task which events have devolved upon us.

Abraham Lincoln, First Annual Message
December 3, 1861, Washington, DC

CONTENTS

Acknowledgments   4

Contributors   8

Foreword   10

Chronology   14

Extremists at the gate   21
Origins of the American Civil War
Dr William A. Blair

I would not be master   41
Governing the War
Professor Richard Carwardine

The power of the land   61
Leadership on the Battlefield
Robert K. Krick

Our hearts were touched with fire   79
The Men who Fought the War
Dr Gerald J. Prokopowicz

Remorseless, revolutionary struggle   97
A People's War
Professor Mark Grimsley

Uncle Sam's web-feet   113
Winning the War at Sea
Dr Craig L. Symonds

They came to butcher our people

The Civil War in the West

Dr Jeffery S. Prushankin

133

That great essential of success

Espionage, Covert Action, and Military Intelligence

Dr William B. Feis

153

We never yielded in the struggle

The Home Front

Professor Victoria E. Bynum

175

The world will forever applaud

Emancipation

Dr Michael Vorenberg

195

One great society

Europe and the Civil War

Dr Hugh Dubrulle

217

A fearful lesson

The Legacy of the American Civil War

Dr Aaron Sheehan-Dean

237

Endnotes 254

Further reading 261

Index 264

CONTRIBUTORS

Dr Aaron Sheehan-Dean is Assistant Professor of History at the University of North Florida. He completed his PhD at the University of Virginia. He has devoted most of his academic career to the study of the American Civil War and has published essays on various themes surrounding the conflict. He is completing a book project titled *Creating Confederates: Family and Nation in Civil War Virginia* (forthcoming). He lives and works in Florida.

Professor James M. McPherson is the George Henry Davis '86 Professor of History at Princeton University and 2003 president of the American Historical Association. Widely acclaimed as the leading historian of the Civil War, he is the author of *Crossroads of Freedom: Antietam* (2002) (a New York Times bestseller), *For Cause and Comrades* (1997) (winner of the Lincoln Prize), and many other books on Lincoln and the Civil War era. McPherson, is widely known for his ability to take American history out of the confines of the academy and make it accessible to the general reading public. His best-selling book *Battle Cry of Freedom: The Civil War Era* (1988) won the Pulitzer Prize in history in 1989. He also has written and edited many other books about abolition, the War and Lincoln, and he has written essays and reviews for several national publications.

Dr William A. Blair is Director of the George and Ann Richards Civil War Era Center at the Pennsylvania State University and editor of *Civil War History*, the journal of the field. His dissertation won the Allan Nevis Prize for Best Dissertation in American History from the Society of American Historians. In addition to articles and chapters in books, Blair has published *Virginia's Private War: Feeding Body and Soul in the Confederacy, 1861–1865* (1998) and *Cities of the Dead: Contesting the Memory of the Civil War in the South, 1865–1914* (2004).

Professor Richard Carwardine is Rhodes Professor of American History at Oxford University and Fellow of St Catherine's College. He has written widely on American politics and religion in the era of the Civil War. His publications include *Evangelicals and Politics in Antebellum America* (1993). He recently completed an analytical political biography of Abraham Lincoln (2003; rev. edn 2006) which in 2004 won the Lincoln Prize, awarded annually by the Lincoln and Soldiers Institute at Gettysburg College for the finest scholarly work in English on the American Civil War era.

Robert K. Krick was Chief Historian of the Civil War battlefields in central Virginia for more than 30 years, during which he was responsible for the sites of Fredericksburg, Chancellorsville, Wilderness, and Spotsylvania Court House. He is the author of 15 books, including *Stonewall Jackson at Cedar Mountain* (1990), which won the Douglas Southall Freeman Award for Best Book in Southern History, and *The Smoothbore Volley that Doomed the Confederacy* (2004).

Dr Gerald J. Prokopowicz is Assistant Professor of History at East Carolina University in Greenville, North Carolina. He earned a PhD from Harvard University, and holds a JD from the University of Michigan. He is the author of *All for the Regiment: The Army of the Ohio, 1861–1862* (2001), and numerous Civil War essays and articles. For nine years he served as the resident Lincoln Scholar at the Lincoln Museum, in Fort Wayne, Indiana.

Professor Mark Grimsley teaches American military history with an emphasis on the Civil War at The Ohio State University. He is the author of *The Hard Hand of War: Union Military Policy Toward Southern Civilians, 1861–1865* (1995), which won the Lincoln Prize. Other works include *And Keep Moving On: The Virginia Campaign, May–June 1864* (2002); *Civilians in the Path of War* (with Clifford J. Rogers) (2001); and *The Collapse of the Confederacy* (with Brooks D. Simpson) (2001).

Dr Craig L. Symonds taught Civil War and naval history for more than 30 years at the US Naval Academy in Annapolis, the Naval War College in Newport and Britannia Royal Naval College in Dartmouth, England. He is author of ten books including, most recently, *Decision at Sea: Five Naval Battles that Shaped American History* (2005). He is currently Chief Historian of the Monitor Center at the Mariners' Museum in Newport News, Virginia.

Dr Jeffery S. Prushankin is a lecturer in military history at Penn State University Abington College. His area of specialization is the American Civil War and particularly the Trans-Mississippi theater. He has lectured on this subject at the United States Military Academy at West Point and at many conferences. He is the author of *A Crisis in Confederate Command: Edmund Kirby Smith, Richard Taylor and the Army of the Trans-Mississippi* (2005) and is active in battlefield preservation with The Friends of the Mansfield Battlefield.

Dr William B. Feis is currently Associate Professor of History at Buena Vista University in Storm Lake, Iowa. In addition to numerous essays and articles on Civil War intelligence, he authored *Grant's Secret Service: The Intelligence War from Belmont to Appomattox* (2002), and is currently working on *The Worst Angels of Our Nature: Guerilla Warfare in the American Civil War* (forthcoming).

Professor Victoria E. Bynum is Professor of History at Texas State University, San Marcos. Her research interests center on dissent in the 19th-century South, with emphases on issues of race, gender, and class in the Civil War era. She is the author of *Unruly Women: The Politics of Social and Sexual Control in the Old South* (1992) and *The Free State of Jones: Mississippi's Longest Civil War* (2001).

Dr Michael Vorenberg is Associate Professor of History at Brown University. He was a Lincoln Prize finalist in 2002 for *Final Freedom: The Civil War, the Abolition of Slavery and the Thirteenth Amendment* (2001). He is currently working on a book provisionally titled, *Reconstructing the People: The Impact of the Civil War on American Citizenship*. He is also at work on a document collection titled *The Emancipation Proclamation: A Brief History with Documents* (forthcoming in 2007).

Dr Hugh Dubrulle is Assistant Professor of Modern European History at Saint Anselm College, New Hampshire. He specializes in the various issues associated with British opinion concerning the American Civil War. His works include articles on the impact of the Civil War on military thought and social criticism in Britain. He is currently working on a book project, *"A War of Wonders": The American Civil War and British Thought*.

FOREWORD

James M. McPherson

As President Abraham Lincoln said during the first year of the Civil War, "the struggle of today, is not altogether for today – it is for a vast future also." Two years later, in his brief address at the dedication of the soldiers' cemetery at Gettysburg, Lincoln defined the stakes of the war for that vast future – whether the nation founded in 1776 would "perish from the earth" or experience "a new birth of freedom" that would ensure its survival into a vast future.

Nearly a century and a half after Lincoln spoke at Gettysburg, we can appraise the meaning of the war for his generation as well as our own. The 12 chapters in this book provide stimulating analyses of essential elements in such an appraisal: the causes and legacies of the war; the political and military leadership on both sides; the men who fought it and their families at home who sustained them and furnished the sinews of war; the far-flung impact of the conflict on the high seas and in foreign lands; the immense destruction of life and property but also the liberation of 4 million slaves and the abolition of the system that had enslaved them. The 12 authors bring a wealth of specialized expertise to these questions and a literary skill that presents their answers with a lucid clarity that makes each chapter a pleasure to read.

Here are a few observations to whet the reader's appetite for the 12-course feast that follows. "The monstrous injustice of slavery," said Lincoln in 1854, "deprives our republican example of its just influence in the world – enables the enemies of free institutions, with plausibility, to taunt us as hypocrites." Lincoln and other members of the new Republican Party, which carried most of the northern states in the presidential election of 1856, were convinced that the growing polarization between the free and slave states was an "irrepressible conflict" between social systems based on free labor and slave labor. The United States, said Lincoln in 1858 at the beginning of his famous campaign against Stephen A. Douglas for election to the US Senate, was a house divided between slavery and freedom.

> But "a house divided against itself cannot stand." I believe this government cannot endure, permanently half *slave* and half *free*... Either the *opponents* of slavery, will arrest the further spread of it, and place it where the public mind shall rest in the belief that it is in the course of ultimate extinction; or its *advocates* will push it forward, until it shall become alike lawful in all the States, *old* as well as new – *North* as well as *South*.

Douglas won the senatorial election in 1858. But two years later, running against a Democratic Party split into northern and southern halves, Lincoln won the presidency by carrying every northern state on a platform pledging to restrict the further expansion of slavery. This was the first time in more than a generation that the South had lost effective control of the national government. Southerners saw the handwriting on the wall. The North had a substantial and growing majority of the American population. So long as slavery remained a festering issue – so long as the United States remained a house divided – the antislavery Republican Party would henceforth control the national government. And most southern whites feared that the "Black Republicans" – as they contemptuously labeled the party of Lincoln – would enact policies that would indeed place slavery on the road to "ultimate extinction."

So to preserve slavery as the basis of their social and economic order, seven Lower South states seceded one by one during the winter of 1860–61. Before Lincoln took office on March 4, 1861, these seven states met in Montgomery, Alabama, adopted a Constitution for the Confederate States of America, and formed a provisional government with Jefferson Davis as president. As they seceded, the states seized the national arsenals, forts, and other property within their borders – with the significant exception of Fort Sumter in the harbor of Charleston, South Carolina. When Lincoln took his oath to "preserve, protect, and defend" the United States and its Constitution, the "united" states had ceased to exist. When the Confederates fired on Fort Sumter and four more states seceded, the two sides made the fateful leap into full-scale war.

These events transformed the principal issue of the sectional conflict from the future of slavery to the survival of the Union itself. But by 1862 Lincoln would become convinced that slavery must die that the Union might live. While the war aim of restoring the Union remained uppermost, giving that Union the "new birth of freedom" that Lincoln proclaimed at Gettysburg became a crucial adjunct. These goals could not be achieved merely by proclaiming them, but only by military victory. Three chapters in this volume appraise the soldiers and their commanders who fought it out over four long years at a cost of more than 620,000 lives. One category of explanations for ultimate northern victory focuses on military leadership. Some historians have argued that by 1864, if not earlier, a group of northern generals headed by Ulysses S. Grant, William T. Sherman, and Philip Sheridan had emerged to top leadership with the skills and determination to prevail, outclassing all Confederate generals except perhaps Robert E. Lee. Several of the South's best commanders – Albert Sidney Johnston, Stonewall Jackson, and J.E.B. Stuart – had by then been killed. Whether the northern commanders won because they were better, or have achieved a reputation as better because they won, is something readers must decide for themselves.

And what about the commanders-in-chief of these armies, Presidents Abraham Lincoln and Jefferson Davis? Do we rate Lincoln more highly only because he won, or did he win because he was better? A broad consensus exists among historians that Lincoln was more eloquent than Davis in expressing war aims, more successful in communicating with the people, more skillful as a political leader in keeping factions working together for the war effort, better able to endure criticism and work with his critics to achieve a common goal. Lincoln was flexible, pragmatic, with a sense of humor to smooth relationships and help him survive the stresses of his job. Davis was austere, rigid, humorless, with the type of personality that readily made enemies. Lincoln had a strong physical constitution; Davis suffered ill health and was frequently prostrated by sickness. Lincoln picked good administrative subordinates and knew how to delegate authority to them; Davis went through five secretaries of war in four years; he spent a great deal of time on petty administrative details that he should have left to subordinates. A disputatious man, Davis sometimes seemed to prefer winning an argument to winning the war; Lincoln was happy to lose an argument if it would help win the war. Were these contrasts a decisive factor in Union victory? Again, several of the following chapters – especially Richard Carwardine's on presidential leadership – will help readers make up their minds.

The legacies of the Civil War have profoundly affected not only the United States, but also the rest of the world. Northern victory in the war resolved two fundamental, festering issues that had been left unresolved by the Revolution of 1776 that gave birth to the United States: first, whether this fragile republican experiment would survive as one nation, indivisible; and second, whether the house divided would continue to endure half slave and half free. Both of these issues had remained open questions until 1865. Many Americans had feared for the republic's survival; many European conservatives had predicted its demise; some Americans had advocated the right of secession and periodically threatened to invoke it; 11 states did invoke it in 1861. But since 1865 no state or region has seriously threatened secession, not even during the decade of "massive resistance" in the South to desegregation from 1954 to 1964. Second, before 1865 the United States, which boasted itself a "land of liberty," had been the largest slaveholding country in the world. Since 1865 that particular "monstrous injustice" and "hypocrisy," as Lincoln described it in 1854, has existed no more.

Before 1865 two socioeconomic and cultural systems competed for dominance within the borders of the United States. Although in retrospect the triumph of free-labor capitalism has seemed inevitable, that was by no means clear for most of the antebellum era. Not only did the institutions and ideology of the rural, agricultural, plantation South based on slave labor dominate the United States government during most of that time, but also the territory of the slave states considerably exceeded that of the free states before 1860 and the southern drive for further territorial expansion seemed more aggressive than that of the North. Most of the slave states seceded in 1861 not only because they feared the potential threat to the long-term survival of slavery posed by Lincoln's election, but also because they looked forward to the expansion of a dynamic, independent Confederacy into new territory by the acquisition of Cuba and perhaps more of Mexico and Central America. If the Confederacy had prevailed in the 1860s, it is quite possible that the emergence of the United States as the world's leading industrial as well as agricultural producer by the end of the 19th century and as the world's most powerful nation in the 20th century would never have happened. That it did happen is certainly one of the most important legacies of the Civil War – not only for America, but also for the world.

At the same time, however, the war left the South impoverished, its agricultural economy in shambles, and the freed slaves in a limbo of segregation and second-class citizenship after the failure of Reconstruction in the 1870s to fulfill the promise of civil and political equality embodied in the Fourteenth and Fifteenth Amendments to the Constitution.

Yet all was not lost. Those Amendments remained in the Constitution, and the legacy of national unity, a strong national government, and a war for freedom inherited from the 1860s was revived again in the civil rights movement of the 1960s, which finally began the momentous process of making good on the promises of a century earlier. Even though many white southerners for generations lamented the cause they had lost in 1865 – indeed, mourned the *world* they had lost, a world they romanticized into a vision of moonlight and magnolias, there can be no doubt that white as well as black Americans, in the South as well as in the North, are better off because the South lost the war than if they had won it.

CHRONOLOGY

1820–59

1820
The Missouri Compromise admits Missouri as a slave state, but prohibits slavery elsewhere in the Louisiana territory above latitude 36° 30' north

1828
John C. Calhoun, the South Carolina politician, advocates nullification in response to the 1828 tariff

1831
The slave rebellion led by Nat Turner sends shock waves through the South; William Lloyd Garrison founds abolitionist newspaper *The Liberator*

1836
Congress adopts the Gag Resolution on slavery, which required all antislavery appeals to be tabled without debate in the House of Representatives

1845
Baptist and Methodist churches split into northern and southern branches

1845
The states of Texas and Florida are admitted to the Union

1846–48
War between the United States and Mexico

1846
The Wilmot Proviso appeals for the eradication of slavery from lands acquired from Mexico

1848
The Free Soil Party fields a presidential candidate

1850
Compromise of 1850 includes admission of California as a free state and enactment of a Fugitive Slave Law

1852
Whig Party fields its last serious presidential candidate, which signifies the breakdown of the two-party system; publication of Harriet Beecher Stowe's *Uncle Tom's Cabin* causes much controversy and creates a widespread sensitivity in the North to the plight of slaves

1854
Kansas–Nebraska Act repeals the Missouri Compromise and inflames sectional tensions

1856
Frémont runs as first Republican presidential candidate

1857
The Supreme Court's Dred Scott decision opens federal territories to slavery, enraging many people in the North

1858
Stephen Douglas defeats Abraham Lincoln in Illinois Senate race

1859
John Brown's raid on Harpers Ferry intensifies sectional tensions

1860

6 November
Abraham Lincoln is elected President of the United States

20 November
South Carolina secedes from the Union

1861

9 January–1 February
The remaining six states of the Lower South secede

4 February–11 March
Convention of delegates from the seceded states in Montgomery, Alabama, writes a constitution and chooses Jefferson Davis and Alexander H. Stephens as provisional President and Vice-President of the Confederate States of America respectively

4 March
Lincoln's First Inaugural Address

12–13 April
Confederate bombardment results in the surrender of Fort Sumter

15 April–8 June
Four states of the Upper South secede in response to Lincoln's call for volunteers

Early May
Winfield Scott briefs President Lincoln about a strategy later known as the Anaconda Plan

11 May
Camp Jackson affair, St Louis, Missouri

14 May
Great Britain issues proclamation of neutrality

20 May
Confederate Congress votes to move national government from Montgomery, Alabama, to Richmond, Virginia; Kentucky declares neutrality

10 June
France issues proclamation of neutrality

21 July
Battle of First Manassas or Bull Run

25 July
US Senate passes Crittenden-Johnson Resolutions, stating that the Union is not fighting to interfere with slavery

6 August
First Confiscation Act approved by US Congress

10 August
Battle of Wilson's Creek or Oak Hills, Springfield, Missouri

30 August
John C. Frémont declares martial law and declares slaves in Missouri free

3 September
Confederate forces under Gideon Pillow enter Kentucky, ending neutrality in that state

10 September
Confederate Albert Sidney Johnston is appointed to command Tennessee, Missouri, Arkansas, and Kentucky

1 November
George B. McClellan replaces Winfield Scott as general-in-chief of the US Army

6 November
Jefferson Davis is elected provisional president by the people of the Confederacy

7 November
Samuel Du Pont captures Port Royal Sound

8 November
USS *San Jacinto* captures British mail packet *Trent*

9 November
Don Carlos Buell and Henry Halleck are appointed to departments in Kentucky and Missouri

2 December
The second session of the 37th US Congress opens

1862

19 January
Battle of Mill Springs or Logan's Cross Roads, Kentucky

6 February
Union gunboats force the surrender of Fort Henry, Tennessee

13–16 February
Battle of Fort Donelson, Tennessee, results in the Union's capture of 15,000 Confederates

25 February
President Lincoln signs the Legal Tender Act, which creates national Treasury notes soon dubbed "greenbacks"

26 February
Don Carlos Buell captures Nashville, Tennessee

7–8 March
Battle of the Pea Ridge or Elkhorn Tavern, Arkansas

9 March
CSS *Virginia* battles USS *Monitor* in Hampton Roads

11 March
Lincoln's War Order No. 3 relieves McClellan as general-in-chief of the Army and consolidates western commands under Halleck

17 March
George B. McClellan begins movement of Union troops to Virginia Peninsula

28 March
Battle of Glorieta Pass

6–7 April
Battle of Shiloh or Pittsburg Landing

16 April
Confederate Congress passes the first National Conscription Act in American history

26 April
Union gunboats force New Orleans to surrender

8 May
"Stonewall" Jackson wins the battle of McDowell, the first of several victories in his Shenandoah Valley campaign; other victories follow at Front Royal (May 23), First Winchester (May 25), Cross Keys (June 8), and Port Republic (June 9)

15 May
US Congress passes the Homestead Bill

30 May
Confederates evacuate Corinth, Mississippi

31 May–1 June
Battle of Seven Pines or Fair Oaks

1 June
Robert E. Lee takes command of Confederate army at Richmond

6 June
Confederates surrender at Memphis, Tennessee

19 June
Lincoln signs a law prohibiting slavery in the territories

25 June–1 July
Seven Days battles reverse a tide of Union military success as Lee drives McClellan away from Richmond in action at Mechanicsville (June 26), Gaines's Mill (June 27), Savage Station (June 29), and Glendale or Frayser's Hill (July 1)

11 July
Halleck is named general-in-chief of the US Army

13 July
General Nathan Bedford Forrest raids Murfreesboro, Tennessee

17 July
Second Confiscation Act approved by US Congress

9 August
Battle of Cedar Mountain

28–30 August
Battle of Second Manassas or Bull Run

30 August
Battle of Richmond, Kentucky, launches Braxton Bragg's invasion of Kentucky

17 September
Battle of Antietam or Sharpsburg ends Lee's first invasion of the North; battle of Munfordville, Kentucky

19 September
Battle of Iuka, Mississippi

22 September
Lincoln issues Preliminary Emancipation Proclamation

4 October
Battle of Corinth, Mississippi

8 October
Battle of Perryville or Chaplin Hills, Kentucky

20 October
Lincoln orders John McClernand to raise troops for an expedition against Vicksburg, Mississippi

24 October
William Rosecrans replaces Buell as commander of Union forces in Kentucky and Tennessee

5 November
Ambrose E. Burnside replaces McClellan as commander of the Army of the Potomac

24 November
Joseph E. Johnston is assigned to the Confederate command in the West

7 December
Battle of Prairie Grove, Arkansas

13 December
Battle of Fredericksburg

20 December
Confederates under Earl Van Dorn raid Holly Springs, Mississippi

31 December–2 January
Battle of Murfreesboro or Stone's River, Tennessee

1863

1 January
Lincoln issues Final Emancipation Proclamation

11 January
Federal gunboats capture Fort Hindman, Arkansas

25 January
Joseph Hooker replaces Burnside as commander of the Army of the Potomac

30 January
Ulysses S. Grant assumes command of the expedition against Vicksburg, Mississippi

25 February
US Congress passes the National Banking Act

3 March
US Congress passes the Enrollment Act, which institutes a national draft

7 March
Nathaniel Banks' Federal force moves to Baton Rouge to cooperate with Grant's Vicksburg expedition

2 April
Women take to the streets in Richmond "bread riot" to protest against food shortages

16 April
David Porter's flotilla runs past Vicksburg batteries

17 April
Confederate Benjamin Grierson launches a raid into Mississippi to draw attention from Grant's expedition

24 April
Confederate Congress enacts the Tax-in-Kind Law, a highly unpopular measure requiring agricultural producers to give a portion of various crops to the national government

30 April
Porter ferries part of Grant's army across the Mississippi River

1 May
Battle of Port Gibson, Mississippi

2 May
Grierson's raiders reach Baton Rouge, Louisiana

1–4 May
Battle of Chancellorsville

10 May
"Stonewall" Jackson dies

12 May
Grant defeats Confederates at Raymond, Mississippi

14 May
Engagement at Jackson, Mississippi, Grant defeats Confederates

16 May
Battle of Champion's Hill, Mississippi, Grant defeats Pemberton

17 May
Battle of Big Black River, Grant defeats Pemberton

18 May–4 July
Siege of Vicksburg, Mississippi

27 May
Banks attacks, besieges Port Hudson; first major engagement for African American soldiers

7 June
Confederate attack on Milliken's Bend

9 June
Cavalry battle at Brandy Station

11 June
Banks's attack repulsed at Port Hudson

14–15 June
Second Battle of Winchester

14 June
Banks's attack repulsed for third time at Port Hudson

23 June
Rosecrans advances on Tullahoma, Tennessee

28 June
General George G. Meade replaces Joseph Hooker in command of the Federal Army of the Potomac

1–3 July
Battle of Gettysburg

3 July
Bragg retreats to Chattanooga, Tennessee

4 July
Pemberton surrenders Vicksburg to Grant

9 July
Fall of Port Hudson

13–14 July
Lee's Confederates recross the Potomac River into Virginia, ending the main phase of the Gettysburg campaign. At the same time, mobs in New York City riot in opposition to conscription, killing or wounding hundreds of victims, many of them African American citizens resented as a visible cause of the war and the draft

19 July
Union attack on Fort Wagner led by 54th Massachusetts (Colored) Infantry

15 August
Burnside begins campaign for Knoxville, Tennessee

16 August
Rosecrans begins campaign for Chattanooga

21 August
Quantrill's raid on Lawrence, Kansas

2 September
Burnside occupies Knoxville

8 September
Battle of Sabine Pass, Texas

8–14 September
Lee detaches General Longstreet with one-third of the army's infantry to go west and reinforce Confederate operations in Georgia and Tennessee. Meade moves south against Lee, but only heavy skirmishing results

9 September
Rosecrans occupies Chattanooga

18 September
Longstreet's men begin to reinforce Bragg's army

19 September
Battle of Chickamauga, Georgia begins

20 September
Longstreet breaks Rosecrans's line

23 September
Bragg lays siege to Chattanooga

24 September
Hooker leaves for Chattanooga with XI and XII Corps

14 October
Battle of Bristoe Station

17 October
Grant made commander of all the Union forces in the West

19 October
Thomas replaces Rosecrans

23 October
Grant arrives at Chattanooga

4 November
Longstreet detached to attack Burnside at Knoxville

7 November
Battle of Rappahannock Station

19 November
President Lincoln delivers the Gettysburg Address

20 November
Sherman arrives at Chattanooga with reinforcements

23 November
Thomas seizes Orchard Knob

24 November
Hooker drives Confederates off Lookout Mountain

25 November
Sherman's attack stalls; Thomas's men storm Missionary Ridge

26 November–2 December
Battle of Mine Run

28 November
President Lincoln issues a Proclamation of Amnesty and Reconstruction, offering pardons to any Confederate willing to take an oath of allegiance

29 November
Longstreet repulsed by Burnside at Knoxville

1 December
Bragg resigns as the commander of the Army of the Tennessee

27 December
Johnston assumes command of Army of the Tennessee

1864

3 March
Sherman leaves Vicksburg on Meridian campaign

4 March
Sherman completes Vicksburg campaign

12 March
Grant is commissioned lieutenant-general, to command all Federal armies. He would make his headquarters with the Army of the Potomac and soon exert virtually direct command over it

18 March
Sherman assumes command of Union forces in the West

25 March
Banks begins Red River campaign

8 April
Banks defeated by Richard Taylor at Sabine Crossroads, Louisiana

12 April
Forrest's massacre of black soldiers at Fort Pillow, Tennessee

4–6 May
Battle of the Wilderness

6 May
Sherman opens Atlanta campaign

8–21 May
Battle of Spotsylvania Court House

9 May
McPherson's flanking movement stalls

11 May
Battle of Yellow Tavern; General J.E.B. Stuart is mortally wounded and dies the next day

13–16 May
Battle of Resaca

15 May
Battle of New Market

18 May
Battle of Yellow Bayou, Lousiana, the last battle of the Red River campaign

23–27 May
Battle of the North Anna River; Sherman outflanks Johnston's position at Allatoona, Georgia

25–27 May
Battle around Dallas, Georgia

1–3 June
Battle of Cold Harbor

5 June
Battle of Piedmont

8 June
Lincoln renominated for president

12 June
Army of the Potomac starts to cross James River

14 June
Lieutenant-General Leonidas Polk killed at Pine Mountain

15–18 June
Opening engagements around Petersburg, while Confederate general Jubal Early arrives near Lynchburg to launch his long and crucial campaign in the Shenandoah Valley

22–23 June
Battle for the Weldon Railroad near Petersburg

27 June
Sherman's assault on Kennesaw mountain repulsed

4–9 July
Sherman maneuvers across Chattahoochee River

9 July
Battle of Monocracy

11–12 July
Early's Confederates stand on the outskirts of Washington; President Lincoln comes under long-range fire

17 July
Hood replaces Johnston as commander of Army of Tennessee

20 July
Hood repulsed at Peachtree Creek

22 July
Hood fails to turn Sherman's army at battle of Atlanta; Major-General James B. McPherson is killed

24 July
Second battle of Kernstown

28 July
Hood's attack at Ezra Church repulsed

30 July
Dramatic explosion of mine at Petersburg turns into the Battle of the Crater

5 August
Farragut wins battle of Mobile Bay

18–25 August
Battles of the Weldon Railroad and Reams' Station

23 August
Lincoln submits to his cabinet a sealed memo stating that "it seems extremely probable that this Administration will not be reelected."

29 August
McClellan nominated for president

31 August
Battle of Jonesboro, Georgia

1 September
Battle of Jonesboro concluded; Hood evacuates Atlanta

2 September
Sherman occupies Atlanta

14–17 September
The Beefsteak Raid

19 September
Third battle of Winchester; Price with 12,000 men crosses into Missouri

22 September
Battle of Fisher's Hill

27 September
Anderson's attack on Centralia, Missouri

28 September
Hood moves to strike at Sherman's supply line

29 September–7 October
Fighting around Richmond and Petersburg at Fort Harrison, Chaffin's Bluff, New Market Heights, Darbytown Road, and Boydton Plank Road

October
Hood fails to capture Allatoona; Sherman in pursuit

9 October
Cavalry fights at Tom's Brook

18 October
Hood crosses into Alabama

19 October
Battle of Cedar Creek

23 October
Price defeated at Westport; begins retreat

27 October
Battle of Burgess' Mill

30 October
Sherman shifts Schofield's troops to support Thomas in Middle Tennessee

8 November
President Lincoln reelected with 55 percent of popular vote

15 November
Sherman's troops burn Atlanta; begin March to the Sea

19 November
Hood opens push into Middle Tennessee

23 November
Milledgville, capital of Georgia, falls to Sherman

29 November
Schofield escapes at Spring Hill, Tennessee

30 November
Schofield repulses Hood at Franklin; Lieutenant-General Patrick Cleburne killed

2 December
Hood besieges Nashville

13 December
Sherman captures Fort McAllister

15–16 December
Thomas routs Hood's army

21 December
Sherman occupies Savannah

25 December
Butler repulsed at Fort Fisher, North Carolina

1865

15 January
Fort Fisher falls to Porter and Terry; Hood relieved of command of Army of Tennessee

31 January
Thirteenth Amendment abolishing slavery passed in Congress

1 February
Sherman begins Carolinas campaign

5–7 February
Battle of Hatcher's Run

6 February
Lee appointed commander-in-chief of all Confederate armies by Congress

17 February
Columbia falls to Sherman

18 February
Charleston seized by Union troops

22 February
Wilmington surrenders to Schofield; Johnston recalled to command Confederate forces against Sherman

2 March
Early's last remnant destroyed at the Battle of Waynesboro

4 March
Lincoln's Second Inaugural Address, "With malice toward none…"

13 March
Confederate Congress approves raising of black troops

16 March
Sherman pushes back Hardee at Averasborough, North Carolina

17 March
Major-General E.R.S. Canby attacks Mobile, Alabama

19–21 March
Sherman repulses Johnston's attack at Bentonville, North Carolina

24 March
Sherman occupies Goldsboro, North Carolina, ending the Carolinas campaign

25 March
Attack on Fort Stedman near Petersburg

28 March
Lincoln, Grant, Sherman, and Porter confer on peace terms

29–31 March
The final campaign in Virginia begins with fighting around the Dinwiddie Court House

1 April
Battle of Five Forks

2 April
Confederate government evacuates Richmond

3 April
Richmond falls

8 April
Sherman resumes march on Johnston

9 April
Lee surrenders to Grant at Appomattox Court House

12 April
Offical surrender of Confederate forces at Appomattox

April
Mobile falls to Canby; Johnston tells President Jefferson Davis resistance is hopeless

13 April
Raleigh falls to Sherman

14 April
Lincoln assassinated at Ford's Theater in Washington

18 April
Sherman and Johnston sign broad surrender agreement

21 April
President Johnston and cabinet reject Sherman's terms

26 April
Johnston accepts same terms as Grant gave Lee

10 May
President Davis is captured at Irwinsville, Georgia

13 May
Last battle of the war, at Palmito Ranch, Texas

23–24 May
Grand Review in Washington, DC

26 May
General Edmund Kirby Smith surrenders Confederate forces west of the Mississippi River

18 December
Thirteenth Amendment takes effect

1868-77

1868
9 July Fourteenth Amendment takes effect

1870
3 February Fifteenth Amendment takes effect

1877
The last enforced military government in the ex-Confederate states is removed and home rule is restored at the state level

"While the people retain their virtue and vigilance, no administration, by any extreme of wickedness or folly, can very seriously injure the government in the short space of four years."

Abraham Lincoln, First Inaugural Address, 1861

Extremists at the gate
Origins of the American Civil War

William A. Blair

In March 1865, President Abraham Lincoln offered a succinct explanation for why the nation had gone to war. In his Second Inaugural speech, the president laid out in a few lines a statement of causation that thousands of words spent since may not have captured better. "One-eighth of the whole population," Lincoln told the crowd at the Capitol Building, "were colored slaves, not distributed generally over the Union, but localized in the southern part of it. These slaves constituted a peculiar and powerful interest. All knew that this interest was somehow the cause of the war." Lincoln cited slavery as the reason for the war, but his explanation contained subtleties easily lost on successive generations. The war came because powerful people strove to protect their interests. He identified them prior to the war in his famous "house divided" speech as a dynasty of slaveholders working in collusion with northern politicians to spread slave labor everywhere and tear down free labor. He added his voice to those who identified this movement as a conspiracy of the Slave Power.[1]

A cotton plantation in the 1850s. Demand from textile manufacturers built the cotton kingdom that made the South the principal supplier of the world's cotton and fed the thirst for expanding slavery into new lands. (Library of Congress)

Lincoln was not alone in emphasizing slavery as a root of the conflict, although southerners blamed a different group of conspirators for creating the disunion. More than four years before Lincoln's speech, delegates to the secession convention in South Carolina issued a written statement to explain their desire to leave the Union. Their Declaration of Secession was by no means as succinct as Lincoln's Second Inaugural; however, one could hardly miss the point. The text claimed that the non-slaveholding states had assumed

> the right of deciding upon the propriety of our domestic institutions; and have denied the rights of property established in fifteen of the States and recognized by the Constitution; they have denounced as sinful the institution of slavery; they have permitted open establishment among them of societies, whose avowed object is to disturb the peace and to eloign the property of the citizens of other States.

It added that the Republican Party's ascendance to the presidency on a minority vote meant that a sectional party had come to power with the purpose of "subverting the Constitution itself," installing a man to the presidency who was hostile to slavery.

> He is to be entrusted with the administration of the common Government, because he has declared that that 'Government cannot endure permanently half slave, half free,' and that the public mind must rest in the belief that slavery is in the course of ultimate extinction.[2]

1859

John Brown: An abolitionist, reared in the partisan violence of Kansas, John Brown led a failed attempt to capture the US Armory at Harpers Ferry, Virginia, and initiate a slave revolt. Brown was executed in Virginia, and northern sympathy for his purpose, if not his methods, alarmed southerners.

Today we generally accept the reasons given by the historical actors who – like Lincoln and the South Carolinians – admitted that powerful interests had lined up behind positions to expand or restrict the growth of slavery. Living in those times, it was also hard not to see the hands of conspirators behind many events, even if no coordinated cabal actually existed. The battles over the territorial expansion of slavery convinced many that there were extremists at the gates: two groups of people attempting to distort democracy in order to advance their peculiar interests. Lincoln had adopted a line of reasoning similar to others in the Republican Party who stressed that a Slave Power dominated the nation. It appeared as if the North always granted concessions to southern Democrats, who enjoyed far more power than their small numbers should have allowed. Until the Compromise of 1850, they dominated the executive branch by holding the presidency for 50 years, and dictated much of the policies of the Congress by supplying the Speaker of the House for 41 years. Their influence extended to the judiciary, with slaveholders providing

18 of the 31 justices of the Supreme Court. Rule by the ballot seemed endangered by oligarchic slaveholders who exercised a tyranny of the minority over the majority in public affairs.

White southerners, meanwhile, increasingly viewed the country as falling under the influence of abolitionists who ignored property rights and resorted to terrorism to further their ends. The resistance to fugitive slave laws that erupted after 1850 made it plausible that northerners were trying, as the South Carolina Declaration of Secession noted, to subvert the Constitution. Abolitionists circumvented the law by helping fugitive slaves via the Underground Railroad, killing US marshals who tried to regain human property, and burning the Constitution in protest. They ignored rulings by the Supreme Court, and men of high means and social position funded the expedition of John Brown to incite a slave insurrection. Southerners increasingly found little consolation in the words of Republicans who vowed that the party would protect slavery, especially when many from this same party had declared that there was an irrepressible conflict facing the nation, and that the country no longer could remain half free and half slave.

The notion that there existed extremists, in the form of a Slave Power and agitating abolitionists, dragged along white moderates who, at first blush, apparently had little in common with activists in both sections. Today we tend to underestimate the way slavery became embedded in the lives of non-slaveholders and the extent of the concern among many from both regions about the fragile nature of democracy in a young republic. The common white man of the antebellum South shared anxieties with planters that abolitionists desired the overthrow of the southern way of life through extralegal means. Northern workers who had little sympathy for antislavery feared an oligarchy that professed that

CHARLESTON
MERCURY
EXTRA:

Passed unanimously at 1.15 o'clock, P. M. December 20th, 1860.

AN ORDINANCE

To dissolve the Union between the State of South Carolina and other States united with her under the compact entitled "The Constitution of the United States of America."

We, the People of the State of South Carolina, in Convention assembled, do declare and ordain, and it is hereby declared and ordained,

That the Ordinance adopted by us in Convention, on the twenty-third day of May, in the year of our Lord one thousand seven hundred and eighty-eight, whereby the Constitution of the United States of America was ratified, and also, all Acts and parts of Acts of the General Assembly of this State, ratifying amendments of the said Constitution, are hereby repealed; and that the union now subsisting between South Carolina and other States, under the name of "The United States of America," is hereby dissolved.

THE
UNION
IS
DISSOLVED!

Charleston Mercury extra announces secession of South Carolina. (Library of Congress)

hierarchies of human beings were natural, that questioned the value of free labor, and that resorted to brute force against white people.

THE GULF OF 'ISMS

Despite the bold statements by Lincoln and the South Carolinians about slavery and the coming of the war, a number of people remain skeptical about this explanation as the cause for the bloodiest conflict in US history. Self-proclaimed southern heritage groups often belittle slavery as the engine driving secession. Their members lean primarily on economics as the cause for war – an agricultural section trying to retain its position against a government employing policies that favored manufacturing. Conflict occurred, in this interpretation, over the tariff and government support of internal improvements that diminished the economic livelihood of the South. Others echo the 19th-century southerners who professed – although more stridently after the conflict began – that the states seceded because they wanted to protect themselves from an aggressive, powerful central government. Finally, even those who admit the importance of slavery as one of the reasons behind secession find it hard to believe that this is the whole answer. They see a region in which three-quarters of the white people owned no slaves and scratch their heads over how these same people could rush to war without seeming to have a vested interest in the "peculiar institution."

1828

Nullification: Under the leadership of John Calhoun, South Carolina attempted to ignore a federal tariff increase. President Andrew Jackson forced the state to back down, but the incident highlighted deep political divisions within the nation.

This skepticism rests on a misunderstanding of the two sections and the context of the time. Economics did have a role in secession, but it was less a concern over the tariffs than over the real problems of what would happen to slave values if the nation suddenly restricted the institution. And without more slave states, southern planters faced an inevitable loss of national power without parity of representatives in the US Senate. It is also true that State Rights and protection of local sovereignty was an important factor driving secession. But this philosophy, too, was deployed as a defense against the assault of northerners on slavery. Finally, it is certainly true that most southerners did not own slaves, but this does not mean they lived in a hermetically sealed universe without contact with the enslaved, without aspirations to own them, and without a desire to feel superior by celebrating white supremacy and paternalistic values they considered different from the greedy, impersonal Yankees.

On the eve of the Civil War, the US South with its 4 million enslaved people stood as the largest modern slave society in the world. In 1860, only Cuba, Brazil, and the United States still practiced African slavery. The US South was a modern slave society because it rested with one foot squarely in the capitalistic world of private exchange, profit, individualism, and desire for progress and liberty, while it accumulated those profits and based that liberty on a system of forced labor enduring from an older world. The South had become something of a hybrid that adopted democratic principles, yet did so by religiously ascribing to a hierarchy of inequality that began with masters and ended with the enslaved. It was a democracy built on the belief in the fundamental inequality of human beings as the organic, natural way of life.

The War of 1812 escalated regional development along disparate paths. The northern economy took a decided turn toward manufacturing, which thrived on the new transportation links taking shape at the same time. Cities formed along these new commercial and social links. In the meantime, the South evolved from a region furnishing tobacco, rice, and sugar into a formidable cotton kingdom whose export constituted 57 percent of the US trade while supplying three-quarters of the world's supply. It accomplished this through western expansion from the East Coast to the Mississippi River fed by an unquenchable thirst from the textile mills of the northern United States and Europe. The region stayed predominantly agricultural and rural, with slave labor growing even more intertwined with the political economy as the century unfolded.

Virtually all forms of measurement describe how divergent the North and South were growing. In 1860, population favored the North, where roughly 19 million white people lived as opposed to 8 million white southerners. About $1/4$ million free blacks lived in the North, nearly the same as the free black population in the South. Of course the South had nearly 4 million enslaved. The North claimed more than 80 percent of the foreign-born residents, swelled during the 1850s because of revolutions in Europe and the potato famine in Ireland. More northerners than southerners lived in urban areas of greater than 2,500 people – about 25 percent versus 10 percent. Concerning the economy, the disparities loomed. The states that would form the Confederacy had a total of 18,026 manufacturing establishments; one state alone in the North had more – New York with 23,236. Not surprisingly, the North held 84 percent of the capital invested in manufacturing. Yet because of the enormous monetary rewards from "King Cotton," the South was famously wealthy. A region with one-third of the white population contained two-thirds of the men worth $100,000 or more.

These regional patterns created societies that shared important commonalities, but contained people who saw themselves as holding disparate values and beliefs. Disruptions to social organization in the free states brought a host of situations that bypassed the South. While transportation and manufactories encouraged new goods and opportunities, it also fostered greater divisions of wealth, labor unrest from changing forms of work and shop arrangements, as well as other problems associated with these kinds of transformations in general. With larger cities came crime and health problems from poor sanitation. Reformers like Horace Mann pushed for public education of the young, and other efforts went toward improving prisons, asylums, public health, women's rights, and drinking habits. Temperance became one of the most successful movements, with 11 states banning the sale of spirited liquor.

Coming with these various efforts to improve society were a variety of somewhat bizarre experiments with social organization that made the South look quizzically at northerners as the purveyors of "isms." Utopian communities formed in western New York and New England, where people dabbled in socialism, free love, or grand philosophical debates about the nature of individualism. More dangerous to southern society, however, was the escalation of antislavery thought. Planters could shake their heads at those strange Yankees practicing transcendentalism, socialism, utopianism, universalism, and other "isms" that tinkered with social arrangements, but they could not treat abolitionism so casually, especially as it transformed into a potent political force that found a home in the Republican Party in the 1850s.

As important as the material divergences were the ways in which people interpreted their idiosyncrasies. Planters and southern whites in general increasingly

The United States in 1860

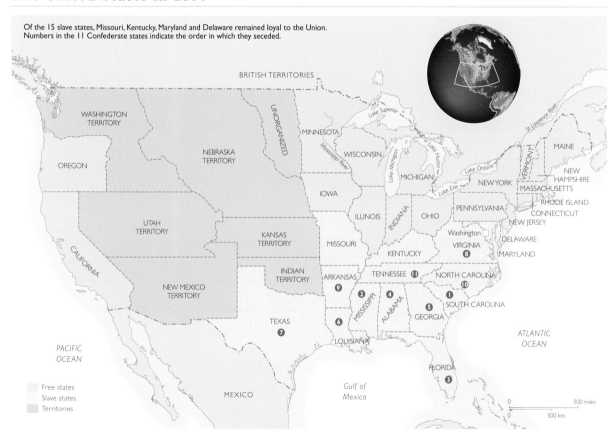

Of the 15 slave states, Missouri, Kentucky, Maryland and Delaware remained loyal to the Union. Numbers in the 11 Confederate states indicate the order in which they seceded.

viewed themselves as the bastion of tradition, defenders of Constitutionalism, adherents to Protestantism as opposed to the North that attracted more Catholics, and practitioners of personal relations that did not place every exchange at the crude level of a balance sheet. While planters spoke out against the antislavery North, their criticisms cut a much wider swath that was in part designed to bring along the non-slaveholder but also reflected their sense of themselves as superior to the men and women who lived across the Mason–Dixon line. As such, they sounded a chorus similar to Ronald Reagan in the 1980s who, like most Americans, did not stop to consider the underlying differences with the Soviet Union over the right to own property individually or communally. The Soviet Union was characterized as an evil empire that threatened democracy.

THE BONDS OF SLAVERY

When first viewing the antebellum South, it is startling how few of the residents owned enslaved Americans. The census of 1850 – the one most available to the public in the moments leading to secession – listed 347,525 owners of slaves among a white population of 6,184,477. Through studies originating in a time when reconciliation was occurring, historians around the turn of the 20th century seized upon such demographics to discredit slavery as a cause of the conflict. How could a region favor disunion over slavery when fewer than a third of its white people – and maybe only one in four – had measurable ties to the peculiar institution? The more that scholars and the public massaged the data, the more it seemed that fewer people enjoyed the benefits of the ownership of human beings.

In an article first published in 1972, historian Otto Olsen took up the task of refuting this logic as he restored the importance of slavery to southern life. Olsen attacked the use of figures in several ways. He first indicated that the statistics themselves were not fully appreciated – that instead of one of four white people being slaveholders the frequency was closer to one of every three. Concentrations of slaveholding, in fact, increased when eliminating the border states and considering only the 11 states that joined the Confederacy. On that basis, the percentages of slaveholding fell in line with the order of secession: South Carolina with 48.7 percent of white families with slaves; Mississippi, 48 percent; Florida, 36 percent; and so on. Then he contrasted this with the percentage of investors and employers in a more recent free society. Using 1949 as his base, he discovered that 2 percent of the people then had a direct interest in the profits generated by business through stocks and bonds and 10 percent were employers, compared with the 31 percent of the white families who owned slaves in the Confederacy. Finally, Olsen reminded readers about the role of racial ideology in committing white people to slavery as a means of reinforcing their common interests.[3]

Slaves ginning cotton. Providing labor and services for farmers who did not have access to such equipment helped give white people a stake in the slaveholding system even if they did not own slaves. Other factors included a common sentiment of white supremacy, shared aspirations to become slaveholders, and fears of retribution from rebellious slaves. (Library of Congress)

There were other intersections of the so-called plain folk with the slave system that bear remembering, for they speak to the way slavery was embedded in the fabric of 19th-century lives. Non-slaveholders had the benefits of a slave in a number of ways. If they lived near planters, those masters friendly to their neighbors might send over an enslaved African American to help with the crop at a crucial time. Or slaves might gin the little bit of cotton grown by a yeoman farmer and the planter might market it through a cotton factor to leverage a better deal for the small farmer. And there was still another way that non-slaveholders entered this system – by renting a person for labor. This typically occurred a year at a time, with an annual fee of roughly $100 to $120 paid to the owner. With a diminished working class from which to draw, artisans in urban areas especially sought this resource. Historians have yet to put together a comprehensive picture of the extent of slave hiring for the entire South, but in the Upper South – specifically Virginia – manuscript census records suggest that in certain areas this practice boosted the direct ties to slavery by as much as 10 percent.

The need for security from insurrection also put slaveowners and non-slaveowners on similar ground. Thomas Jefferson perhaps articulated this issue best when he stated that even if planters wished to free their laborers they faced possible retribution by the enslaved for their bondage. Jefferson used the vivid metaphor that the region held a wolf by the ears, unsure of what would happen if it released the grip. Although few in number, slave uprisings occurred sufficiently enough to remind planters and plain folk of a fate that all might share if they were not vigilant.

Even religion reinforced the importance of slavery to southern society. Recent work by scholars such as Mark A. Noll has demonstrated how the abolition critique had to avoid a literal interpretation of the Bible because passages in the Old Testament too often endorsed the ownership of human beings and no passages in the New Testament featured Christ speaking out against human bondage.[4] Ministers ranked among the most important proslavery ideologues in the states that became the Confederacy, with their Sunday messages from the pulpit increasingly endorsing slavery as the underpinning of the region's character and economic might. They praised the institution for its beneficial influences on white and black people. In this interpretation, white people allegedly treated the enslaved as members of their families, providing them with material goods they could not otherwise achieve, caring for them beyond their years of productive labor, and supervising them in a life of Christian worship.

Congregations can show a remarkable facility for seemingly hearing ministers without really listening to them, yet dramatic evidence suggests that non-slaveholders internalized their concerns about the antislavery movement. During the antebellum period, two church denominations that drew the most non-slaveholders into their pews split into northern and southern wings over the agitation by abolitionists. Three-quarters of the southern whites belonged to Baptist and Methodist denominations. The abolition movement heated up in the 1830s and strengthened in the next decade, with abolitionists lobbying churches to take stands against the ownership of human beings. The rupture among Baptists came in May 1845 during a convention of Southern Baptists in Georgia. Delegates from eight southern states set up a separate governing body that recognized slavery – the only fundamental difference between the two wings. The Methodist Episcopal South followed almost exactly the same course and time frame. Delegates met in May 1845 to set up a southern organization, declaring:

> The Northern Methodist Church... is so mixed up with the whole machinery of abolition and anti-slavery agitation and invasion, by its recent proclamation of hostility to the South, in so many forms of bitter and malignant assault, that its own chosen colors will not allow us any longer to distinguish it from the common enemy... It is an *Abolition* church.[5]

Even admitting that there was a material and social base in common with planters, how can we account for non-slaveholders' internalizing messages geared toward propping up the slave regime? Like the residents of the antebellum South, most people adopt the values of the world into which they are born. Revolution is an exceptional event, not the norm – as is the desire to challenge the system. Something as horrible as slavery can, in its own context and time, appear to the oppressors as natural, desirable, and worth defending, even to the ones who are not yet the direct beneficiaries.

Imagine asking the question to a room full of primarily 18- through 21-year-olds, "How many of you are homeowners?" The predictably few hands that go up might provoke the following question: "Then does that mean you are against homeowning?" The absurdity of the question strikes them almost immediately. They understand that they have grown up in a society based on property owning by individuals, with homeowning as a means of measuring success. Although listed on a census as non-homeowners, most have grown up in domiciles owned by parents and, even if they begin their independent adult lives as renters, wish to find property reflective of their social stations as soon as conditions allow. Those who were raised in apartments admit to the power that homeowning holds on the culture. Furthermore, while renters derive no benefit from the tax code that credits expenditures for interest rates on mortgages, few of them storm the tax office and cry for an end to the advantage, even if they grumble on tax deadline day about the lack of a similar break for themselves. Similar to our ancestors, we can overlook the contradictions within our society. Many of us can walk by the homeless on the street and believe that a character flaw contributes to their condition, rather than challenge the individualism that undergirds our society or question whether we ought to accept the poverty-stricken as unfortunate, if inevitable casualties of a free-market system.

1846–48

Mexican–American War: Initiated by President James K. Polk and the Democrats, this relatively brief war led to a massive territorial expansion of the United States. The question of whether this new land should be slave- or free-territory exacerbated sectional divisions.

The students in this exercise come to realize that they might have homeowning as a basis for a war someday. They can see how, if threatened by a country that proclaims the individual holding of property to be wrong – a country, say, like the former Soviet Union – they might rally against such a threat. Only in this case, they rarely would reduce their concerns to the crass materialistic base of a house as the reason for their action. Instead, they would proclaim how communal property owning tends to prop up an aggressive, totalitarian regime that disrupts the right of self-determination. And they admit they would fight tooth and nail against the evil empire that attempted to challenge their own way of life.

None of this discussion should be construed as saying that the antebellum South consisted of harmonious white people in perfect agreement with each other. Nor should anyone think that no one in the South ever expressed reservations about slavery. It would be a mistake to believe that all white people loved each other then any more than all white people in America today love Bill Gates or Donald Trump. In fact, they may envy the success of these rich people, and perhaps in their darkest moments even wish for their comeuppance. But most would not want to deny themselves the same ability to amass wealth and power on the terms set by their society. They might even be tempted to go to war if an external foe appeared that seemed bent on obliterating life as they knew it.

THE SLAVE POWER WRIT LARGE

When the United States went to war with Mexico in 1846, antislavery supporters immediately suspected the hand of the Slave Power lay behind the conflict. For years they had warned of the growing menace of the slaveholding Democracy. During the 1830s white abolitionists had flooded the South with antislavery tracts, but planters met this problem by having the postmaster-general, with the blessing of slaveholding President Andrew Jackson, refuse to deliver this mail. Protests lodged in Congress went nowhere. Beginning in 1836, the Congress instituted a gag rule on abolition petitions that automatically tabled them without a hearing. War with Mexico, which acquired territory predominantly below the Missouri Compromise line, seemed just another step toward protecting the political power of the slaveocracy.

The war that broke out in 1846 attracted more than abolitionists to this interpretation. To some northern Whigs, and even some Democrats, it appeared that the conflict had begun through an unjust pretext by a slaveholding, Democratic president. In 1847, Congressman Abraham Lincoln of Illinois issued his Spot Resolutions, demanding that President James K. Polk prove that the first shot of the Mexican War had been fired on US soil. The skirmish between US and Mexican forces had occurred on disputed territory. It was possible to think that US forces had instigated the first shots, thus bearing culpability for the war. Opponents believed that Polk wanted the additional land to create more room for the slave empire – a point underscored when he vigorously pursued the Mexican lands but gave in to a compromise over the border with the British over the Oregon territory. Lincoln was joined in his suspicions by abolitionists, free soilers, and northern Democrats who had tired of bowing to the southern oligarchy.

Consequently, the country emerged from the Mexican War as a greater power with its current territorial posture on the North American continent, yet this new might came at the price of internal divisions that could have torn the nation apart. A crisis was delayed only through strenuous legislative efforts that resulted in the Compromise of 1850. The components of this agreement, however, contained the seeds of bitter fruit that would feed the perceptions that a slaveocracy existed that was intent on spreading slavery everywhere.

The key provision for discontent involved the enhanced federal posture to enforce the capture and return of fugitive slaves. The Constitution of 1787 gave the federal government the power to return laborers who fled from a variety of work arrangements, including indenture, apprenticeship, and slavery. As early as 1793, the Congress enacted a Fugitive Slave Act, but resistance was

1857

Dred Scott: US Supreme Court decision that ruled African Americans did not have a right to bring cases before a federal court. Chief Justice Roger Taney's decision excluded blacks from the protections of citizenship and drew deep protest from many northerners.

Destruction in Lawrence, Kansas, caused by proslavery forces. Coming in 1856, the incident was one of many violent outbreaks over whether to make the Kansas territory a free or slave state. This particular incident led to a speech by Senator Charles Sumner who angered proslavery forces and was caned in retribution by a US congressman. (National Archives)

1854

Kansas–Nebraska Act: Federal legislation that organized the territories that became Kansas and Nebraska. The legislation struck down the Missouri Compromise, reached in 1820, that restricted slavery south of the 36° 30' line, and this action inspired a new generation of activism around antislavery politics in the North.

relatively easy. The Compromise of 1850 changed this, but in the process it brought to communities in the North the visible hand of the Slave Power. The new laws established federal commissioners to hear cases, instead of the state courts that had supervised these laws. And the new system hardly provided fair justice. Slaveowners could testify and bring witnesses, but the African American defendants could not. The commissioners who heard the cases received double the pay if defendants were found guilty. White citizens could be imprisoned and fined if they obstructed capture or refused to help when deputized. Although the controversy during the 1850s concerned the expansion of slavery in the territories, the fugitive slave laws brought the sectional crisis to a personal level for residents of states such as Ohio and Pennsylvania, the natural escape routes for the enslaved. To people along the border of freedom, it appeared that the slaveholders' democracy – one that threw out the usual forms of justice – had impinged on the freedom of white people.

The desire to organize the territories of Kansas and Nebraska – as well as attempts by the Congress and the Supreme Court to resolve the issue of slavery in the territories – contributed to northern concerns. Stephen Douglas, the Democratic senator from Illinois, had become a new force in national politics with his efforts surrounding the Compromise of 1850. Shortly,

Douglas became an advocate for organizing the new territories of Kansas and Nebraska on the basis of popular sovereignty, in other words, for letting residents of the region decide whether to become a free or slave state. Douglas was motivated to organize the territories in part by the need to court southern support for the construction of a transcontinental railroad, with a terminus in Chicago. The passage of the Kansas–Nebraska Act of 1854 made it appear once again that northern Democrats had sold out to their southern brethren.

Kansas became the bloody foreshadowing of civil war. Proslavery and antislavery forces recognized immediately the importance of the region and flooded the territory, bringing with them arms and the resolve to use them. They soon established rival governments, one with a proslavery constitution and the other a free state. Shooting inevitably broke out. In the spring of 1856, proslavery forces demolished the town of Lawrence, Kansas. Eight hundred men poured into town with five cannon, demolished two newspaper offices, burned a hotel and the home of the free-soil governor, and plundered shops and homes. Antislavery supporters conducted their own atrocities, most notably John Brown who, with his followers, brutally murdered five proslavery settlers by hacking them to death with broadswords. Ignoring the abolitionist transgressions, Senator Charles Sumner of Massachusetts stood on the Senate floor and condemned the proslavery forces in a speech titled "The Crime against Kansas." Sumner identified whom he thought was responsible:

Dred Scott. His case struck northerners as providing more cause for suspecting that a Slave Power dominated public affairs. Antislavery people believed that this decision by the Supreme Court meant that Congress could not restrict slavery and that slaveholders could take the peculiar institution into free states. (Library of Congress)

> Even so the creature, whose paws are now fastened upon Kansas, whatever it may seem to be, constitutes in reality a part of the slave power, which, in its loathsome folds, is now coiled about the whole land.

He called what was happening in Kansas a "Tyrannical Usurpation" and urged the masses to help "redeem the Republic from the thralldom of that Oligarchy which prompts, directs, and concentrates the distant wrong."[6]

One more incident registered on Abraham Lincoln. In 1857, the Supreme Court issued a ruling concerning a slave who had been taken to a free state for a time. In the Dred Scott case, the court declared that the case had no standing: enslaved Americans could not file actions because they were not citizens. Then the court went a step further. It declared that the Congress could not restrict slavery in the territories because the institution was protected by the US Constitution. In effect, the court had overturned the 36° 30' line and blocked legislative measures to curb slavery. Although the court had spoken specifically about the territories, antislavery

The four conspirators identified by Lincoln in the "house divided" speech. From left are Senator Stephen Douglas, President Franklin Pierce, Supreme Court Chief Justice Roger B. Taney, and President James Buchanan. Antislavery opponents derisively referred to northern men who sympathized with slaveholders as "dough faces." (National Archives)

OPPOSITE *Anthony Burns. He became a famous case involving the federal government's desire to prove to southerners that fugitive slaves would be returned from the North. Burns's recapture by federal authorities led to violence and angry protest that helped convince southerners that antislavery forces were willing to use extralegal means to achieve their ends. (Library of Congress)*

people figured that it was a rather small step toward a more sweeping understanding of the law that allowed masters to take slaves into the existing free states.

A few more elements about this case reinforced that a Slave Power lay behind the decision. The court itself consisted of a majority of men from the slave states, including the chief justice who had issued the majority opinion. The newly elected President of the United States – James Buchanan of Pennsylvania – had endorsed the ruling rather quickly. Later it became known that he had used his influence on the justice from Pennsylvania to become a sixth vote for the majority to make the ruling appear to be less sectional. In accordance with the Kansas–Nebraska Act, it was easy to argue that northern sympathizers – pejoratively called "dough faces" – had climbed into bed with the Slave Power.

This, at least, was what Lincoln conveyed in his famous "house divided" speech. Issued in 1858 as he campaigned for his new Republican Party, Lincoln's speech has been better known for its poetic statements concerning the need to end slavery. "'A house divided against itself cannot stand,'" Lincoln said in quoting the Bible. "I believe this government cannot endure permanently half slave and half free." However, the speech was intended to build the circumstantial case against the slaveholding dynasty. He implicated four men as conspiring to spread slavery: Stephen Douglas, his rival for an Illinois Senate seat; Franklin Pierce, the former president; Roger B. Taney, the Supreme Court chief justice; and Buchanan. Douglas had orchestrated the Kansas–Nebraska Bill, thus opening a greater portion of the territories to slavery. Pierce had pushed the legislation. Taney issued the court ruling that made the entire territories open to slavery. "We cannot absolutely know that all these exact adaptations are the result of preconcert," Lincoln admitted.

ARREST IN BOSTON.

THE ESCAPE ON SHIPBOARD.

DEPARTURE FROM BOSTON.

THE SALE.

THE ADDRESS.

THE PRISON.

Anthony Burns

35

But when we see a lot of framed timbers, different portions of which we know have been gotten out at different times and places and by different workmen – Stephen, Franklin, Roger and James, for instance – and when we see these timbers joined together, and see they exactly make the frame of a house or a mill, all the tenons and mortices exactly fitting … we find it impossible not to believe that Stephen and Franklin and Roger and James all understood one another from the beginning, and all worked upon a common plan or draft drawn up before the first blow was struck.

He added with his typical twist of a phrase:

We shall lie down pleasantly dreaming that the people of Missouri are on the verge of making their State free, and we shall awake to the reality instead, that the Supreme Court has made Illinois a slave State.[7]

ABOLITION AGITATION

Southern whites watched the same events and arrived at different conclusions. Secessionists in South Carolina characterized the conflict as coming from persistent agitation by abolitionists that took place over 25 years. It seemed compelling to them that the key institutions of the country that dictated future government policy had been infiltrated by abolitionists who would disobey the law or the Constitution to achieve their ends.

The sensitivities always had been there, but they increased as northerners resisted the new fugitive slave law. Boston provided the most notorious examples. In 1854, abolitionists stormed the courthouse where authorities held runaway slave Anthony Burns. In the process, a deputy was killed. When federal troops escorted Burns to the ship returning him to Virginia, a crowd estimated at 50,000 lined the streets. Buildings were draped in black bunting and American flags hung upside down. Local authorities thwarted attempts to prosecute the leading rioters, and, on July 4, noted abolitionist William Lloyd Garrison publicly burned the Constitution in protest. This was not the only violent episode. Three years earlier, African Americans had resisted federal attempts to capture two fleeing slaves in Christiana, Pennsylvania. The slaveowner who accompanied the federal deputies was killed. The fugitives escaped to Canada and, despite federal efforts to prosecute, no one was convicted for the death.

Violence was not the only response: northerners conducted resistance through their state legislatures. During the 1850s, more states in the North began passing personal liberty laws to combat the Fugitive Slave Act. Vermont's, enacted in 1858, stipulated that no human being in the state could be considered property, that any slave that had entered its borders was free, and that African Americans had the right

OPPOSITE *Angry Bostonians watch the procession of Burns back to slavery in Virginia. They also draped buildings in black bunting and hung US flags upside down in protest of the event. Later one of the leading abolitionists in the country, William Lloyd Garrison, burned a copy of the Constitution. (The Granger Collection, New York)*

William Henry Seward, senator from New York, whose speech prophesying an "irrepressible conflict" raised concerns among southerners that Republicans were pressing for a fight over the issue of expanding slavery. Seward forecast that the two sections were on a collision course and that the nation could not contain two societies devoted to different social and labor organizations. (National Archives)

to due process of the law. These laws ignored the federal statute that had existed since 1793, and they ignored a court decision in the 1840s that had rendered these codes as unconstitutional.

It was the participation by respectable men and women that especially concerned secessionists. If the Slave Power had its presidents, congressmen, and Supreme Court justices, the abolitionists had ministers, lawmakers, prominent philanthropists, and manufacturers on their side. A minister had helped lead the charge in the mob that killed the federal deputy in Boston during the attempt to free Burns. Henry Ward Beecher, another minister, covertly shipped guns to abolitionists in Kansas. Lincoln, a former congressman and prominent Illinois attorney, sounded chilling warnings of a future conflict, in which a divided house was supposed to cease being half slave and half free. He was joined by William Henry Seward, a senator from New York, who spoke out against the growing power of the slave aristocracy in an 1858 address that proclaimed that two antagonistic systems were heading on a collision course. "It is an irrepressible conflict between opposing and enduring forces," he said, "and it means that *the United States must and will, sooner or later, become either entirely a Slaveholding nation, or entirely a Free-labor nation*."[8] It hardly consoled white southerners that the Lincolns and Sewards of the North, both respectable men, represented the moderate segment of the new Republican Party. Men such as they had helped construct a party of social experimenters, abolitionists, financiers, humanitarians, racists, politicians, and supporters of free labor around the platform of prohibiting slaves in the territories – a gradual approach that depended on constricting slavery so it might die gradually in some distant future.

Other respectable men, however, took a more militant approach. Frustrated with the slow progress toward emancipation, the so-called Secret Six supported the raid by John Brown on the government's arsenal at Harpers Ferry in 1859. Even though Brown had touched the worst fears of white southerners by trying to foment a slave uprising, the region endured the abortive episode and subsequent hanging of Brown with some relief. After all, no slaves rallied to his side and justice was served on the gallows. But then investigators uncovered mail and documents at the Kennedy Farm in nearby Maryland, which Brown had used as a headquarters. The materials tied the raid to Bostonians and a New Yorker: ministers, a philanthropist-former congressman, a manufacturer of lead pipe, and a protégé to Ralph Waldo Emerson. These were hardy marginal members of society. Southerners also heard accolades to Brown mouthed by northerners such as author Henry David Thoreau. Although many other northerners decried the raid as wrong, southerners overlooked these more temperate expressions, seeing in the more extreme reactions affirmation that there was an effort under way to assault slavery by people who supported the Republican Party.

Small wonder that when Lincoln was elected president, the seven states of the Lower South seceded. In 1860, he received just shy of 40 percent of the popular vote – 1.8

million of 4.4 million cast. He would have defeated the other three candidates combined. The quirks of the Electoral College awarded him a majority determined by the population of the states he won. Sectionalism defined the balloting. Lincoln captured every county in New England, 109 of 147 counties in the mid-Atlantic, and 252 of 292 counties in the Old Northwest. He took exactly two counties in the entire Lower South. For that last region, the time had come to leave the Union. Their vote mattered little in this sectional alignment and it seemed pointless to continue in a political arrangement with people who had shown little respect for the law, and promised that an irrepressible conflict lay ahead between slave and free societies.

Lincoln and the North could not let them go. The democracy that took root in this republic was imperfect, exclusive by race and gender, yet it was one of the only functioning systems of its kind in the world. There were other reasons for forcing the South to return to the Union. People realized that the country would have been weaker economically if the Confederacy achieved independence, and the territorial question surely was not resolved by secession. Further conflict undoubtedly lay ahead. Too many concessions had been granted to the Slave Power already. The fact remained, however, that the European powers welcomed the demise of the United States, this upstart that bragged about its political freedoms without an aristocracy. To many northerners, it was embarrassing to have this great democratic experiment discredited by disunion that occurred over a presidential election that everyone knew had been legally conducted. Alongside the economic and nationalistic reasons for going to war was the potential that a democracy could be blown apart by the very thing intended to hold it together – the ballot.

Consequently, the problems that resulted in the Civil War appeared at the time to threaten a way of life for people on both sides of the divide. On one level, these problems were rooted in a real material base of economics and social-political organization. The South faced a power struggle with actual consequences for the place of slavery in the nation and the southern master class that it supported. On another level, this struggle occurred in the hothouse climate of the sectional crisis that contributed to an exaggerated sense of conspiracy on both sides, a tension inflamed and exacerbated by party politics. The notions of what lay behind the sectional crisis helped radicalize the situation, drawing moderates into the same orbit as extremists. And although slavery lay at the heart of these problems – or at least the conflict between champions of free and slave labor – the articulation of grievances often sought the higher plane of a people acting to protect democracy and liberty. Or, put more simply, to protect their way of life.

> "*As I would not be a* slave, *so I would not be a* master. *This expresses my idea of democracy. Whatever differs from this, to the extent of the difference, is no democracy.*"

Abraham Lincoln, August 1, 1858 fragment on democracy

I would not be master

Governing the War

Richard Carwardine

Early in 1861 the president-elect left home for his inauguration. At each railroad stop on his roundabout route to the capital he tested support for the new administration, inspired a surge of popular patriotism, and declared his peaceful intent. War having broken out, he threw himself unselfishly into the larger cause: sustaining an American nationalism erected on the principles of the Declaration of Independence. Previous administrations offered him little useful guidance for the crisis: Andrew Jackson and James Knox Polk had shown how to be an assertive national leader, but their party, the Democrats, whose laissez-faire and states' rights philosophy had set the tone at Washington since the advent of mass democracy, provided no blueprint for the strong central government and enhanced bureaucracy which an all-consuming civil war demanded. The United States' most recent military engagement, the Mexican War, fought by a small army against a weak foe, also offered few useful lessons.

Jefferson Davis's inauguration as president on February 18, 1861, at the Capitol, in Montgomery, Alabama, marked the bright morning of the Confederacy. (Library of Congress)

Quite simply, the chief executive had to learn on the job. He strove to fashion a balanced cabinet, but could not rely on every minister's ability or loyalty. Weighing military command in eastern and western theaters, he found it easier to appoint more successfully in one than the other. Suspension of habeas corpus, and the introduction of conscription, prompted growls of criticism from hostile newspaper editors, congressional factions, and state-level critics, and fed burgeoning peace movements that capitalized on war-weariness and hardship. An ascetic, he worked without regard for his health and had little concern for his personal safety. He ate poorly, but had remarkable physical stamina. Prone to periods of low spirits and depression, he labored long hours at his desk, hindered by a reluctance to delegate key tasks, and by streams of visitors who distracted him and bombarded him with unwanted advice. His intelligent but strong-minded and sharp-tongued wife alienated many. His children provided a happy diversion, but the death of a beloved young son almost crushed his spirit. He gave more thought to the purposes of God than ever before. By April 1865 the president's haggard features bore eloquent testimony to four years' unceasing and faithful toil.

This is an ambiguous passage, interchangeably applicable to the leaders of both sides in the American Civil War. I have contrived it less to tease than to suggest striking similarities between the circumstances of Jefferson Davis and Abraham Lincoln, some superficial, others substantial. It serves as a reminder of the common problems facing the two presidents who, as chief executives in republican–democratic systems, operated within certain common traditions during a time of internecine war. Yet if it tells a truth, the passage by no means tells the *whole* truth, for the key to understanding presidential leadership within the Union and Confederacy does not lie in what Davis and Lincoln had in common. They faced very different challenges. They operated within dissimilar if not wholly different political systems and cultural traditions, and they confronted divergent social and economic realities. Most important, for present purposes, they revealed contrasting characteristics and qualities in leadership.

CHALLENGES AND CONSTRAINTS

As the newly installed president of the Confederacy, Davis recognized the challenge ahead of him in February 1861. He had to implement a new constitution, construct an administration from scratch, erect a bureaucracy, sustain a *de facto* independence, broaden the basis of support beyond the Lower South, build and equip an army and navy, and – once the initial battle lines were established – defend a thousand-mile northern border from possible attack. For his part, Lincoln

Dating from the summer of 1861, this cartoon intimates an early end of the rebellion, with Jefferson Davis holed up in Richmond as Winfield Scott, the Union commander, traps the Confederates, east and west, at Manassas Junction and Memphis. The optimism was misplaced, but the role of loyalist graphic art in sustaining Lincoln's administration throughout the war should not be underestimated. (Library of Congress)

THE OLD GENERAL READY FOR A "MOVEMENT".

confronted no less daunting a challenge, whatever his advantage in inheriting a functioning government. The regular armed forces immediately available to the Union were quite inadequate for its needs, but so too, foreign observers judged when war broke out, was the mass army under construction. Forcing the seceded states back into the Union looked to them to be a near impossible task, demanding the invasion of some 800,000 square miles of hostile territory and the subjugation of some 9 million people, almost one in three of the prewar nation.

Politically, Davis would operate under a constitution little different on paper from the Union's, but within a dissimilar political culture: one that celebrated localism, state sovereignty, and weak government, and that judged the absence of party conflict a measure of popular patriotism. He would deal with a Confederate public suspicious of centralized authority, sensitive to slights to its honor, proud of the region's agrarianism and mythic martial traditions, overconfident of its international advantage as the self-styled Cotton Kingdom, hostile to even modest levels of taxation, and increasingly unsure about how best to accommodate within the war effort an enslaved population whose loyalty to the cause of southern independence could by no means be relied on. As the war advanced, he would have to contend with ever deeper invasions by Union armies; with Lincoln's proclamation of freedom to the slaves of rebels; with other aspects of an increasingly hard war – one to which his own family's slave-run plantations were not immune; and with the unenviable task of holding together a "nation" threatening to split along the geopolitical faultline between Upper and Lower South.

By contrast, the Union's president operated within a society where citizens were generally more tolerant of the Federal government's taking an activist and centralizing role, and where patriotic "antiparty" sentiment did not run to the point of erasing all inter-party conflict. Lincoln looked to an essentially free-labor economy whose agricultural, manufacturing, and industrial elements were more evenly balanced and open to wartime growth than those of the Confederacy. However, the Union's war effort was served by a free population that was more culturally mixed than the Confederacy's, and that encompassed elements, immigrant and native-born, with divergent, even conflicting, understandings of the Union's meaning. And, as the Union armies advanced, Lincoln had to confront a problem that whatever the Confederacy's fortunes, would never trouble Davis: how to deal with the unprecedented and divisive issue of reconstructing the nation.

In addressing these different challenges and constraints, Lincoln and Davis displayed contrasting characteristics and qualities of leadership, which would significantly shape the course followed by each side. To each man, as chief executive and commander-in-chief, fell three major responsibilities: establishing and sustaining effective political and military strategies; developing a productive mode of wartime management; and, as the democratically accountable leader, communicating the administration's purposes to the wider public and mobilizing it behind the war during dark times as well as good. Exploring their leadership from these three perspectives allows for some reflections on how far they were merely reactive to larger forces. Were they – in the words Lincoln famously used to describe his own course to Albert Hodges in 1864 – "controlled" by events?[1]

Their leadership also calls for some comparative assessment. While in each case the balance of achievement lies with Lincoln, the Confederate president's record was by no means negligible: it should be read less in the knowledge of the South's defeat, than in view of the Confederacy's remarkable fight against the odds and of the hard reality of Davis's limited options at any given moment. Equally, the Union's victory does not of itself provide evidence of its leader's unfailing political wisdom: we should recall the depth of popular anxiety over the apparent rudderlessness of the administration during the first year or so of the war, and the sense amongst radical critics in particular that, for most of the conflict, Lincoln was

The Confederate president is here recognizably the same figure described by the London Times *correspondent, William Howard Russell, during the first month of the war: "his head is well formed, with a fine full forehead,… features regular, though the cheek-bones are too high, and the jaws too hollow to be handsome… The expression of his face is anxious, he has a very haggard, care-worn, and pain-drawn look." (GLC 05153 The Gilder Lehrman Collection, courtesy of The Gilder Lehrman Institute of American History, New York)*

simply not up to the job. Some historians have rightly remarked that had he been operating under a parliamentary system, his party would surely have ditched him during 1862.

STRATEGIC VISION

For both sides there were four key strategic concerns: exerting control over the rich and essential resources of the "border" slave states, tugged in two directions by ties of blood, economy and culture; securing international support, notably from Great Britain, the most powerful nation of the day and master of the seas; devising a military plan that would minister to one's own strengths while exploiting the enemy's limitations; and mobilizing to the full the human and natural resources of the country.

The border

Neither Davis nor Lincoln needed instruction in the enormous significance of the border. Taking office, the Confederate president immediately reached out to the eight slave states still loyal to the Union, signing a law that declared the Mississippi open to all states' commercial traffic. He fashioned his policy towards Fort Sumter, still in Union hands, to prevent South Carolina zealots acting unilaterally and alienating middle-state opinion. For Lincoln, too, preventing a second wave of secession became a paramount objective, though one that had to be squared with holding on to the forts as symbols of Union. His eventual masterstroke of policy – openly resupplying Fort Sumter by means of an unarmed relief effort – aimed to advertise his peaceful intent and throw onto the Confederates the odium of firing the first shot. Both presidents could take some satisfaction in the outcome. Davis's ordering of force at Sumter and his immediate dispatch of envoys to the Upper South secured the support of Virginia, North Carolina, Tennessee and Arkansas as well as the neutrality of Kentucky. Lincoln, however, had not lost the northernmost tier of slave states, on which the outcome of the war would almost certainly hang. Cede Delaware, Maryland, Kentucky, and Missouri, and the Confederacy would expand its population to over 12 million, Washington's days as the Union's capital would be numbered, the Ohio River would provide the South with a natural defense, and the domain of slavery would stand undivided in its mortal struggle with freedom.

In the ensuing effort to cement the loyalty of the border, Lincoln's determined pursuit of the Union's strategic interest prompted in Maryland the brilliant use of an iron fist – the threat of military force, the suspension of habeas corpus – in a gloved hand. Less well judged was his handing over military authority in Missouri to Nathaniel Lyon, the impulsive agent of the Radical Unionists, who hastened the state's decline into guerrilla warfare. It was Kentucky, however, with its command of the Ohio river, that provided the strategic crux. "I think to lose Kentucky is nearly the same as to lose the whole game," Lincoln declared.[2] Respecting the state legislature's proclamation of "neutrality," he resisted pressure from neighboring Union governors to send in forces. His waiting game seemed humiliating, but by August 1861 the tide had so turned that Unionists easily dominated the legislature. This was the point at which Davis, confronted by a crisis concocted by his field commander, undermined his own strategic purpose. When the president's friend General Leonidas Polk occupied Columbus, to preempt its seizure by Ulysses S. Grant, the Kentucky legislature declared it an act of invasion. Yet Davis ignored the pleadings of local Confederates that he order his general to withdraw. He left Polk to make the final decision. Polk stood firm. Grant moved Union forces across the Ohio into Paducah. Neutrality was at an end. Further Union troops pushed in to secure the balance of control.

Davis's decision here contrasts pointedly with Lincoln's almost simultaneous repudiation of the actions of one of his own western commanders. When John C. Frémont issued a proclamation to free the slaves of rebels, he won fame, but stunned conservative slaveholding Unionists in Kentucky and presented Lincoln with a great political challenge. Lincoln knew the proclamation could torpedo his border strategy, at the very time Polk's actions at Columbus promised a successful denouement. When Frémont refused to rescind the proclamation himself Lincoln "very cheerfully" modified it.[3] Unlike Davis, Lincoln would not allow *his* key political strategy to be derailed by his commanders' actions in the field.

Foreign relations

Winning the border states was important, but no more so than securing the respectful support of the great European powers, especially Britain. For Lincoln, and his accomplished secretary of state, William Henry Seward, this meant persuading European nations not to intervene. Lincoln was inexperienced in foreign affairs, but he understood that civil wars left nations exposed to interference. Foreign powers should recognize that the Union was involved in suppressing an internal insurrection, accept that the Confederate "government" was illegitimate, offer the rebels no support, and respect his blockade of southern ports. Above all, war must be avoided.

A breakdown in British–Union relations was, of course, precisely what Confederates prayed for. Davis expected from the outset that the Europeans would welcome the fracture in the American Union and seek friendship with an

independent Confederacy, above all because of their supposed dependence on "King Cotton." He immediately sent commissioners to Europe to announce his government's commitment to peace and commerce. In May 1861, the British government issued a proclamation of neutrality, recognizing the Confederates as belligerents. Other European powers followed suit, but this fell far short of the full diplomatic recognition that Davis desired. The fact was that he and other southern leaders had for some years been on the road to a self-imposed cultural isolation, had lost their feel for the pulse of European opinion, and now failed to understand that British national interest, including economic ties with the Union, would keep her clear of intervention – at least until it was clear that southern independence would be, not a project in progress, but a permanent reality.

This was a lesson driven home by the *Trent* crisis of December 1861, when the Union navy's seizure from a British mail packet of Confederate commissioners bound for diplomatic service in Europe prompted the British government into ordering naval and military reinforcements to Canada and the western Atlantic. Davis could only watch in impotence, however, his hopes melting into deep disappointment, as Lincoln's dawning awareness of the seriousness of the crisis, and his firm grasp of national interest, produced an outcome of wary peace and a gradual strengthening of British–American ties.

This Harper's Weekly *cartoon targets a point of real Confederate vulnerability: the Davis administration's inflationary financial policies and – against a background of the Union blockade and a hubristic faith in "King Cotton" – the more general economic weakness of the South. (Library of Congress)*

Other perils lay ahead in the Union's international relations, especially relating to the blockade, the construction of Confederate raiders in European shipyards, and British and French efforts at mediation. Lincoln was determined that he would not have "two wars on his hands at a time."[4] Calculation of national self-interest, and the implications of Lincoln's emancipation proclamation, made conflict inconceivable. Davis could do little about it. "King Cotton" may have contributed an arrogance to Confederate perceptions, and a concerted attempt to export cotton early in the war might have challenged the efficacy (and thus the legal status) of the blockade, but it is doubtful that any commercial or diplomatic policy pursued by Davis could have changed Britain's stance. When in the final months of the war he made an offer to the British of gradual emancipation in return for recognition, they rightly saw it as the last throw of the dice, but it is unlikely that the same overture at an earlier date would have elicited any other response.

This pro-Lincoln cartoon of 1864 exploits the contrasting military reputations of George B. McClellan and Ulysses S. Grant. Only the bull dog commander can be relied upon to capture the kenneled and cowering Jefferson Davis: elect McClellan and the lieutenant-general will be pulled off. (Library of Congress)

Military strategy

If Davis had any real room for maneuver in securing foreign recognition, it existed not in overseas corridors of power but on the battlefields of North America. Sustained Confederate military success, and taking the fight to the enemy, had the

capacity to achieve what the diplomatic dance of statesmen could only propose. This is in part why Davis has scored good marks from Civil War historians for not only endorsing but also encouraging the aggressive, risk-taking military strategy of Robert E. Lee. With his West Point training, experience during the Mexican War, and service as secretary of war, Davis enjoyed a confidence in this arena that he did not instinctively enjoy in other domains. Determined to get "at the Enemy," Davis and Lee knew they did not have the resources to sustain indefinite offensive action, but they knew that invading the North would make foreign powers sit up, help nurture a peace movement within the enemy's midst, and speak to the Confederate temperament. Davis also deserves credit for recognizing that the era's military orthodoxy of the concentration of forces worked against the needs of nation-building: a broad-based military presence along the line of Confederate defenses would counter "dissatisfaction, distress, desertion of soldiers, opposition of State Govts." Moreover, he understood the strategic significance of the Mississippi Valley and the need to defend the river.[5]

Although Lincoln's military inexperience meant that he initially lacked Davis's self-confidence, he applied himself as commander-in-chief with every bit as much diligence, and would eventually outrun most of his generals in his strategic thought. His blockade of southern ports showed his quick grasp of the value of the Union's naval superiority. He built the western theater into his strategic framework. Operating from first principles, rather than the textbooks of Napoleonic warfare, he came early on to see the best means of exploiting the Union's advantage in numbers. While McClellan planned a concentration of massive force against Richmond, Lincoln was telling his western commanders that his "general idea" was that – since "we have the *greater* numbers, and the enemy has the *greater* facility of concentrating forces upon points of collision" – the best way to exploit the Union's superiority was by menacing the enemy "with superior forces at *different* points, at the *same* time." To this insight he added another: that the tracking and destroying of Confederate armies, not places, was the key to victory.[6] But to destroy armies one had to deny them food, ammunition, and other supplies. With Lincoln's encouragement, the North moved from a war of conciliation toward white southerners into a "hard war" against them. By late 1864 Union troops were destroying railroads, seizing crops, burning buildings, plundering homes, killing livestock, and freeing slaves.

Mobilizing resources

Behind Lincoln's military aggression stood a statistical ruthlessness. After the grievous defeat at Fredericksburg in December 1862, Lincoln remarked "that if the same battle were to be fought over again, every day, through a week of days, with the same relative results, the army under Lee would be wiped out to its last man, the Army of the Potomac would still be a mighty host, [and] the war would be over."[7] The advantage Lincoln identified would have remained merely theoretical without an effective means of organization. Human resources, and the other materiel of war, had to be mobilized. Both presidents showed a lively understanding of this need, notably in their "modernizing" embrace of an expanded, more intrusive government, and an unprecedented centralization of power.

1862

16 April

Confederate Conscription Act: With most enlistments set to expire in April, the Confederate Congress passed a national draft (the first in US history) that also automatically reenlisted all one-year men for a three-year term. The act ensured a large army but exemptions and other draft-related policies created social and political divisions within the nation.

Lincoln's circumstances gave him opportunities for broadening presidential power in ways undreamt by his predecessors. All now understood executive authority to be a key lever in the wartime mobilization of Union resources, as administration initiatives took effect in the arena of black enlistments, conscription measures, and taxation. But Lincoln left much to Congress, knowing that – now freed from the shackles of the Slave Power – it would stimulate wartime economic growth by implementing a Whig–Republican program: railroad construction, high tariffs on imported manufactures, homestead and land-grant laws, scientific agriculture, and a national banking structure. Together, executive and legislature announced the arrival of a new dispensation, one pledged to a liberated commercial order.

Far more startling was the Confederacy's own ambitious centralizing program. Nothing prepared southerners for the wrenching change overseen by the Richmond administration from a traditional small-government, states-rights confederation to the Confederacy's (short-lived) precursor of a modern state. Davis, as his most authoritative biographer explains, knew his material resources did not match the enemy's, that the Union could call on a vast reservoir of men of military age, supply the armies from its superior industrial capacity, and rely on a far better developed communications and transportation network than that available to the South.[8] He was ready, much earlier than Lincoln, to embrace conscription. He also pursued policies – the suspension of habeas corpus; the impressment of property (including slaves) by government agents at official prices; government funding of railroad construction; direct government involvement in shipbuilding and other war necessities – that allow one to see the Confederacy as *more* statist than the Union, where the war effort was more reliant on the mobilization of private corporations. According to Frank E. Vandiver:

> The techniques of administration and business management Davis adopted during the war, the experiment he conducted in rudimentary economic planning, in social control, in national mobilization, all represented fundamental changes in the South – changes which wrenched it rudely into modern times.[9]

In this regard, then, Davis deserves credit for his grasp of a key element of strategy.

POLITICAL AND MILITARY MANAGEMENT

Strategic vision was a necessary but insufficient condition of successful wartime leadership. Equally required was a capacity for the deft handling of the available political and military levers. How well, then, did each president pursue his day-to-day business? How sure a judge of people and appointments was he? How effectively did he respond to new administrative needs? How well did he relate to the different loci of power? What acumen, what personal strengths and defects, did he bring to his political dealings?

Neither Lincoln nor Davis was a natural administrator. Neither knew the art of delegation, and each worked himself to self-punishing exhaustion. John Hay, Lincoln's young secretary, found him "extremely unmethodical."[10] The Union president was, however, the superior of Davis in sifting out the trivial from the important, in avoiding suffocation from an avalanche of paper, and, in rationing his cabinet meetings, keeping them focused, and preventing them from meandering unprofitably for hours.

In making his key cabinet appointments Lincoln sought to surround himself with able men, and had the self-assurance to include his chief rivals for the presidential nomination in 1860. Not every choice was well judged, but mostly Lincoln collected an outstanding team, with superb ministers in the key departments of state, war, navy, and the treasury: Seward, Edwin Stanton, Gideon Welles and Salmon Chase. Davis's cabinet, constrained by his policy of keeping a geographical balance, and tending to measure an appointee's suitability more by his loyalty to the Confederate cause than to his personal qualities, proved less distinguished.[11] In Stephen Mallory and John H. Reagan he had a fine secretary of the navy and postmaster-general; he also had a dependably wise presence in Judah P. Benjamin. Davis himself served as *de facto* secretary of war, but the quality and turnover in the formal holders of that portfolio did the Confederacy few favors: he was never blessed with the remarkable partnership that Lincoln forged with Stanton. The most serious cabinet shortcoming, however, was at the treasury, from where the inadequate Christopher Memminger, endorsed by the uncomprehending Davis, pursued disastrous policies based on borrowing and fiat money, and surveyed a gothic landscape of paper and rampant inflation. The contrast with Chase's masterly handling of the Union finances – and the support that Lincoln gave him, despite his wavering loyalty to the president, in the knowledge that Chase was far better at the job than he would have been – could not have been starker.

Even allowing for the limitations of planter society and the shortage of well-qualified personnel, Davis's appointments to diplomatic posts lacked imagination. His early trio of commissioners to Europe contained a fire-eating ideologue and a lightweight; none was a match for Lincoln's wise appointment to Britain of the urbane Charles Francis Adams. When Davis chose to replace them, his choice for the key London post was the unsuitable, tobacco-juice spitting James Mason, the author of the reviled Fugitive Slave Law. In the military arena, neither president had a monopoly of wisdom, each made some poor appointments under political pressure, and – given the limits of talent and experience – both were bound to promote some who would fail to make the grade. But in several of Davis's least successful appointments "hope and faith prevailed over perceptive appraisal."[12] Lincoln's own sad experience of failing generals in the Army of the Potomac paralleled Davis's failure to find a suitable commander in the western theater, but eventually Lincoln found an answer in George Meade and Grant, while Davis – perhaps more limited for choice than Lincoln – persisted for too long with a general, Joe Johnston, in whom he had lost confidence.

Both presidents necessarily found themselves striving to exercise control over an unwieldy war machine that evolved by trial and error as much as by good planning. It was to the discredit of neither that a degree of impromptu experimentation marked the early stages of the war. But the Union president's lesson-learning was faster and more complete than his Confederate counterpart's. Thus, for example, the Union eventually benefited from the evolution of an effective military command structure that was discernibly modern, with Henry Halleck as chief-of-staff liaising between Lincoln as commander-in-chief and Grant as general-in-chief. Davis's departmental structure, by contrast, left cooperation between neighboring commanders to depend on their voluntary coordination, respect for rank structure, and common patriotism.

In his relations with other branches of government and key individuals, judgment on Davis has to be mixed. On the whole he had good, constructive relations with congressmen, a majority of whom were loyalists or, as representatives of areas most immediately affected by the conflict, ready to endorse the radical measures the administration proposed; he met them regularly and gave a strong executive lead. His relations with several state governors were much more troubled, notoriously so in the case of Joseph E. Brown of Georgia, and broke down over such issues as the enlistment and organization of volunteers, the appointment of officers, and the arming of units and their deployment. Exploiting fears of centralization and the erosion of liberties, Brown sucked other dissenters into his circle, including fellow Georgian, and vice-president, Alexander Stephens.

Lincoln was more deft in political management. A lesser figure would have been ground between the upper and nether millstones of Republican radicals and conservative Unionists, each essential to the war coalition. Lincoln shrewdly played

Now, Marshal, sing us 'Picayune Butler', or something else that's funny.

off these forces. "He handled and moved men remotely as we do pieces upon a chessboard," an associate remarked.[13] He left Congress to its own devices in some policy areas, notably its economic program, but he kept firm control over emancipation, reconstruction and – the Joint Committee on the Conduct of the War notwithstanding – management of the war. He drew political strength from his relations with the Republican governors who dominated the northern states, a reflection of his influence over his party. He gave his cabinet secretaries room for maneuver in their own departments but he remained their master. This was a command that as a congressional radical explained, made Lincoln "the virtual dictator of the country." [14]

Davis's leadership was undoubtedly compromised by personal defects. The record of deteriorating relationships cannot be explained exclusively by the over-sensitivity, pride, self-importance, and related shortcomings of others, legion though these traits were. The Confederate president's austerity in manner and lack of a sense of humor were no doubt related to his dyspepsia, neuralgia, and recurrent malarial symptoms, but they provide a jarring contrast with Lincoln's self-control, and use of story-telling and jokes to lubricate and turn conversation. Despite his bouts of

Part of the Democrats' assault on the Lincoln administration during the 1864 election campaign, this cartoon plays on Lincoln's fondness for jokes and places a callous president amongst the Union casualties at Antietam. He asks Marshal Lamon to "sing us 'Picayune Butler' or something else that's funny." Lincoln is clad in the garments – Scottish cap and military cloak – he was said to have worn when he furtively entered Washington in February 1861. (Library of Congress)

dark depression, Lincoln could often be good company; Davis – though he could be charming and gracious – generally was not. And whereas an oversensitive Davis might hit back with savage remarks, Lincoln knew how to control his anger and disappointment with others. Regarding quarrels as unprofitable, Lincoln withheld letters – as when Meade failed to press his advantage after Gettysburg – he had written at the height of despair. He could admonish and rebuke without giving offence. While Davis might put self-justification before results, and find it difficult to admit he was wrong, Lincoln's self-worth allowed him to admit his mistakes to others.[15]

It oversimplifies the issue, however, to reduce the contrasting achievements in political management to the leaders' personal capabilities. We must recognize differences in political systems that presented Lincoln with an institutionalized opposition of a kind the Confederacy lacked, one that brought benefits as well as disadvantages. The Democratic opposition could be dangerous, powerful, and extreme, but it also provided a political channel for hostility, which helped identify and contain dissent, and gave Lincoln a target he could work on. He could appoint Democrats to political and military posts, and engage in a kind of "recognition" politics that helped bring opponents on board. His "antipartyism" differed from that of the Confederate states; he used the "Union" party in a nationalist effort to delegitimize his partisan opponents.

Davis faced no anti-administration party. No rival force stood in the congressional elections of 1863. Davis and his opponents shared the view that "they who engage in strife for … party aggrandisement deserve contemptous [sic] forgetfulness."[16] Yet the administration's critics – the upholders of the politics of liberty against the centralizing politics of national unity – grew ever more venomous in their sniping at the tyranny of Richmond.[17] And the voices of a disenchanted elite threatened to resonate amongst those less articulate common folk for whom tax policies, the exemptions of large planters from war service (the "Twenty-Negro law"), and substitutions gave evidence of a rich man's war. But this amorphous opposition could not be challenged, corralled, and delegitimized in the way that Lincoln's administration handled its Democratic foes.

THE PRESIDENT AS COMMUNICATOR: MOBILIZING THE PUBLIC

That Lincoln headed a powerful political party gave him a further advantage over Davis in an area critically important for them both: maintaining morale on the home front and amongst the fighting men. Military force and an organized economy would not alone secure victory. Essential to success was the nourishing and mobilizing of popular patriotism. Lincoln in particular pushed the Constitution to its limits, but the coercive means that both leaders were ready to sanction to combat disloyalty – the suspension of habeas corpus, military arrests, enforcement of the draft – were far less significant to each side's operations than the public's willing responses to appeals for loyal service.

Lincoln appreciated that, whatever the North's material superiority and success in preventing foreign intervention, without a regenerating patriotism his administration would founder on war-weariness. The pressure of war, however, gave him few opportunities to shape sentiment through long set-piece speeches. He spoke in public nearly 100 times, mostly modest remarks addressed to troops, or to well-wishers who came to "serenade" him. His two inaugural addresses and his celebrated speech at Gettysburg were rare exceptions. But Lincoln reached out by other means. The mass-produced lithographs and photographs carried his image into thousands of homes. His carefully crafted public letters addressed issues crucial to the conduct of the war: emancipation, conscription, treason, military arrests, and the suspension of habeas corpus. His prose had color and energy: Harriet Beecher Stowe praised language that had "the relish and smack of the soil."[18]

Mathew Brady's photograph of Lincoln, taken in January 1864, suggests an assured and confident president. That assurance would be severely tested by the Union's military experience during the spring and summer. (GLC 05111.02.0015 The Gilder Lehrman Collection, courtesy of the Gilder Lehrman Institute of American History, New York)

In setting out the meaning of the war, offering his vision of a Union founded on the universal principles of the Declaration of Independence, and explaining how that ideal had to embrace a new role for African Americans, Lincoln tapped the Union's deep well of patriotic and religious sentiment. Also, in seeking out the most potent agencies to mobilize that opinion, Lincoln looked beyond the official institutions of government to the most powerful of the nation's voluntary networks: the political party, the churches and their philanthropic agencies, and the citizen army. Tapping their steadfast loyalism, the president projected his cause into the heartland of the Union.

As war-weariness grew, Lincoln looked to Republican congressmen, governors, local leaders, and newspaper editors to sell each new statement of policy and national purpose. Systematic news management lay in the future, but Lincoln controlled the press's access to his meetings, and rewarded loyal editors with lucrative jobs and printing contracts. The churches, too, provided Lincoln with a

OPPOSITE *Lincoln and his vice-presidential running-mate, the Tennessee War Democrat, Andrew Johnson, are presented as the harbingers of freedom and national well-being: above their portraits is a "Temple of Liberty," below a scene of bucolic prosperity. (Library of Congress)*

potent weapon. He met editors of religious newspapers, influential preachers, and representatives of humanitarian bodies. He wanted to show that the nation's chief executive recognized his dependence on Divine favor. In his proclamations for days of fasting and thanksgiving, and in speeches summoning a moral understanding of the nation (the Gettysburg Address; the Second Inaugural) observers perceived a "deep religious feeling." For their part, the majority of Protestant leaders put their full-blooded Unionism at the service of the administration's patriotic politics. Lincoln also turned to the Federal army to rally support. Most Union soldiers were, or came to be, staunch Republicans, loyal to "Father Abraham" and dedicated to the values symbolized by their flag. Federal citizen-soldiers played an essential role in mobilizing the wider Union public behind the president's reelection in 1864.

If Davis did not match Lincoln's power in mobilizing support, he still worked impressively to deliver meaning to the conflict. With an eye on both domestic and foreign opinion, he sought to show that Confederates were united by something more elevated than defending the slave system. Shrewdly recognizing the socially divisive potential of apologias for slavery, Davis instead sought to "bind [and] ... cement ... together" all southerners behind the Founders' ideals of liberty and self-government, in resistance to tyranny and political slavery: "will you be slaves or will you be independent?" he demanded.[19] Making a public profession of faith during the second year of the war (through confirmation in the Episcopal Church), and breaking radically with southern convention by calling for days of public fasting and prayer, Davis cast the Confederate cause as holy and righteous. Even in the last desperate months of the rebellion he asked his people to believe that while God "may chastise us for our offences, ... in doing so He is preparing us, and in His good Providence will assist us, and never desert the right."[20] By that late point in the war, the president was beginning to prepare the public for the dramatic logic of his unwavering commitment to independence: proposing the government's purchase and ownership of slaves, the use of slaves as soldiers, and even the possibility of emancipation.

In contrast to Lincoln, largely pinned in Washington, the Confederate president made time to leave his own capital and carry a message into the southern heartland. Making three protracted trips westward within two years, Davis seized the chance to deliver an abundance of short speeches and longer addresses, to review troops, and to make himself generally visible. He was particularly at ease amongst his fighting men. Only during the last of these excursions, after the fall of Atlanta, did he encounter a significantly mixed response. Even then, his addresses, circulating widely in the press, seem to have worked as something of a tonic: parading the president's confidence in ultimate success, calling for the return of deserters, appealing to Confederate women to use their

1864

2 September

Sherman occupies Atlanta: By capturing Atlanta, Sherman seized the second-most important city still in Confederate control. The strategic significance of the victory was nearly overshadowed by the political importance, which resuscitated Lincoln's flagging electoral hopes in the fall election.

TEMPLE OF LIBERTY.

ABRAHAM LINCOLN.

ANDREW JOHNSON.

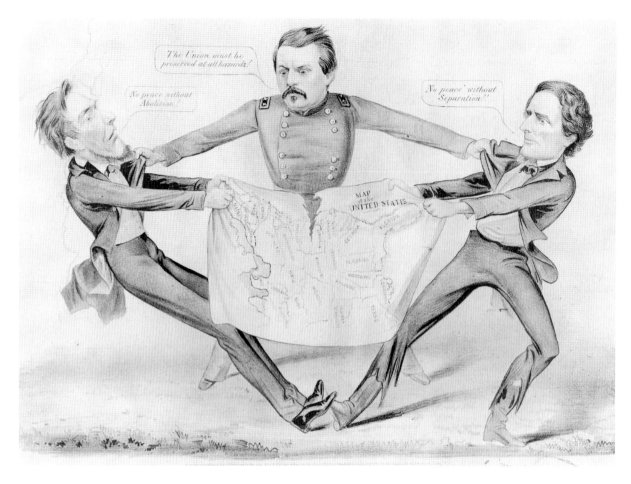

Here Democratic propagandists present their presidential candidate, George B. McClellan, as a true conservative who can preserve the Union: Lincoln's insistence on emancipation and surrender as the basis for reunion makes him as much as Davis an obstacle to national restoration. (Library of Congress)

influence, and insisting that only victory on the battlefield would secure a permanent independence. Davis retained a high degree of personal loyalty for the duration of the war, despite growing unrest. Insofar as the war saw the forging of a Confederate nationalism – fragile though it was – he played an essential part in its construction, though after 1863 Lee's army probably did more than the Richmond government to sustain it.

As a communicator, however, Davis lacked the Union president's common touch. His addresses and public letters lacked the striking metaphors of Lincoln's prose; a 52-page pamphlet was probably not the most effective means of responding to Joe Brown's accusations of tyranny. Davis – upper-class planter and Episcopalian – was respected but rarely loved by ordinary folk. In the judgment of one historian, the president simply did not have the language or the empathy to fashion a popular ideology able to speak for those suffering from the effects of inflation, impressments, and shortages. And to Davis's personal shortcomings should be added circumstances that denied him an organized political party that could operate as an engine of propaganda and mobilization; and which left him with a dwindling of those resources – paper and skilled labor especially – necessary for the sort of substantial and loyal newspaper presses on which Lincoln could rely.

Several conclusions should follow from this brief analysis of the two Civil War presidents. First, we should be wary of taking as an explanation for either president's approach to government Lincoln's statement that he had been controlled by events. Each president had a seam of fatalism (a valuable source of self-protection during the darkest days of war), but neither acted as if he lacked the power to shape the course of the conflict. Activism, not passivity, was the prevailing creed of each. It is worth noting that Lincoln's words to Hodges were written to persuade conservative Kentucky Unionists – electorally important in 1864 – that his emancipation policy had been forced on him by the changing circumstances of war. It overstated the crushing limits within which all leaders must act, and deliberately understated his own remarkable capacity for recognizing choices and seizing the moment to act.

Second, however, we have to guard against granting so powerful an influence over events to each president that the quality of his leadership is deemed the element that defined the war's outcome. Great historian though he was, it is hard to go along with David Potter's verdict that Davis's leadership presents such:

> a record of personal failure [that] … it hardly seems unrealistic to suppose
> that if the Union and the Confederacy had exchanged presidents with one
> another, the Confederacy might have won its independence.[21]

Leadership mattered, but so too did political systems, human and material resources, economic organization, military capabilities, the interests of foreign powers, and – powerfully evident in time of war – contingency and the law of unintended outcomes.

Finally, it is important to erase from the mind that by which it is too easy to judge presidential leadership during the Civil War: the image of emancipationist victor *versus* defeated slaveowner. Lincoln's reputation, variable in the wartime Union, was subsequently transformed by national rebirth, the death of slavery, and his own assassination; in contrast, Davis's unsuccessful struggle on behalf of a people mired in a moral enormity has understandably done him few favors. In fact, as this essay suggests, Lincoln rose remarkably to the crisis he faced: his was the achievement of a political master whose capacities bordered on genius. But Davis's qualities in the realms of strategic vision, political management, military grasp, and encouragement of public morale were evident, too, as were his courage, resolve, and dedication to the cause. They were, certainly, mixed with serious inadequacies in judgment and temperament. But perhaps what he lacked most was luck. It is his bad fortune that he will always be measured against the most exacting of standards: those set by his opposite number in Washington, perhaps the most accomplished wartime leader of modern history.

> *"I find myself in a new and strange position here: President, cabinet, Gen. Scott, and all deferring to me. By some strange operation of magic I seem to have become the power of the land."*
>
> George B. McClellan to his wife, 1861

The power of the land
Leadership on the Battlefield

Robert K. Krick

"There is in every battlefield a decisive point," Antoine Henri Jomini wrote in *Précis de l'Art de la Guerre* (1838), "the possession of which, more than any other, helps to secure victory by enabling its holder to make a proper application of the principles of war." A quarter-century later, American officers serving the United States and the Confederate states proved the axiom again and again. Leaders who won battles skillfully identified crucial positions, and inspired their soldiery to hold and exploit them: Marye's Heights at Fredericksburg, Snodgrass Hill at Chickamauga, Culp's Hill at Gettysburg, Fort Sanders at Knoxville.

At the beginning of 1861, the United States Army mustered an authorized strength of only about 15,000 of all ranks. Barely more than 1,000 of those were commissioned officers. Within a scant few months hundreds of thousands of men were carrying muskets in the ranks of armies, North and South, and their numbers continued to swell. Eventually some 3,250,000 men served, about 1 million of them as Confederates.

During the Civil War, General R.E. Lee carved out an unexcelled record, but in 1861 he had little battle experience on which to draw. During three decades of service in the United States Army, Lee had enjoyed much success in staff roles, but had never led any substantial body of troops in combat. (Author's collection)

THE FORMATIONS OF WAR

Since 1865, counting numbers and losses and arguing about them has been a popular pastime. Books and articles on the subject, most poorly written and full of jingoism, became a veritable cottage industry soon after the war. The once-warring sections looked askance at everything published in enemy country. Even among friends, states calculated their contributions of soldiers generously, and discounted the numbers of their out-of-state brethren. A thorough computer-based index to all official Compiled Service Records (CSRs) at the National Archives, done during the 1990s, has vanquished most of the doubt. Confederate CSRs number 1,373,000, and Federal CSRs fall just short of 3 million.

Those records, meticulously arranged by name and unit, include a good bit of duplication as individuals moved from one organization to another. The perceived joys of cavalry service triggered the most pronounced tides. The apparently less dangerous, more glamorous, less onerous mounted duty appealed to weary infantrymen. "If you want to have a good time," General "Jeb" Stuart sang as he bestrode a gaily caparisoned steed, "jine the cavalry." Men who could manage the switch did so. Extensive work in the original CSRs suggests that at least 20 percent of men have records with more than one unit. The proportion surely does not exceed 30 percent. Applying a 25 percent duplication factor equally to both sides suggests that just a few more than 1 million men wore Confederate uniforms, first and last, and about 2.25 million Federals. Partisans will avidly, joyously argue about the numbers as long as ink lasts, but those round numbers unmistakably come amply close to the truth.

Where could combat leadership for the swarms of citizen-soldiers be found? The trained and experienced officers in the US Army had been no more than adequate to manage 14,000 men. They obviously, therefore, must have been less than $1/200_{th}$ capable of leading more than 3 million. Even those professional leaders had seen little, if any, duty at the head of sizable units in battle.

Coping with that logarithmic expansion, absolutely unparalleled in scope throughout American history (before or since), dreadfully strained the capacity of each side in 1861. The cozy notion that the citizen yeomanry could simply be armed and pointed at an enemy had never borne much relation to actual military verities over the years, despite the fondness of Americans for a mythical militia mystique. In 1861, on the eve of what aptly has been called the first modern war, circumstances overtook the militia concept and drowned it in a sea of raw levies utterly unprepared for what they faced.

The earnest young Americans who flocked to enrolling stations all across both countries organized into companies, to which they proudly attached names such as the "Clinch Mountain Boomers," "Tyranny Unmasked Artillery," and "Mississippi Yankee Hunters." That lowest tactical unit on Civil War battlefields (platoons did not appear on 1860s organization tables) consisted almost always of men from a locality. Most men in a company had known their mates before the war, and would live amongst them after 1865. Their neighbors and kinsmen signed them up for service; others became their officers.

Infantry companies numbered 100 men when mustered into service. By the time most units faced heavy combat in midwar, company strength had dwindled markedly. At Chancellorsville in May 1863, with the war approximately one-half over, Confederate companies averaged about 41 men, and Federal companies 45.

Modern auditors must adjust to the absence of battalions in Civil War tactical formations. The triangular system so familiar from later wars – three rifle companies in a battalion, three rifle battalions in a regiment – had not yet taken hold. The tiny handful of battalions on Civil War rolls were regiments that did not quite muster enough companies. In an important wartime adjustment, Confederates did cluster artillery into battalions, and Federals then did likewise. Infantry regiments did not include component battalions, however: regimental leaders commanded the entire unit, dealing directly with captains and their companies. Three field-grade officers of the line led each regiment: a colonel, lieutenant-colonel, and major. When all three were present, a by-no-means certain occurrence, the two junior officers played subordinate leadership roles, usually without direct tactical command.

Captains led companies, whether of infantry, cavalry, or artillery. Colonels commanded ten-company regiments. Brigades made up of four or more regiments answered to a brigadier-general. "Troops furnished by the same State" a Confederate brigadier explained, "were, as far as possible, brigaded together, in order to stimulate State pride, and a spirit of healthy emulation."[1] The United States War Department did not adopt that system. Federal brigades routinely included regiments from two states, if not more.

Divisions, usually of about four brigades, warranted a major-general. Confederate lieutenant-generals commanded corps (made up of multiple divisions), but Federal armies of the 1860s never adopted that practice, which led to some confusion – then and now.

Regiments constituted the most important tactical building block during the Civil War, and usually elicited the greatest loyalty from the troops. A man amply proud of his company, and perhaps of his brigade or division too, still would first identify himself as a member of, say, the 14th Indiana Infantry. Regimental leadership therefore ranked high on the list of requirements for military success.

SKILL AT ARMS

Most Americans with demonstrable ability, in both the North and the South, who had military training and/or experience advanced to general-officer rank. Whence, then, came the colonels? Most of them had occupied prominent roles in civilian life, and hoped to parlay talents in those lines into military leadership. The transition rarely came easily, and in all too many cases proved to be impossible.

Among the nearly 2,000 men who held field-grade rank in one large army (R.E. Lee's Army of Northern Virginia), fewer than 5 percent had attended the United States Military Academy at West Point. Another 10 percent had some military education at one of the South's state-operated military schools, notably the Virginia Military Institute. That admixture of leaders with military education certainly stood the army in good stead, and gave it a leavening of professionals well beyond the average in Civil War armies. Even so, those trained men still mounted up to not much more than a tincture amidst a sea of abject amateurs: in that army, six of every seven field officers did not have any military training.

The one notable pre-Civil War military proving ground had been the campaigns in Mexico in 1846–47. Only one in 15 field officers in the same army sample cited above had been in Mexico. Given the typical age profile of the field officers, most of that handful of Mexican War veterans obviously had been subalterns or even private soldiers a decade and a half before. Experience at that level must have been of some value as preparation for the general rigors of war, but it would not have involved much leadership background, if any at all.

Furthermore, the revolution in arms and techniques during the interval rendered many Mexican War lessons moot. At the battle of Buena Vista in 1847, Colonel Jefferson Davis of Mississippi performed well at the head of a regiment. Some have postulated that the Confederacy was lost on February 22, 1847, on the unkind premise that Davis's success in that minor role convinced him of his own military genius, to the detriment of the country he attempted to lead years later. The notion is simplistic, but it does illustrate the chasm between military affairs of 1847 and 1862.

Wars always have been fought by young people. Civil War colonels averaged only 32 years of age, and the median age (a measure less affected by extremes) was not much more than 30. More of them were lawyers or politicians than followers of any other profession, and by a wide margin. Many of the rest had been farmers and planters, or businessmen and clerks. Turning young men, successful in civilian pursuits, into regimental leaders proved to be difficult indeed, on both sides of the Potomac River. Some proved to be born to the role; others manfully did their level damndest, and proved to be capable in most instances; a great many more simply failed, at great cost to their troops and to their respective causes.

By the time that green citizen-soldiers serving as regimental and company officers began to grasp the requirements of battlefield leadership, politicians on both sides interrupted the maturation process in a fashion that strains credulity. Early in 1862 the Confederate Congress passed the first-ever nationwide "draft," and their counterparts in Washington soon followed suit. Leaders on both sides faced a new problem: how to blend conscripts with volunteers into a cohesive unit. The new system imposed an even more fundamental change. As a dose of sugar to help the conscription medicine go down, the law allowed enlisted men to elect their officers by popular vote. That device knocked the entire system of command into the proverbial cocked hat.

Implementing this revolution in the selection of officers varied in different organizations and at different times, but everywhere and always the politicizing of army command led to the electioneering excesses customary in such processes. Good officers who imposed necessary discipline often were ousted as a penalty for their responsible demeanor. In the famous old 1st Virginia Cavalry (the renowned Jeb Stuart and Fitzhugh Lee had been its first two colonels), an orderly sergeant aspiring to win a lieutenancy allowed the men to lie in their bedrolls while he called the morning muster. He also promised them that if elected he would have the company reorganized as artillery and have it transferred to duty near their homes. Neither thing, of course, lay remotely within his power to achieve, but promising impossibilities always has seemed attractive to candidates. (As an American pundit said of a presidential candidate in another century: "If there had been any formidable body of cannibals in the country he would have provided them with free missionaries fattened at the taxpayers' expense.")

1862

1 June

Lee assumes command of Confederate army at Richmond: Lee reversed Joseph Johnston's policy of careful retreat by attacking McClellan's larger army while it was divided. He successfully pushed Union forces back to the James River, fundamentally altering the momentum of the conflict.

A Georgian repulsed by the electioneering atmosphere wrote home in May 1862:

> It is a time replete with feelings of disgust and contempt... A man is perfectly bewildered by the intensity of the affection that is lavished upon him. I never dreamed before that I was half as popular, fine looking and talented as I have found out I am, during the past few days.[2]

Even if the new, elected, leaders afforded better potential than the supplanted commanders (and they probably in fact did not), the hard-earned experience of the original officers now went for naught. In the Confederate army defending Richmond early in 1862, the elections replaced more than one-third of the regimental officers, and probably an even larger proportion at the company level. (Neither side ever elected officers above the rank of colonel.)

With a large enemy army thronging at the gates of its capital, the Confederate army's elections hamstrung its efficiency. Richmond survived thanks to Federal lassitude, some good luck, and a skilled and determined resistance led by General R.E. Lee. For the remainder of the war, leaders on both sides had to cope with the challenge of pleasing an electorate. Generals had to rely upon the judgment and leadership of regimental officers elevated not because of ability, but rather due to electioneering skills.

LOSSES AND LOGISTICS

Officers directing citizen-soldiers in battle often led from the front – literally at the forefront of battle. One of the Civil War's most famous images is that of General Lewis A. Armistead, his hat impaled on a waving sword, charging at Gettysburg on July 3, 1863. Armistead paid for his bravery with his life, as did scores of other generals, and fully one-quarter of regimental officers. (Painting by Don Troiani. www.historicalartprints.com)

Regimental leaders – whether appointed early in the war or elected later – died in astonishing numbers. The necessity of inspiring citizen-soldiers in battle often obliged Civil War commanders to lead from the front, literally advancing with the front line, sometimes waving swords or flags. A worse prospect from the actuarial perspective would be hard to imagine. The advent of rifled muskets had rendered such leadership moot, but military and societal norms only adapted slowly. Even though rudimentary tactical evolutions began to adjust to the deadly range of rifles, expectations of officers' demeanor only slowly ceased being wedded to a past era. As a consequence, the war killed fully one-quarter of the field-grade officers in line regiments. That ghastly harvest of dead colonels numbered about 50 times greater mortality than among Americans of like ranks and duties during World War II.

In addition to the dire human consequences of such casualties – staggering loss of life, shattered homes, vanished potential – the military effect of dead leaders complicated military operations. Without forgetting the horrible losses in human terms, we can recognize also their impact upon military operations. Every officer killed or invalided out of service exacerbated the problem of finding and training leaders. On average, it is impossible to avoid the conclusion that many of the bravest and best shed their blood doing their deadly duty. Replacing any experienced general or field officer would be difficult, successively more so as the war dragged on, for both armies.

Military men are prone to say, in referring to the interests of modern students: "Amateurs study tactics, professionals study logistics." Supply functions necessarily underpin everything that armies do in preparation for higher-profile activities in conflict with an enemy. Napoleon Bonaparte summarized the matter famously: "An army marches on its stomach."[3] An old military saying carries the same theme: "biscuits are more important than bullets."

The contending forces in the American Civil War faced markedly different logistical challenges. Northern leaders enjoyed access to a vast cornucopia of resources of almost every kind, and employed a strong railroad network to distribute the riches. Federal commanders still had to arrange the intricate matter of carrying that materiel from depots to points of need, but they rarely wanted for the basic sinews of war.

Southern logisticians could only envy their enemy's mechanical and industrial wealth, which far exceeded Confederate capacities. The crucial matter of arming, feeding, and equipping Confederate armies vividly revealed the vital impact of leaders on military affairs. In a country bereft of large industrial works, chief of ordnance Josiah Gorgas somehow contrived to keep southern soldiers steadily supplied with arms and ammunition. By stark contrast, Confederate Commissary-General Lucius B. Northrop failed egregiously at his task of keeping those same men fed. Gorgas's brains and energy conquered a staggering challenge. Northrop, querulous and quarrelsome and widely loathed, never managed to convey enough of the produce of the lush agricultural South to a starving soldiery. Among the problems he never recognized was the startling fact that the president of an immensely important Virginia railroad, a prewar immigrant from the North, spent the war as a spy and saboteur in the pay of the United States. It would be hard to draw a more telling picture of the impact of individual leaders on a national cause than by comparing those two men who occupied essential logistical billets. The man with an almost insuperable task succeeded. The man with plenty of raw material close at hand failed miserably.

LEADERSHIP AND TERRAIN

The immense northern advantages in materiel proved especially useful in the war's western longitudes. The two primary military theaters in which the American Civil

FORT DARLING ON DREWRY BLUFF BELOW RICHMOND

War unfolded varied dramatically in extent and configuration. What historians customarily call "the western theater" stretched far across the trans-Alleghany region to the Mississippi River. Mighty rivers played a crucial role, cutting their courses through that vast stretch of mountains and valleys in directions detrimental to Confederate defensive plans. All-but-uncontested control of navigable waters by the US Navy condemned southern defenders to a nervous existence, with no flank permanently secure. Federal logistical might poured supplies down rivers and railroads to armies that moved steadily forward.

Northern hegemony in all things naval of course affected military affairs in "the eastern theater" too, but not as profoundly as in the West. Most operations in the East focused on Virginia, sometimes moving into Maryland and southern Pennsylvania. Fortunately for southern defensive options, the rivers along the mid-Atlantic littoral ran nominally west to east (most typically, somewhat atilt from northwest to southeast). Accordingly they afforded barriers to invasion, instead of serving as convenient corridors for intruders as in the west. Rivers in Virginia and adjacent states, however, widened as they neared the Chesapeake Bay and the sea. As far upstream as they were tidal and navigable, the United States Navy controlled them. The fall lines of the region's primary rivers marked the western edge of that naval fiefdom: Washington on the Potomac; Fredericksburg on the Rappahannock; Richmond on the James; and Petersburg on the Appomattox. In the case of Richmond, powerful fortifications at Drewry's Bluff, a few miles downstream on the banks of the James, succeeded in extending Confederate control a few crucial miles below the capital city.

Federal shipping roamed deep into inland rivers. In this view, Admiral D.D. Porter's warships have penetrated far up the Red River. (Public domain)

Through the war's four years, the power of the land, especially the influence of the coastal geography and of the rivers that ran through the land, formed an imperative feature in prosecution of operations. A naval officer contemplating the war's evolution concluded:

> The transcending facts of the American Civil War are the military genius of Robert E. Lee and the naval superiority of the North... Lee's tactical opponent was the Army of the Potomac, but his strategic rival was the Union Navy.[4]

Thus the power of the land and its rivers configured the stage upon which military operations transpired. In the East, the navigable rivers and the looming mountains beyond the Shenandoah Valley left a usable front that stretched in some places only about 70 miles wide. Armies in the West regularly moved in zones that offered maneuver options – and defensive headaches – stretching across many hundreds of miles of width.

In Virginia and its environs, General R.E. Lee spent three years operating in masterful fashion across the narrow stage imposed by geography. With hindsight, it is easy to speculate that Lee's prowess in maneuver might have been even more useful in the broad western theater than in the straitened terrain in the East. Federals focused on defeating Lee and his army by getting to Richmond ground forward repeatedly, and repeatedly came back unsuccessful and battered. General George B. McClellan had two chances at Lee, while commanding the Federal Army of the Potomac. Generals John Pope, Ambrose E. Burnside, and Joseph Hooker

Eastern Theater of Operations, May 1861–June 1863

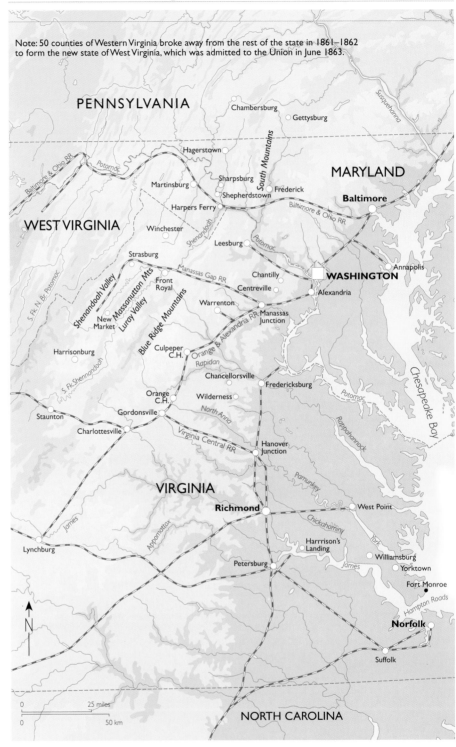

Note: 50 counties of Western Virginia broke away from the rest of the state in 1861–1862 to form the new state of West Virginia, which was admitted to the Union in June 1863.

Western Theater of Operations

failed once each. When the calmly competent George G. Meade assumed command of the Army of the Potomac, he won at Gettysburg a few short hours after taking control and led that seasoned organization on to Appomattox.

In Tennessee and Georgia, the Confederate cause did not enjoy leadership anywhere close to the caliber that Lee supplied in Virginia, nor even a faint simulacrum. The wildly unpopular General Braxton Bragg exercised Confederate command there longer than any other officer, at the head of the Army of Tennessee. Later Joseph E. Johnston grudgingly assumed responsibility for much of the western theater, and eventually the government in Richmond selected John B. Hood to take command of a forlorn hope. Early in the war, the southern cause in that region held on in the face of Federal leaders ranging from poor to mediocre – men such as Don Carlos Buell, Henry W. Halleck, and William S. Rosecrans. At midwar, the brilliant campaign to reduce Vicksburg, Mississippi, engineered by General Ulysses S. Grant, fractured the backbone of the Confederacy, and eventually Grant's protégé William T. Sherman then ran roughshod over a region prostrated by a long war.

The unusual, complex blend of personal characteristics that yield a man capable of leading a large army to victory appears only infrequently. Those occasional instances of military prowess fascinate students of history. Only R.E. Lee clearly displayed that capacity during the pivotal year of 1862. Late in the war, several northern leaders shone at a time when powerful advantages in manpower and war materiel had created a strikingly different military environment. General Philip

General Winfield Scott, far past his years of glorious field service but still a perceptive leader, recognized that the best means for restoring the Union was to isolate the Confederacy and squeeze its boundaries. (Public domain)

Sheridan, for instance, defeated a Confederate army in Virginia's Shenandoah Valley late in 1864, at a time when he had as many cavalrymen in his command as his foe had troops of all arms – infantry, artillery, and cavalry combined. Winning out in such a setting required energy and determination, to be sure, but it hardly warrants comparison to the strivings of leaders on both sides before the war had reached that penultimate stage.

One of the most impressive figures in all of America's military annals, now largely forgotten, is General Winfield Scott (1786–1866). After displaying magnificent front-line heroism on the Canadian frontier during the War of 1812, and becoming a youthful general officer by 1814, Scott led an American army from Vera Cruz to triumph at Mexico City in 1846–47. His observations on R.E. Lee in Mexico had prompted the prescient Scott to call the Virginian "the very best soldier that I ever saw in the field."[5]

Although a Virginian himself, General Scott stayed north at the beginning of the Civil War. He had feuded bitterly with Jefferson Davis when the latter had been United States secretary of war, in 1856 writing to him a gorgeously dismissive sentence: "Compassion is always due to an enraged imbecile."[6] In 1861, physically doddering and spectacularly obese – but still amply acute – Scott recognized the solution to conquering the rebellious Confederacy. He proposed that the North's long naval reach should establish firm control of the coastlines and allow Federal might to overwhelm the nascent southern republic. Scott's "Anaconda Plan," named for the South American serpent that crushes victims within its powerful coils, foresaw the national policy that would win the war.

BATTLEFIELD EXPERIENCE

Professional soldiers who adapted to war's demands provided most of the successful leadership on both sides. None of them, however, despite excellent military educations and a bit of experience, in Mexico or on the western frontier, had led large formations into action before 1861. R.E. Lee's gaudy compliment from Winfield Scott came after important staff duty, but Lee's role had involved no actual command responsibility whatsoever. After long service on the frontier, Richard S. Ewell admitted in 1861, he "had learned all about commanding fifty United States dragoons, and forgotten everything else."[7] Soon he would be sending 20,000 Confederates into battle as a lieutenant-general directing an infantry corps.

Adaptation proved to be the key ingredient in battlefield success, as so often is the case in human affairs – adaptation to leadership demands, to the tactical impositions of terrain, and to the changing face of weaponry. Some men with no hint of military education or experience in their background proved themselves capable of meeting such challenges and advanced to high rank. Generals Wade Hampton, John B. Gordon, and Nathan Bedford Forrest typify that class within the Confederate armies. They had been before the war, respectively, a wealthy planter, a mine operator, and an uneducated planter and slave trader. John A. Logan (a lawyer and politician) and Francis C. Barlow (a journalist) forged similar careers in the Federal armies.

In some battlefield matters, southerners managed at least temporarily to offset shortages in men and materiel with élan. Confederate cavalrymen, born and bred to mounted life, kept the upper hand over their blue-clad counterparts through the first half of the war by virtue of their skill and dash. Unionist artillerymen benefited from the outset of the war from a huge advantage in both weapons and ammunition for the "long arm," and from sterling leadership by such men as the brilliant General Henry J. Hunt, chief of artillery of the Army of the Potomac. Southern gunners contrived to hold their own, until late in the war, as a consequence of energy and ardor. Confederate artillerists such as Edward Porter Alexander, Willie Pegram, R. Preston Chew, and John Pelham became legends as the leaders of bands of daring cannoneers.

Popular lore suggests that the military mind adjusts even more sluggishly than the human norm – that soldiers stubbornly fight each war with the strategy and tactics of its predecessor. Whether that maxim bears up generally may be debatable; Civil War leaders certainly adapted well in some instances to altered battlefield verities. Rifled shoulder arms of course doomed tactics of the Napoleonic stripe. The evolution took time, and thousands of soldiers died during the gradual transition to open-order tactics. Thoughtful leaders, however, began to react empirically by the spring of 1862, before most of the war's major engagements erupted. The creation of "sharpshooter" battalions in many brigades signaled the beginning of the shift.

To a modern reader, the word "sharpshooter" suggests a skilled rifleman attempting to hit a specific target, probably at long range. Civil War sharpshooter battalions included such men, and of course encouraged marksmanship, but their genesis and primary function was to screen an infantry line on both offense and defense. A better label, in modern usage, would be to call these new formations "skirmisher" battalions. They picketed in front of a line, and warned of approaching attackers. In an attack mode, they preceded the main infantry line to drive in the opposing skirmishers and develop intelligence about the enemy's position. Good military leaders had employed light troops in similar fashion in the age of smoothbore musketry; it now became essential and universal. This eminently practical evolution in tactics revealed the pragmatism of leaders on both sides, as they came to grips with a changed face of battle.

General Francis Channing Barlow (1834–96) graduated first at Harvard, studied law, and edited a New York newspaper. His steady rise through the ranks made him an archetype of the class of citizens-turned-soldier who found a calling in leading men in battle. (Public domain)

Major John Pelham fought a lone gun with such distinction at the battle of Fredericksburg that General Lee called the 24-year-old Alabamian "the gallant Pelham." He typified the dashing young officers whose élan helped bridge the gap in materiel between Confederate and Union artillery. A few months after his famous moment at Fredericksburg, Pelham died in action at Kelly's Ford. (Painting by Don Troiani. www.historicalartprints.com)

Even in units that did not form official sharpshooter battalions, the use of regular companies to discharge that vital duty quickly became tactical doctrine. A seasoned Confederate brigadier general, veteran of many famous battles, described how the system worked:

> The regiment was formed… in line two-deep, covered by skirmishers… Sometimes two companies were extended as skirmishers; sometimes one company… In rear of the skirmishers, at a distance ranging from three hundred to one hundred and fifty paces, came the remainder of the regiment.

In wooded or confusing country, he noted, "the line of battle was greatly aided in maintaining the direction by the fire of the skirmishers."[8]

The power of rifled weapons also prompted the steady, sometimes rapid, evolution of earthworks. Good leaders mastered the changing science of field fortifications.

Similarly, innovative cavalry leaders came to recognize the potential, in an age of new weapons, for employing their troops in the fashion of mounted infantry. The better commanders routinely began to exploit that concept to good effect. Utilizing their horse-borne high mobility, troopers could move rapidly to decisive positions. Dismounting, leaving one man in four to hold the horses, the soldiers could then employ rifled shoulder arms – instead of the traditional cavalry armament of pistols and sabers – to establish control of the ground. Federals equipped with the repeating weapons that came into use late in the war proved especially effective. Mounted men would continue to operate, steadily less practically, on battlefields for many more decades, but the Civil War marked the end of a long era in which cavalry fought primarily from horseback.

Commanding positions on good ground served intelligent leaders well. Sometimes, though, even the most powerful land fell prey to determined men under good leaders. Federals successfully stormed the apparently unassailable Missionary Ridge near Chattanooga; bypassed the towering bluffs at Columbus, Kentucky; and conquered Marye's Heights (which had been impregnable in an earlier battle) during Second Fredericksburg. Confederates won the battle of Port Republic by overwhelming an apparently invincible battery atop the formidable "Coaling" ridge. Far more typically, though, the power of the land ruled battlefields: Hazel Grove at Chancellorsville, Little Round Top at Gettysburg, the Hornet's Nest at Shiloh, the Round Forest at Murfreesboro, Nicodemus Heights at Antietam.

Troops accustomed to victory under good officers usually coined fond appellations for them, often akin to family nicknames: "Uncle Billy" Sherman, "Marse Robert" Lee, "Uncle John" Sedgwick. When death of a leader broke the bonds forged in battle, soldiers faced a personal adjustment just as armies and governments attempted to fill the void. Some of the most frequently discussed counter-factual theorems about the Civil War turn on the question of the impact that dead officers might have made on later events. "What if" – General Albert Sidney Johnston had not bled to death at Shiloh in April 1862? Would the popular, experienced, charismatic Johnston have been able to defend the western Confederacy had he lived? Anyone would have been better than Braxton Bragg, but Johnston had not yet had an opportunity to exhibit his abilities on a broad stage, so the question will always remain open. "What if" – General John F. Reynolds had not been killed early on the first day at Gettysburg, or General Phil Kearny had not died near Manassas in the late summer of 1862? Both men had supporters who envisioned them successful at the head of an army. Neither general had the chance to prove them right or wrong.

The officer's death that generated the most comment about impact, with good cause, was that of "Stonewall" Jackson. When a mistaken volley by maladroit North

1862
17 September

Battle of Antietam: This battle denoted the high-water mark of Lee's 1862 invasion of the North, and his army's repulse provided a crucial boost for northern morale. It was also one of the deadliest single days of fighting in the war, or the nation's history, with more than 24,000 total casualties.

1863
10 May

Death of Stonewall Jackson: Shot accidentally by Confederate pickets following the battle of Chancellorsville, Jackson's death deprived Lee of one of his most trusted corps commanders. In death, Jackson became a symbol for all that was noble about the Confederacy.

1863

25 November

Battle of Missionary Ridge: The last phase of the battles around Chattanooga, the battle is remembered as one of the only in the war where attacking troops scaled an elevated position against artillery successfully. The victory enabled northern forces to begin pushing Confederates back into Georgia.

Carolinians of his own command laid Jackson low, southerners believed they had lost an invaluable military asset. They recognized the fear that Stonewall had inspired in his foes, and relished it. The Yankees "fear Jackson … as the little quadrupeds of the forest does the Lion," a Louisianian wrote.[9] When Jackson's replacement equivocated below Cemetery Hill at Gettysburg a few weeks later, the troops bewailed the absence of their resolute leader. "There we missed the genius of Jackson," an enlisted man wrote at the time. "The simplest soldier in the ranks felt it."[10] R.E. Lee himself endorsed the notion, telling an aide that he often thought that "if Jackson had been there he would have succeeded."[11] No one can say what Jackson would have achieved at Gettysburg or elsewhere had he lived; we will never know. Unmistakable, however, is the fact that no one stepped up to take his place as the reliable executor of Lee's imaginative military designs.

During the Civil War and in its aftermath, just as now and always in human affairs, perceptions often outweighed substance. Some superb leaders disappeared from view for no good reason. General George G. Meade took command of the Army of the Potomac mere hours before the largest battle ever fought in North America. Leading that sturdy but perpetually mismanaged army, he defeated Lee and herded the Confederates back across the Potomac, then capably commanded his army for the rest of the war. President Abraham Lincoln began grumbling immediately after Gettysburg that Meade had not completely destroyed Lee, and that impossibly shallow view took hold. Meade did not much like journalists, who did not help his access to public opinion. To this day, the competent Meade remains relatively unknown and unhymned, with no strong new biography in print or in prospect, despite being perhaps the best Federal general officer who fought in Virginia.

By contrast, exaggerated reputations embellish the reputations of others. George Armstrong Custer looms far out of proportion to his actual Civil War role, on the basis of gaudy uniforms and superficial plash – and especially because of the fantastic way he stumbled upon his just reward in Montana Territory a few years later. Joshua Lawrence Chamberlain today is among the most famous Union officers of his middling grade less because of what he accomplished than because he

Sometimes even the most powerful ground succumbed to determined men. The Union charge up Missionary Ridge near Chattanooga in November 1863 defied all of the odds by succeeding. (Public domain)

lived for many decades, hurling autobiographical bouquets to himself the while. His superior in a dramatic moment at Gettysburg remains virtually unknown, having died in action and thus missed the postwar publicity opportunities. One colleague bewailed Chamberlain's "robbing the dead" in that fashion, and described a congenital "inability to tell the truth."[12] The legendary power of the pen over the sword affects every era. Napoleon is quoted in that regard: "Four hostile newspapers are more to be feared than a thousand bayonets."

Virtually all of America's mid-19th-century males fought for their home states. The entire nation of that era went to war, and what they did changed the country fundamentally and permanently. Leaders of American armies in subsequent epochs grew out of the generations that faced the great battlefield tests of the 1860s, sometimes as direct descendants. The highest-ranking United States Army officer killed during World War II was General Simon Bolivar Buckner, Jr, whose father had surrendered Fort Donelson to Ulysses S. Grant in 1862. General Nathan Bedford Forrest III, a graduate of the United States Military Academy, died in June 1943. Stonewall Jackson's great-grandson, Colonel Thomas Jonathan Jackson Christian, Jr (also a West Pointer), remains missing in action over Arras, France, since August 1944. All of America's modern armed forces study their ancestral roots in the country's dreadful Civil War, and recognize their heritage growing out of that national ordeal.

ABOVE LEFT *Many southerners believed that the popular, charismatic General Albert Sidney Johnston would lead Confederate armies to success in the war's western theater, but he bled to death at Shiloh in April 1862. (Public domain)*

ABOVE RIGHT *General George Gordon Meade took command of the Federal Army of the Potomac in June 1863, just a few hours before the largest battle ever fought in North America – and won at Gettysburg. His success never translated into resounding fame, largely because of President Lincoln's ill-considered lack of enthusiasm, and hostility from the press corps. The sword never has been able to outshine the pen. (Public domain)*

> *"We have shared the incommunicable experience of war... we have felt, we still feel the passion of life to its top. In our youths, our hearts were touched with fire."*

Civil War veteran, Oliver Wendell Holmes, Jr, 1884

Our hearts were touched with fire
The Men who Fought the War

Gerald J. Prokopowicz

VOLUNTEERS

Perhaps the most remarkable characteristic of the armies that clashed at Shiloh, Gettysburg, and dozens of other battlefields from 1861 to 1865 was that none of them existed in 1860. When the Civil War began in April 1861, the Federal government had a tiny standing army of some 15,000 men, while the newborn Confederacy had no military force at all. Each state was supposed to have a ready militia, but by the 1850s most of these were moribund organizations whose annual assemblies had degenerated into parodies of military ceremony.[1] Rarely in history have two such large societies (19 million northerners and 9 million southerners, plus 3 million in the border states) gone to war with so little preparation.[2]

The first step in creating the armies that were to struggle with one another for four years was to call for volunteers. By the end of 1861, the governments of

The 7th New York Regiment parades down Broadway in April 1861. *Enthusiasm ran high in the first months of the war. (Collection of the New-York Historical Society)*

Abraham Lincoln and Jefferson Davis had requested 975,000 men to join the colors, and more than that number answered. They enlisted for many reasons. Some sought adventure; some were swept up in the excitement of the moment; some hoped to prove their manhood by emulating the deeds of their forefathers against the British in 1776 and 1812.[3]

Most, however, were motivated at least in part by their views on the issues that had increasingly separated the North and the South over the previous 30 years. Americans were intensely interested in politics, as evidenced by voter turnout percentages in presidential elections from 1840 to 1860 that far exceeded those of the 20th century. In the decade that followed the Compromise of 1850, sectional tension heightened to the point that many greeted the outbreak of war in 1861 with relief. At last, it seemed, here was a chance to put those perfidious Yankees or arrogant rebels in their place once and for all.

The armies of the Civil War were organized from the bottom up. Because the Federal government was so small (and the Confederate government non-existent) before the war, the process of organizing volunteer units was delegated to the individual states. The state governors, in turn, delegated the task of raising companies and regiments to their political allies and other prominent citizens, by giving them provisional commissions that were contingent on their success in recruiting. As soon as one of these would-be officers managed to enlist a hundred or so of his friends and neighbors, enough to form a company, he took them to the state capital or other rendezvous point, where he negotiated with other recruiters to form a regiment of ten companies. The volunteers also considered themselves entitled to play a role in the process, and insisted upon their right to conduct elections for their company and regimental commanders. Currying favor with voters proved incompatible with enforcing military discipline, however, and officer elections generally disappeared by the end of 1862.[4]

Whether elected or appointed, the officers who were responsible for turning their citizen volunteers into soldiers were almost entirely innocent of military knowledge. Of the 977 living graduates from the US Military Academy at West Point, 259 joined the Confederacy while 638 remained loyal to the Union.[5] Even after adding the graduates of state academies like the Virginia Military Institute and South Carolina's Citadel, as well as any volunteer officers with experience of fighting in Mexico, there were scarcely enough to meet the need for commanders of regiments, brigades, and divisions. The field and company-grade officers who conducted day-to-day training of the recruits were no more than recruits themselves.

Though they lacked professionalism, the volunteers of 1861 were not short of enthusiasm. They practiced close-order drill for hours, day after day. An Alabama soldier complained that his colonel "has the drill-mania, for I think he would rather drill than eat a good dinner" but admitted "I suppose however it is to our advantage."[6] Each regiment undertook its own training, some using the tactical manual authored by Union general Winfield Scott, others the tactics of Confederate general William Hardee. Regiments of German-speaking immigrants like the 42nd Indiana adopted the drill of the Prussian army, and both sides had numerous companies of Zouaves who mimicked the *pas gymnastique* of fashionable French light infantry units.

The endless hours of drill had multiple purposes. One was to break down the individuality of the volunteer, who believed that he was fighting for a society in which every free white male adult was politically equal, at least in theory. Saluting, standing at attention, and instant obedience to orders were alien behaviors, especially when the officers who were supposed to be accorded such deference were the friends and relatives of the rank and file. "Have we enlisted to secure freedom for others only to give up our own?" asked a private of the 17th Maine in his journal.[7] It often took weeks of drill before the men began to see themselves as soldiers and to take more pride in their unit's performance than in their individual political or social status.

Another purpose of drill was to prepare for battle. While modern armies use close-order drill simply as a way to instill the value of teamwork, Civil War regiments expected to employ on the battlefield the same maneuvers that they practiced on the parade ground. The most common infantry company formation was a line of two ranks, with the men standing shoulder to shoulder, each occupying a space as narrow as twenty inches. Such a compact arrangement kept the men together, allowed their captain to shout his orders to the entire unit, and produced a devastating volume of fire when every musket was discharged at once. Little attention was paid to marksmanship; instead, the troops were taught to load quickly and to fire volleys on command.[8]

After a unit had trained itself for anywhere from a few days to several months, it was formally mustered into national service. The ceremony was a significant moment in the transition from civilian to soldier. From this point, there was no turning back, at least for the next three years (the most common term of enlistment in Federal service), or for the war (as it turned out for many Confederates, whose government unilaterally extended their one-year enlistments).

Another important ceremony, sometimes combined with mustering, was the presentation of a flag by representatives of the regiment's home community. Regimental flags played a vital role on the battlefield, marking the unit's position amid the smoke produced by thousands of muskets and cannon, but their importance went beyond their tactical value. The flag symbolized both the identity of the regiment, and the connection between the soldiers and the people for whom they were fighting. There was no greater shame than to lose a flag to the enemy, and many color bearers gave their lives trying to protect their units' banners. Conversely, when Brigadier-General Alexander Hays and his aides tied captured rebel flags to their horses' tails and dragged them in the dust to celebrate the repulse of Pickett's

Charge, or when southern cavalrymen boasted of wiping their horses down with the enemy's "starry rag," they were expressing their deepest contempt, not so much for the other side's soldiers as for its entire way of life, as represented by its flags.[9]

Once a soldier joined a regiment, in theory he stayed with it throughout his service; official transfers from one regiment to another were rare. The regiment itself, however, might serve in the same brigade (consisting of four or five other regiments) through the war, or it could be shuttled from brigade to brigade as needed. In some cases, especially in the Confederate armies, all the regiments of the brigade were from the same state. The famed Stonewall Brigade, for example, consisted of the 2nd, 4th, 5th, 27th, and 33rd Virginia infantry regiments. Such brigades often developed the same kind of *esprit de corps* that characterized their component units. The practice in the Union armies, in contrast, was to combine regiments from different states, which made it harder for northern brigades to attain the same level of cohesion. A notable exception was the Iron Brigade (2nd, 6th, and 7th Wisconsin, 19th Indiana and 24th Michigan), which developed a very strong sense of unit pride, because although they came from different states its men were conscious of their regional identity as the only brigade in the Army of the Potomac made up entirely of Midwestern regiments.

Brigades were grouped into divisions, divisions into corps, and corps into armies. These larger units were subject to frequent reorganization. With no permanent standing, they rarely had the same grip on the loyalty of their members as did Union regiments or Confederate brigades. Union major-general Joseph Hooker used insignia to try to increase his men's identification with their corps; in March 1863 he introduced cap badges that designated the wearer's corps (by shape) and division (by color: 1st division red, 2nd division white, 3rd division blue). The system had some success, reflected for example in the slogan "Clubs are trumps" adopted by men of the II Corps in honor of their trefoil emblem. When the members of the III Corps objected to its consolidation with another unit in 1864, army authorities defused the situation by allowing the men "to retain the old diamond-shaped, flannel badges on their caps, a prudent concession under the circumstances."[10]

More commonly, however, whatever feelings soldiers had about their corps or army were directed toward its commander, and not the institution itself. Soldiers of Lee's Army of Northern Virginia demonstrated their intense loyalty to "Marse Robert" throughout the war, most notably when they followed his instruction to surrender in April 1865 rather than obey President Jefferson Davis's call for continued resistance.[11] The men of the long-suffering Army of the Potomac idolized George McClellan for the magnificent job he did in training, clothing, and equipping

Reading the news – off duty by Edwin Forbes. The typical volunteer was not lonely, serving with friends and relatives in a company (numbering 30–101 men) that functioned as his military family. Even so, soldiers were always eager for news from home. (Library of Congress)

them, and never fully got over their collective infatuation with him even after his weakness as a battle commander had become manifest.

LIFE IN THE RANKS

The experience of soldier life rarely met the expectations of the soldiers. In his postwar novel *Corporal Si Klegg and His "Pard,"* Union general Wilbur F. Hinman caricatured the naïve recruits and their families who could not imagine that military service would require doing without the comforts of civilian life.[12] The fictional Josiah Klegg, like many of the real boys of '61, went to war laden with books, extra clothing, cooking utensils, sewing kits, hair oil, umbrellas, and other impedimenta. When he was ordered to fall out to "get mustered," Klegg reacted with delight at the thought of an issue of mustard, which he imagined would go well with the ham he expected as part of his ration.

Ham, unfortunately for the Josiah Kleggs of both armies, tended to find its way to the officers' mess, leaving the enlisted men with less desirable cuts of meat. Their main source of protein was salt pork, commonly called "sowbelly." This was taken from the sides or back of a pig, like bacon, but was preserved with salt instead of being cured, and was almost entirely fat. Boys who were accustomed to meals of cooked bacon at home soon found themselves eating slices of raw salt pork straight from the haversack, when the vicissitudes of campaigning did not allow time to stop and build a fire.

Traffic between the lines by Edwin Forbes. Confederate soldiers often lacked coffee but had ample supplies of tobacco, of which little was grown in the North. It was not uncommon for opposing pickets in quiet sectors to declare informal truces and meet to trade these prized commodities. (Library of Congress)

SI AS A RAW RECRUIT.   SI AS A VET.

In addition to salt pork, hardtack was the other staple of the soldier's diet. A piece of it resembled a large, thick soda cracker, but it was in fact rock hard and almost impervious to the tooth, which gave rise to the common wisecrack about biting into something soft in a piece of hardtack and finding a ten penny nail. Old hardtack often did in fact contain something soft, such as insect larvae, making it still more unpalatable. To eat hardtack, a soldier might pound it into fragments with the butt of his musket, cook it in the copious grease produced by frying a piece of salt pork, or soak it in his coffee. The latter was the most prized item in the soldier's standard ration, especially in the South where the Union naval blockade made imported coffee beans a scarce commodity. James Kidd of the 6th Michigan Cavalry wrote to his mother, "I can do without anything to eat but can not dispense with coffee."[13]

If army food was inferior in quality (and quantity, for more and more southern units as the war progressed), army clothing represented an even more abrupt break from what most recruits had enjoyed at home. In the mid-19th century, civilian clothes were made for the wearer individually, either sewn at home by family members or manufactured by skilled tailors. Ready-to-wear clothing was regarded as a badge of servitude, produced only for slaves and sailors. Joining the army of course meant submitting to wearing a uniform, but the independent-minded volunteers initially resisted the anonymity and uniformity of mass-produced military attire by going to war in outfits of their own design. Military fashion ranged from the finely tailored cadet look of the Clinch Rifles (Company A, 5th Georgia Infantry) to the kilts and sporrans of the 79th New York Cameron Highlanders. Not until after the First Battle of Bull Run, in July 1861, did a consensus arise that Union troops would wear blue and Confederates gray. By 1862 most of the prewar finery of Zouave units and militia companies had worn out and been replaced, in the North, by government issue sky-blue trousers and dark-blue blouses or jackets, all made of wool. In contrast, Confederate units tended to wear cotton, and in many cases to become less uniform in appearance as the war went on, especially in the western theater.

Regardless of its color or material, almost all military clothing of the Civil War had several things in common. One was that every item seemed to be issued in two sizes, either too large or too small. Another was that after it had been worn on campaign, it was infested with vermin. Soldiers took what opportunity they could to bathe in streams, or to boil their clothes in camp kettles, but most of the time they were subject to the constant torment of lice. As civilians, they would have regarded such a condition with horror, but as soldiers they soon became accustomed to the evening ritual of "skirmishing," taking off their shirts to better hunt for the insects and kill them between the nails of the thumb and forefinger.

Although the soldiers regarded lice as a nuisance and valued cleanliness, medical science had not yet progressed to the point of understanding the causal link between

Rebels and Yankees began the war wearing a wide variety of uniform styles. This Harper's Weekly illustration from 1861 shows a range of Confederate military fashion. (Courtesy of HarpWeek)

unsanitary living conditions and the spread of disease. In green, undisciplined regiments, little care was taken to dispose of human and animal waste in an orderly manner, with the result that local water supplies were often contaminated. Doctors ministered to patients and even performed surgical operations without taking care to wash their hands or instruments. Under these conditions, it is not surprising that many soldiers died of disease, more than were killed in battle.[14] Epidemics of childhood illnesses like measles, mumps, and chicken pox, which are merely uncomfortable for young children but potentially fatal for adults, swept through many new regiments and claimed as victims men who had grown up on farms in isolation from large numbers of other children, and thus had never developed immunities. Only after these and other diseases had run their courses, killing the weak and immunizing the strong, was a regiment considered "seasoned" and capable of serving without losing too many men to the sick list.

Most regiments traveled by train from their home states to an active theater of operations, but once they arrived almost all further movement was on foot or horseback. The first long road march was another landmark in the transition from civilian to soldier, as each weary step prompted the recruit to reconsider the need to carry all the items so lovingly bestowed upon him by friends and relatives when he enlisted. Throughout the war, whenever a newly raised regiment undertook its first significant march, it left behind a trail of discarded overcoats, blankets, books, utensils, mementos, and other baggage that seemed necessary to a life of minimal comfort as a civilian, but merely weighed down the soldier.

Veteran infantrymen learned to make do with a blanket roll, a haversack for food, a canteen, a tin cup, two small boxes worn on the belt (one for cartridges and the other for percussion caps), a musket, and a bayonet (used as an all-purpose tool more than as a weapon). Cavalrymen and artillerists could take advantage of their horses to carry a bit more personal gear, but they too learned to travel light. In 1861 a typical infantry regiment marched with as many as a dozen wagons laden with officers' trunks and other luggage, but by the end of the war it was not unusual for four or five regiments to go on campaign sharing only a single wagon.[15]

Marching was the primary military activity for most soldiers. The months that might elapse between battles were often filled with long and difficult marches. Ten miles was a good day's march for a corps of 20,000 men, resting every third or fourth day. An individual regiment could cover 20 miles a day for several days without undue strain. In emergencies, troops could move faster for short periods. A.P. Hill's Light Division marched 17 miles from Harpers Ferry to the battlefield of Antietam in just eight hours on September 17, 1862, arriving in the nick of time to save the Confederate right flank from crumbling. In the same month, the Union Army of the Ohio covered more than 300 miles in 27 days from Chattanooga to the Ohio River, outmarching by a narrow margin the rebel Army of Tennessee and preventing Braxton Bragg from capturing Louisville. These were exceptional accomplishments, and required great sacrifices of the troops. The experience of marching on blistered feet was described by one Union officer as "an incessant bastinado applied to oneself, from morning to night."[16]

SEEING THE ELEPHANT

The first year of service did much to strip away whatever romantic illusions of war the men may have held before enlisting. The real test of the soldier, and the experience that created an unbridgeable gulf between him and the civilians he left behind, was that of battle. Most new soldiers were extremely eager to "see the elephant," but few had any idea what it would look like. In the mid-19th-century American mind, Waterloo with its serried ranks of horse, foot, and guns was the paradigm of battle, and many popular visual representations of Civil War battles portrayed what the public expected.

On occasion, life imitated art and presented the grand spectacle of closely packed formations crossing an open field: there was Ambrose Burnside's attempt to send the Army of the Potomac up Marye's Heights at Fredericksburg, Pickett's Charge at Gettysburg, and John Bell Hood's desperate advance of the Army of Tennessee at Franklin, among others. But these attacks, and others like them, were bloody failures. Better generals tried to use more subtle tactics, taking advantage of terrain to outflank the enemy (as Stonewall Jackson did at Chancellorsville) instead of offering a mass target.

1864
4 May
Battle of the Wilderness: This was the first battle in the Overland campaign, and marked a new style of fighting in the Civil War. Confederates and Federals would fight nearly continuously for the next six weeks, producing over 90,000 total casualties.

Most Civil War soldiers thus did not see entire armies laid out before them in Napoleonic fashion. Some battlefields, like Shiloh, Chickamauga, or the Wilderness, were so heavily wooded that most men could see nothing but their immediate surroundings. Even on the relatively open plains of Manassas, "a man that is in the battle cannot tell much about it," as a survivor of First Bull Run wrote to his wife.[17]

Sound became as important a part of the experience of battle as sight. A distant booming meant that artillery was dueling with the enemy, which might or might not signal an impending engagement. A rapid series of smaller popping sounds indicated that infantry skirmishers were at work, while an almost indistinguishable mass of gunshots, comparable to the sound of an endless piece of canvas being torn, was the sign that lines of battle were blazing away at one another. Those who were in the front ranks of such a battle were soon enshrouded by heavy white smoke from their muskets, limiting visibility further. Under these conditions, men simply loaded and fired into the haze as fast as they could, and learned to judge the course of the battle by the rising or falling sound of the enemy's fire.

Battle as imagined. This postwar image reflects the public's lingering conceptions of battle: both armies are clearly visible, men march in straight lines, and heroic individuals like the officer in the lower left can determine the outcome of the event. (Library of Congress)

The weapon used by most infantrymen was a muzzle-loading rifled musket. It resembled the smoothbore musket that had dominated European and American battlefields for the previous 200 years, but it differed in that its barrel was rifled, meaning that it contained a spiral groove that imparted spin to the bullet as it was fired. This made the rifled musket far more accurate than the smoothbore, which could rarely hit a man-sized target beyond 100 yards. In the hands of a trained marksman, a Springfield or Enfield rifled musket could hit its target at ranges of 600 yards and beyond.

Since the mid-20th century, many historians have focused on the rifled musket as the cause of the high casualties and indecisive results of most Civil War battles. With such an extended field of fire, the argument runs, no attacking force could hope to close with the enemy and execute a decisive bayonet charge. Thus no Civil War army was ever destroyed on the field of battle, as Napoleon's was at Waterloo, with the exception perhaps of Hood's gravely weakened Army of Tennessee that dissolved after the battle of Nashville in late 1864. In dozens of other major encounters, attempts to use Napoleonic tactics against defenders equipped with long-range rifled muskets caused both sides to suffer heavy losses, and left the victors in little better shape than the vanquished, unable to exploit whatever success they had gained.

This explanation, however, does not withstand close scrutiny. Battles early in the war, including First Bull Run and Shiloh, conform to the pattern of high casualties and indecisive results, but they were fought by troops largely armed with old smoothbore muskets. Many other battles were fought in terrain where the full range of the rifled musket could not come into play, as woods and hills prevented troops from seeing the enemy until they were well within smoothbore range. Moreover, in later conflicts like the Franco–Prussian War in 1870, the defenders' use of rifled weapons did not prevent attacking forces from achieving decisive battlefield victories.

Even more significant is that the after-action reports submitted by field commanders show that they routinely discouraged their men from shooting at long range. They preferred to hold their fire until the enemy was close enough to be shattered by a sudden, deafening volley fired at the closest range possible, in order to deal the strongest emotional as well as physical shock to the enemy.[18] Ambrose Bierce, who served in the 9th Indiana at Shiloh, tried to capture the experience of advancing against a line of infantry "coolly holding its fire till it could count our teeth:"

Then – I can't describe it – the forest seemed all at once to flame up and

Battle as the soldiers saw it. Smoke obscures the enemy and even the unit's own front rank; the faceless men are not in step and wear variations of the standard uniform; and the prominent casualties in the foreground suggest that any victory will come at a high cost. (Library of Congress)

disappear with a crash like that of a great wave upon the beach – a crash that expired in hot hissings, and the sickening 'spat' of lead against flesh.[19]

For the purpose of close-range volley fire, the smoothbore was quite as effective as the rifled musket.[20]

While the technological impact of the rifled musket has been overstated, a more likely key to the bloody indecision of Civil War battles can be found in the social characteristics of the armies. Battles (in any war) are lost not necessarily by the army that has suffered the most casualties, but by the one whose will to resist first gives way. Military forces very rarely fight to the last man; instead, at some point those who have not been killed or wounded decide that their survival as individuals is more important than further resistance as a unit, and they begin to surrender, run away, or otherwise cease fighting.

In the Civil War, locally raised companies, regiments, and brigades often maintained their cohesion despite extraordinary losses. The numbers are almost legendary: the 26th North Carolina lost 714 out of 800 men at Gettysburg (89 percent of its strength); the 2nd Minnesota in the same battle suffered 82 percent casualties; in one charge at Cold Harbor, the 25th Massachusetts lost more than 71 percent of its men. By way of comparison, the destruction of the Light Brigade at Balaclava entailed a casualty rate of 37 percent.[21]

Why did these men stand and fight long after suffering casualties that in other wars would have driven most units from the field? In part, they fought for the same reasons for which they had enlisted. They were well informed on the issues that divided the nation, and believed deeply that they were fighting for the kind of America that the Founding Fathers had envisioned. Even in private letters to their wives, soldiers wrote with passion for or against the constitutionality of secession, the merits of free labor, and other points of political debate that might seem like mere abstractions to future generations, but were of vital importance to the men who fought for them.[22]

Religion, like politics, motivated Civil War soldiers. The Second Great Awakening, which lasted from roughly 1800 to 1840, made evangelical Protestantism the dominant religion throughout the United States, and a substantial majority of the men in blue and gray alike professed some form of Protestant Christianity. They found comfort in the idea that the cause for which they were fighting was just and holy, and that if they were to die, it would not be in vain. In late 1863 and 1864 a religious revival swept through the armies of both sides. If there was irony in the fact, as Abraham Lincoln observed in his Second Inaugural Address, that "both read the same Bible and pray to the same God, and each invokes His aid against the other," this did not lessen the importance that individuals attached to their faith.[23]

1865

4 March

Lincoln's Second Inaugural Address: With the end of the war in sight, Lincoln's brief address pointed toward a generous reconstruction. He called on Americans to pursue peace with "malice toward none; with charity for all."

Beyond politics and religion, the men fought for one another. Joshua Chamberlain, colonel of the 20th Maine during its heroic stand on Little Round Top, wrote that the soldier's deepest motivation to stand and fight was comradeship: "Here is Bill, I will go or stay where he does."[24] Studies of soldiers in more recent wars have confirmed that men will take great personal risks rather than be seen as letting down their fellow soldiers.[25] In the Civil War, this factor was compounded by the fact that a man's fellow soldiers were also likely to be his life-long friends, neighbors, and relatives. The option of running away in the face of danger was simply unavailable, unless the soldier was willing to lose his reputation for manhood not just within his company, but within his entire world, civilian as well as military. Word of a soldier's cowardice would inevitably reach his home community, bringing shame on his family and making it impossible for him to face his former comrades, to hope to marry a respectable woman, or even to find a decent job. If leaving the firing line meant the end of life as one knew it, standing and fighting no matter the cost was simply a rational choice. The social organization of companies, regiments, and brigades made it almost impossible to destroy a Civil War army, regardless of the weapons used.

VETERANS

In 1884, Oliver Wendell Holmes, Jr, said of his fellow Civil War veterans, "In our youths, our hearts were touched with fire."[26] For many of those who served, the touch was fatal. The 600,000 lives lost in the war are almost equal to the total lost in all of the United States' other wars combined. For those who survived, the verb "touched" seems a trifle too delicate. They were burned, seared, and forever changed by the experience.[27] They went from citizens to soldiers, and from soldiers to veterans. As the war progressed, their understanding of it evolved from innocent romanticism and patriotic idealism into a different and sometimes much harsher outlook, toward the enemy, toward civilians, and particularly toward the African Americans whose enslavement was "somehow" (in Lincoln's word) the cause of it all.[28]

One symptom of the war's increasing brutality was the poor treatment of prisoners. When the war began, neither side had any facilities for holding prisoners of war. Mass surrenders, like those of the Confederate army at Fort Donelson in February, 1862, or the Union garrison of Harpers Ferry in September the same year, presented the captors with enormous logistical problems. The solution was to parole captured soldiers and release them, trusting that they would not betray their promises not to fight again until duly exchanged. The system was obviously vulnerable to abuse; at the battle of Richmond, Kentucky in August, 1862, some 4,000 Union troops surrendered to a small Confederate force, knowing that their paroles would afford them a safe and honorable way out of the war. To crack down on such conduct, the Federal government began to imprison its own parolees at

In Prisoners from the Front, *Winslow Homer portrayed not only accurate uniform details but also characteristic attitudes, in the unrepentant young Confederate aristocrat and the supercilious Federal officer confronting each other after a battle. (Courtesy of Metropolitan Museum of Art, New York)*

1864

12 March

Grant commissioned to lieutenant-general: Grant's success at Vicksburg, and the West in general, convinced Lincoln that he could manage all the Union forces. Grant came east, where he brought a more aggressive strategy to the Army of the Potomac.

camps in Ohio and Maryland, holding them under guard until their names appeared on one of the lists of captured men that the warring governments periodically exchanged, after which the men were free to rejoin their regiments.

The parole and exchange system began to break down in 1863. Some Union officials argued against it after Confederate prisoners paroled from the capture of Vicksburg in July turned up in the ranks at Chickamauga in September, without having been properly exchanged. The system collapsed altogether following the large-scale enlistment of African American soldiers in the Union armies, authorized by the final Emancipation Proclamation of January 1, 1863. The Confederate government announced that it would treat all captured black men as escaped slaves rather than legitimate prisoners of war, and would prosecute their white officers for the capital crime of inciting servile rebellion. President Lincoln threatened retaliation, and both sides suspended any further exchanges. When Ulysses S. Grant became Union general-in-chief in 1864, he recognized that the return of prisoners was of much greater benefit to the manpower-starved rebel armies than to his own massive forces, and determined that the practice would not be resumed under any circumstances.

The end of prisoner exchanges led to one of the ugliest aspects of the war, the inhumane treatment of prisoners. Names like Camp Douglas (in Chicago), Elmira, NY, Point Lookout, Maryland, and most notorious of all, Andersonville, Georgia, became watchwords for horror, where thousands of prisoners died from inadequacies in food, sanitation, housing, and medical care. Andersonville's commandant, Henry C. Wirz, was executed for war crimes in 1865, the only person to be tried and found guilty of such conduct after the war.

That only one person was convicted and executed for war crimes should not disguise the fact that atrocities were committed by soldiers of both sides in increasing numbers as the war went on. From the start, areas where public loyalty was divided, like Kentucky and Missouri, were the scenes of brutal guerrilla warfare that pitted neighbor against neighbor. Events like the Shelton Laurel Massacre in 1863, when Confederate soldiers executed 14 pro-Unionist civilians in the mountains of western North Carolina, left scars that lasted long after the war's end.[29] Early in the war Federal soldiers were held under a tight rein by commanders like George McClellan and Don Carlos Buell, who forbade any destruction of civilian property, but as guerrilla resistance to Union occupation of the South increased, Federal officers began to give their troops more license to destroy property, take hostages, and even kill civilian or military prisoners in retaliation for guerrilla violence.[30]

In 1864, generals William T. Sherman in Georgia and Philip Sheridan in Virginia's Shenandoah Valley made the destruction of civilian property a formal policy. Sherman's "bummers," as even they came to call themselves, were ordered to take or burn everything in their path that could be of military use to the Confederacy. The legacy of Sherman's march through Georgia and the Carolinas is still bitterly recalled by many southerners, but neither side held a monopoly on cruel behavior. In Pennsylvania, civilians attacked a wagon train carrying wounded rebel soldiers from the battle of Gettysburg in 1863, and Confederate troops burned the town of Chambersburg to the ground in 1864; had more of the war taken place in the North, there surely would have been just as much bushwhacking by northern civilians, and property destruction by southern soldiers, as occurred in the South.

One factor contributing to the deterioration in conduct toward civilians as the war continued was the introduction of unwilling soldiers into the ranks. The initial rush of volunteers subsided by 1862, and in April the Confederacy enacted the first conscription law in American history. The Federal government passed a similar measure in March 1863. Both draft laws were filled with loopholes; one could hire a substitute, or pay a fee of $300 to escape the current draft, or (in the South) claim an exemption for one white man per 20 Negroes owned by the household. Districts that met their volunteer quotas were exempt from the draft, so localities began to offer large bounties to convince willing men to enlist, sparing the rest the risk of conscription. In contrast to the enthusiastic and politically motivated volunteers of 1861, the draftees often made poor soldiers, and were shunned by the old hands of

1864
15 November

Sherman begins March to the Sea: After burning Atlanta, Sherman launched a sustained raid through Georgia. Building on previous raids, his army lived off the land, destroying what they could not consume. Sherman intended the movement to demonstrate the weakness of the Confederate government to protect its citizens and their property.

their units. A Confederate artillerist wrote, "The pride of the volunteers was sorely tried by the incoming of conscripts – the most despised class in the army – and their devotion to company and regiment was visibly lessened."[31]

Of all the changes in attitudes wrought by the war, none was more significant than that inspired by the participation of African American soldiers. In 1861, most northern volunteers saw themselves as fighting for the restoration of the Union, not the abolition of slavery. White racial superiority was an almost universal assumption among European Americans of the North as well as the South. The war, however, brought many northern soldiers into contact with slavery for the first time. Some felt sympathy for its victims, some anger at its perpetrators. As they recognized the importance of slavery to the southern war effort, many came to support emancipation simply as a way to weaken the Confederacy, regardless of their feelings about the slaves themselves.

The war similarly eroded resistance to the enlistment of African American soldiers. Both governments prohibited black men from serving as soldiers at the start of the war, but by 1863 the Union was actively recruiting them, ultimately enlisting 180,000. The heroic charge of the black 54th Massachusetts against Battery Wagner in August 1863 was widely reported in the North, lending support

The veterans' reunion at Gettysburg in 1913, 50 years after the battle, symbolized the reconciliation of the former enemies. (National Park Service, Gettysburg National Military Park)

to those who believed that black men could fight as effectively as white ones. Northern opponents of the war and the draft came to accept the idea of black volunteers, on the grounds that each meant one fewer white man conscripted. Even a few southern leaders, notably General Patrick Cleburne, came to the conclusion that the Confederacy would have to enlist black soldiers to survive, but the majority southern view remained that of Georgia's Howell Cobb: "If slaves will make good soldiers our whole theory of slavery is wrong."[32] Only in the last month of the war, long after any possibility of victory had disappeared, did the Confederate Congress agree to begin enlisting slaves as fighting men.

Regardless of the reasons for accepting black enlistment, the political implications were inescapable:

> Once let the black man get upon his person the brass letters 'U.S.,' … and a musket on his shoulder and bullets in his pocket, and there is no power on earth which can deny that he has earned the right to citizenship.[33]

1865
14 April
Lincoln assassinated at Ford's Theater: Coming on the heels of the euphoria over northern victory, Lincoln's murder embittered many northerners against the South. The assassination gave northerners a martyr who was both human and sacred, their "captain," in Walt Whitman's words.

By 1865, antislavery sentiment was widespread throughout the Union armies, and the idea of granting political equality to African Americans had become a serious possibility. In his last public speech, three days before his fateful trip to Ford's Theater, Abraham Lincoln recommended that black veterans be given the right to vote.

WE HAVE DRUNK FROM THE SAME CANTEEN

For many years after the war, the soldiers who made it back home tended to say little about their experiences. By 1890, however, a flood of published recollections was pouring forth in the form of memoirs, articles, regimental histories, and other accounts, many of them tinged with the romanticism that attaches to recollections of one's youth, no matter how horrific the reality may have been. The veterans, and the nation as a whole, came to emphasize the heroism, comradeship, and shared sacrifices of the men in blue and gray alike. They reconciled over the shared memory of a glorious military past, marked by memorials throughout the North and the South that featured the image not of Lincoln or Lee, but of the common soldier. To remember the war in this light meant putting to one side the memory of the unresolved issues that had caused the conflict, and allowing the freedmen and their descendants to suffer under a formal system of second-class citizenship for another half century. The cost paid by the men who fought the war had been high; the cost of their reconciliation was high as well.[34]

"In considering the policy to be adopted for suppressing the insurrection… I have been anxious and careful that the inevitable conflict for this purpose shall not degenerate into a violent and remorseless revolutionary struggle."

Abraham Lincoln, December 1861

Remorseless, revolutionary struggle
A People's War

Mark Grimsley

Arguably the most successful general of the mid-19th century was neither Ulysses S. Grant nor Robert E. Lee but Helmuth von Moltke, the Prussian chief-of-staff who served as the architect of victory in the three Wars of German Unification. Of the Civil War he is said to have had disdain. Reportedly he quipped that it offered only the spectacle of "two armed mobs chasing each other… from which nothing can be learned."[1] However, General William T. Sherman, who visited Moltke in 1872, doubted that Moltke "was such an ass as to say that," and even if Moltke did not give much study to the Civil War, as a dedicated student of war he certainly would have understood its nature.[2] It was what the Prussian general staff regarded as "a people's war" – one in which the passions of ordinary people were fully engaged – in contradistinction to the "cabinet wars," or wars fought by professional armies for limited objectives, which were the norm in post-1815 Europe.

His Supreme Moment, by Mort Kunstler, depicts the reunion of General Robert E. Lee's army after its division in order to deliver the famous flank attack at Chancellorsville in May 1863. Recalled a staff officer: "He sat in the full realization of all that soldiers dream of – triumph; and as I looked upon him, in the complete fruition of the success which his genius, courage, and confidence in the army had won, I thought that it must have been from such a scene that men in ancient times rose to the dignity of gods." Even so, Chancellorsville was nowhere near the sort of war-ending blow that Napoleon had achieved at Marengo, Austerlitz, Jena-Auerstadt, and other fields. It simply paved the way for the next battle: Gettysburg. (Courtesy of Kuntsler Enterprises)

Helmuth von Moltke (1800–91), chief of the Prussian general staff, was regarded by most contemporaries as the greatest soldier of the 19th century. A number of American generals, including Philip H. Sheridan and William T. Sherman, visited Europe to observe the army he created. Said Sherman, "It is unquestionably the finest army in the world … a perfect machine of war." The US Army studied the Civil War not so much for its own sake as to find American illustrations of Moltke's military doctrines. (Courtesy of TopFoto)

Moltke feared the specter of people's war. Europe had seen such conflicts during the French Revolution and throughout the reign of Napoleon Bonaparte. In 1890 he warned:

> The age of cabinet war is behind us – all we have now is people's war… The greatest powers of Europe, armed as never before, will be going into battle with each other; not one of them can be crushed so completely in one or two campaigns that it will admit defeat, will be compelled to conclude peace under hard terms, and will not come back, even if it is a year later, to renew the struggle.[3]

With only slight modification, Moltke might have been speaking of America's Civil War, a conflict that killed 620,000 men out of a population of just over 31 million.

Such a struggle sounds like a forerunner of World War I, and, considered simply in terms of carnage, a fair case can be made for the comparison. The Civil War was by far the bloodiest conflict in American history. It achieved a scale and level of intensity that have led many historians to view it as a harbinger of 20th-century total warfare. The use of railroads and repeating rifles, ironclad warships and telegraph communications, land mines and entrenchments, all helped to produce this impression, as did such operations as General William T. Sherman's fearsome marches through Georgia and the Carolinas.

Even so, it must be noted that, though certainly destructive, the conflict remained chiefly a contest between governments and armies. Each recognized the belligerent rights of the other. Civilians lost property but seldom their lives. Rapes and sexual assaults were few. Both sides took prisoners. And at the end of the war, despite the Federal government's steadfast insistence that the Confederacy had no legal existence and that its public officials and military officers were, in a formal sense, guilty of treason, only one Confederate officer was executed, and then for war crimes, not for his participation in the rebellion.

This record remains unusual in the history of civil wars. At the end of the American Revolution, for example, over 100,000 British loyalists had their lands seized by the victorious revolutionaries and were forced into exile. In May 1871 a French army brutally crushed the Paris Commune and executed some 30,000 participants. In China the Tai-ping Rebellion of 1851–64 claimed the lives of at least 20 million people, many of them civilians. Furthermore, the conduct of the Civil War involved a measure of conscious forbearance on the part of both sides, for the Confederacy fought most of the war on its own soil, while the principal northern war aim – the restoration of the Union – required some measure of restraint so as not to alienate the South more than necessary.

"In considering the policy to be adopted for suppressing the insurrection," wrote President Abraham Lincoln in December 1861, "I have been anxious and careful that the inevitable conflict for this purpose shall not degenerate into a violent and remorseless revolutionary struggle."[4] In some respects, Lincoln succeeded. For example, his most dramatic war measure, the emancipation of over 3 million African American slaves, was achieved without unleashing the titanic interracial war that some observers, North and South, feared would be the sequel. Yet in many ways, "a violent and remorseless revolutionary struggle" aptly describes the nature of the contest from mid-1862 onward. By its end, the war, despite killing almost exclusively combatants, had claimed the lives of 2 percent of the country's population. It had destroyed billions of dollars in property, eliminated the institution of slavery, and greatly if temporarily expanded the scope of government power.

Indeed, not a few Americans of the Civil War years saw their times as analogous to those of the French Revolution of 1789–99. When the war began, a Maryland congressman warned that if the Federal government adopted high-handed measures in his state, "we shall hear of scenes that only find a parallel in the bloody records of the French Revolution when the people fought and conquered the trained soldiers of their king behind barricades."[5] After the defeat at First Bull Run, Major-General George B. McClellan called for redoubled efforts with the comment, "The rebels have displayed energy unanimity & wisdom worthy of the most desperate days of the French Revolution – should we do less?"[6]

In reality, both sides displayed the kind of energy seen during the French Revolution. Moreover, their efforts to mobilize depended on harnessing the same forces unleashed during the revolution, forces that brought a protean change into the military dimension of human affairs. Prior to the French Revolution, few commoners felt any sense of identification with the state whose laws they obeyed and whose taxes they paid. The stakes for which their monarchs fought had scant relevance for them. During the revolution, the passions and aspirations of the common people decisively entered the picture. The age of mass politics was at hand.

When the revolution promised liberty, equality, and brotherhood, and the monarchies of Europe threatened to extinguish that dream, the leaders of revolutionary France had little trouble tapping the full resources of its people. Many Frenchmen shouldered muskets voluntarily, fired by a combination of patriotism and republicanism. Even conscripts largely accepted the idea that the French republic represented the direct will of the people and therefore had a legitimate claim to their services that no dynastic monarch could match. This contributed to a new dynamic on the battlefield, for three reasons. First, although revolutionary soldiers initially lacked training, they more than made up for it in devotion to the cause, something rare in *ancien régime* armies. They could be trusted to march, fight, and even forage at a distance without close scrutiny. Second, through its system of volunteers and conscription, revolutionary France could field armies much larger than its monarchical adversaries, while the ease with which new recruits could be summoned enabled revolutionary commanders to dispense with the *ancien régime* fear of heavy combat losses. (Indeed, the fact that the revolutionary leadership often imprisoned or executed unsuccessful generals gave them a positive incentive to fight to the utmost.) Third, it became fashionable to assert that the patriotic and republican spirit of French soldiers made them unusually formidable, even irresistible. "What a difference there is, general, between free men and slaves!" marveled one revolutionary commander to another.[7]

The wars of the French Revolution were followed by even greater struggles during the reign of Napoleon. But after his final defeat at Waterloo in 1815, Europe entered a long period of conservative backlash. Far from seeking to tap the passions of the people, the European monarchies regarded them as a devilish menace. They created standing armies intended as much for internal control as for war. It was the Union and Confederacy who in 1861 revived the revolutionary idea of the "people in arms" and pursued it with great success. The North managed to place 2.25 million men – over half of its population of military age – under arms, all but 10 percent of them volunteers. Proportionately the South did even better: 1 million men, or over 80 percent of its military population – 12 percent of these were conscripts. On both sides, most men enlisted from the conviction that they were fighting for political ideals in which they felt a personal stake.

So, of course, did the generation that marched to war in 1914, but with this exception: by then, most of Europe had adopted a very different system for mobilizing armies. Moltke had foreseen this back in 1870 when the fledgling French Third Republic, in the wake of severe defeats that destroyed the armies of Napoleon III, attempted to create new forces using a method similar to that of the Union and Confederacy in 1861. "We are now living through a very interesting time," Moltke observed:

> when the question of which is preferable, a trained army or a militia, will be resolved in action. If the French succeed in throwing us out of France, all the Powers will introduce a militia system, and if we remain the victors, then every State will imitate us with universal service in a standing army.[8]

The quick Prussian victory in the conflict sent European nations scrambling to create a substantial peacetime army backed by a structure of first-line, secondary, and tertiary reserves and generated by universal conscription.

GETTING THE ARMY ON THE MOVE

Once mobilized, Civil War units generally reached the front by way of steam power. Often this power propelled riverine or ocean-going vessels, and although it tends to get short shrift in Civil War studies, waterborne transportation carried far more

supply tonnage, and perhaps more troops, than the oft-studied railroads. Even so, it remains fair to say that the railroads were the single biggest factor in Civil War operations. The goal of most campaigns was to secure key railroad junctions or defend them, the goal of much military labor was to construct or repair tracks, and the goal of most raids was to destroy them.

In 1860 the United States had 31,000 miles of track, all but 9,000 miles of it in the North. Yet because most of the war was fought in the South, those 9,000 miles mattered a great deal. By and large the South had a tough time keeping its railroads in good working order even when they were not being captured or wrecked by the Yankees. It had few spare rails and scant capacity to manufacture new ones. By contrast, northern management of its railroads was good, and the United States Military Railroad, the organization that managed occupied railroads in the South, was nothing short of superb.

Further, the United States had an industrial capacity the South could not even begin to match. Historian Bruce Catton once noted that in the planning stages of the Fredericksburg campaign, a US Military Railroad administrator ordered 10 miles of spare railroad rails just in case the Union army should need them. The administrator thought nothing of it, yet at that time, there were not 10 miles of spare rails in all the Confederacy.[9]

The engine Firefly *crosses a trestle on the Orange & Alexandria Railroad in northern Virginia. Both sides made extensive use of railroads. Fortunately, many officers had significant prewar experience with this new form of transport and understood how to exploit it. When war broke out in 1861, for example, Major-General George B. McClellan was superintendent of the Ohio & Mississippi Railroad. Before that he worked for the Illinois Central Railroad, where he met a prosperous Springfield attorney who sometimes did legal work for the firm: Abraham Lincoln. (National Archives)*

THE ARTS OF WAR

The Civil War took place near the end of a long period of stability in the grim arts of the battlefield. A British musketeer from Blenheim or a French *tirailleur* from Tourcoing could have looked down upon the struggles at Shiloh or Spotsylvania and comprehended what he was seeing. For that matter, if a grizzled Civil War veteran had somehow found himself in 1914 Belgium, the sight and sounds of the opening battles of World War I – though punctuated by many novelties – would have resonated powerfully with memories of his own service. Were any of these old soldiers to visit the Western Front in 1918, however, only the fear, chaos, and squalor would have been familiar. The dispersion of infantry formations, massive use of indirect artillery fire, chemical weapons, and ponderous primitive tanks would have transformed the battlefield into a strange new land.

Hovering above the armies of the 19th century, as it hovered above the armies of the Edwardian era until the bitter exorcism of 1914–18, was the ghost of Napoleon, the greatest of Great Captains, the god of black-powder warfare. In Civil War America his presence was mighty. Generals exhorting their troops modeled their proclamations on the emperor's charismatic addresses to his *grognards*. Posing for photographs, officers (and even some private soldiers) stuffed their right hand into their jackets, as Napoleon had done. The Corsican was the final authority on all things military. If one wished to clinch a point beyond possibility of rebuttal, one invoked his name. An engineering officer used the imprimatur of Napoleon to confirm the number of troops required to defend Washington, DC. The Union army's chief quartermaster used it to establish the correct number of supply wagons needed for every thousand soldiers.

Civil War commanders, however, arguably understood Napoleonic lore better than Napoleonic methods. The tale that Moltke remarked that the Civil War was fought by armed mobs may be apocryphal, but it contains a grain of truth. It is not inappropriate to think of the conflict as, in terms of tactics, a badly fought Napoleonic war.

For some 30 years after the Napoleonic Wars, tactics altered scarcely at all. Then improvements in the infantry musket led the Europeans to revisit the issue. These improvements centered on the percussion cap, which replaced the flint as the musket's ignition mechanism because it resulted in fewer misfires, and the Minié ball, which for the first time enabled a rifled musket to be loaded as rapidly as a smoothbore. Recognizing that a defender armed with the rifled musket could fire accurately at 300 to 400 yards – double the effective range of a smoothbore musket – armies now revised their tactics in order to accelerate the speed of an infantry attack and reduce the exposure time of troops as they "crossed the deadly ground." The French devised such tactics in the 1840s; the Americans shamelessly copied them in the 1850s. Using the revised tactics an attacker would typically step off at a "quick time" pace of 110 steps per minute (about 85 yards per minute). Once under serious fire the rate of advance would increase to a so-called "double-quick time" of 165 steps per minute (about 150 yards per minute). Only when the regiment was within a few dozen yards of the defending line would they be ordered to advance at a "run," a very rapid pace but still not a sprint, since an all-out dash would completely destroy the shoulder-to-shoulder formation on which linear tactics depended.

Thus a regiment might easily take about ten minutes to charge 1,000 yards, even if it did not pause for realignment or execute any further maneuvers en route. This was considered adequate to offset the introduction of the rifled musket, but critics since the Civil War have argued that this was a terrible miscalculation; that the rifled musket in fact revolutionized the battlefield and ought properly to have been countered by the adoption of the dispersed infantry tactics only devised years after the war. A recent American history textbook faithfully reflects this orthodoxy when it asserts:

> Whereas [smoothbore] muskets had a range of only about eighty yards, rifles propelled spinning bullets four times as far. The rifle's greater range and accuracy, along with cannons firing canister filled with flesh-ripping, bone-breaking steel shot, made sitting ducks of charging units and gave enormous advantage to entrenched defensive forces.[10]

Of course, this description overlooks the fact that grape shot, an early form of canister, had been a normal feature of Napoleonic battlefields. It may also exaggerate the impact of the rifled musket, for two reasons. First, some authorities have maintained that a massed smoothbore volley was effective at ranges of up to 150 yards, not 80. Second, and much more importantly, the description assumes that because Civil War defenders *could* shoot as far as 320 to 400 yards, they *did* shoot at such ranges. In fact, an analysis of the actual ranges of engagement severely undercuts this assumption.

An examination of after-action reports from six pre-1864 eastern theater battles yielded 90 unambiguous references to ranges at which defenders opened small-arms fire or attackers first received small-arms fire. Of these, in only 13 instances (14.4 percent) was the range beyond 200 yards. The average range was 136 yards, while half the references indicated ranges of less than 100 yards. The reasons for this varied. Frequently the presence of woodlands or undulating terrain played a role; one or two engagements occurred at twilight when visibility was limited; and in a few cases, undoubtedly, the defenders were armed with smoothbores. A common reason, however, was a deliberate decision to withhold fire until the enemy had closed the range. During Pickett's Charge, for example, the Confederates attacked across nearly a mile of open ground, but according to Union corps commander Winfield S. Hancock the defenders permitted them to come within musketry range without firing, "our men evincing a striking disposition to withhold it until it could be delivered with deadly effect."[11]

Whatever the reason, it is difficult to lay the carnage and indecisiveness of Civil War battles at the foot of the rifled musket. Some analysts have noticed the sharp contrast between these engagements and their Napoleonic counterparts. Whereas Napoleonic battles featured massed artillery and cavalry operating in concert with infantry, Civil War infantry usually attacked on their own, with limited (and often ineffective) support from artillery and virtually none whatever from cavalry. Further, the infantry usually attacked in line formation, not column, thereby sacrificing shock and also multiplying the problem of controlling the assaulting troops laterally. Finally, as tactical historian Paddy Griffith has noted, attacking Civil War infantry often halted at some point to return the defenders' volley, thereby draining momentum from their assault and resulting in a standup firefight at murderously close range.

The Civil War witnessed the deployment of a number of new technologies, among them rifled artillery and breech-loading firearms, but neither of them had great impact on the course of the war. Rifled field artillery, although it had a longer range than smoothbore cannon – and, to be sure, could batter down casemate forts, obliging the belligerents to turn increasingly to earthen forts – was still a direct-fire weapon. Artillery was not yet the killing arm it would become in World War I, when much longer ranges, more powerful explosives, and indirect-fire techniques enabled it to inflict 70 percent of all casualties suffered.

The breech-loading rifle was another matter. In a war where small-arms fire was by far the most lethal thing on a battlefield – "it is that," Robert E. Lee remarked at Cold Harbor of an unbroken crackle of rifle volleys, "that kills men" – rifles that could fire more quickly might have been fervently coveted.[12] Indeed, a number of soldiers purchased such weapons with their own funds, and one wealthy colonel bought them for his entire brigade. But only the Union cavalry was extensively armed with breech-loaders, and many of these were single-shot rifles, not repeaters like the seven-shot Spencer. Mindful of the logistical demands their appetite for ammunition might pose, most Civil War commanders regarded breech-loaders with a degree of skepticism.

Sherman remarked after the war, "The only change that breech-loading arms will probably make in the art and practice of war will be to increase the amount of ammunition to be expended, and therefore to be carried along." He also thought, correctly, that rapid-firing weapons would force troops to attack in more open order, and incorrectly, that they would "reduce battles to short, quick, decisive conflicts."[13] Neither he nor anyone else understood how fundamentally infantry tactics would have to change in the future.

ENTRENCHED

A common misconception of the Civil War holds that it was the first to see the extensive use of field fortifications and/or that these appeared only late in the war. In fact, both European and American armies had entrenched in previous conflicts, and Civil War armies consciously emulated previous practice. When Lee's Army of Northern Virginia entrenched its position along the Rappahannock River in the winter of 1863, for example, a Confederate officer noted proudly that the fieldworks rivaled the famous lines at Torres Vedras, constructed by British engineers with Portuguese labor in 1809–10 to defend Lisbon against an attack from Napoleon's armies. (Although the officer deserves credit for a learned analogy, he did not have a clue as to the size and sophistication of the lines of Torres Vedras. Even today their eroded remnants are massive.)

Field fortifications were used even earlier – from the beginning of the war, in fact. There were earthworks at Big Bethel, Virginia, the site of the war's first significant skirmish, in June 1861, and earthworks atop the Confederate position at Rich Mountain, western Virginia, captured by Union troops in July 1861. The rebel army constructed extensive fieldworks after its victory at First Manassas. The use of such fortifications would have been familiar to any West Point graduate from the doctrines of Dennis Hart Mahan, professor of military science at the US Military Academy.

These fieldworks, constructed after the battle of First Bull Run, were abandoned when Confederate forces evacuated Centreville and Manassas Junction in March 1862. Though modest by the standards of 1864–65, they nevertheless show that Civil War armies used fortifications from the outset of the conflict. Fortifications like these often deterred attack. Unwilling to assault this strong position, for example, Union Major-General George B. McClellan took his army by sea to the tip of the peninsula formed by the James and York rivers. There he found a belt of entrenchments almost equally strong, and spent a month besieging them. (National Archives)

Photographer George N. Barnard captured this view of Union field fortifications at Kennesaw Mountain, Georgia, one of the major battles of the Atlanta campaign. As soldiers dug the trench they threw some of the clay in front, facing the enemy. But most of it was piled perpendicular to the trench as a defense against potential artillery and small-arms fire from the sides – "enfilading fire" in military parlance. The perpendicular mounds were called traverses. Engineering officers sometimes supervised the siting and construction of earthworks, but by mid-1864 veteran troops could – and did – construct them with little prompting or instruction from their superiors. (National Archives)

Mahan thought they steadied raw troops and militia. "It was one of Prof. Mahan's maxims," Sherman recalled, "that the spade was as useful in war as the musket."[14]

That said, it remains true that initially earthworks were used principally to guard fixed points. They tended not to be used on battlefields until 1863. Lee, as we have seen, fortified his position after the battle of Fredericksburg. Hooker constructed breastworks at Chancellorsville, and the Union army built them at Gettysburg, especially to shield the flanks. By the close of the year, fieldworks had become commonplace, and they would dominate the campaigns of 1864.

The construction of field fortifications followed a well-established pattern. The troops would start with (fairly shallow) rifle pits. Next they would construct breastworks in front using two rows of logs stacked horizontally. They would then fill the intervening space – often 4ft thick – with earth. The works were supplemented at intervals by traverses running perpendicular to the main line in order to reduce the damage from enfilade fire. Barbed wire had not yet been invented, so *abatis* – felled trees with their branches interlocked to hinder an attacker – would be placed in front. Topped by "head logs," laid horizontally a few inches

above the breastwork, with just enough room left to aim a rifle, the earthworks shielded defenders from direct fire very effectively.

Though present throughout the conflict, the use of field fortifications – especially on campaigns of maneuver – greatly accelerated in 1864, and as Civil War soldiers grew utterly convinced of the life-saving value of earthworks, they constructed them readily, sometimes even without orders. Not just shovels but also axes and even cups and mess plates came into play as thousands of men sweated to create a barrier between themselves and the enemy's bullets, shot, and shell. Theodore Lyman, a staff officer in the Union Army of the Potomac, noted during the Overland campaign how quickly Confederate infantry could construct field fortifications, and Union infantry could match this pace as well:

> Within one hour, there is a shelter against bullets, high enough to cover a man kneeling, and extending often a mile or two. When our line advances, there is the line of the enemy, nothing showing but the bayonets, and the battle-flags stuck on top of the work. It is a rule that when the Rebels halt, the first day gives them a good rifle-pit; the second, an infantry parapet with artillery in position; and the third a parapet in front and entrenched batteries behind. Sometimes they put this three days' work into the first twenty-four hours.[15]

Such extensive fortifications made Civil War armies, already difficult to trap, almost impossible to destroy in battle. With the accession of Ulysses S. Grant as commander of all Union forces in 1864, northern units widely adopted a practice already pioneered by Grant and his subordinates in the western theater. War upon the southern economy supplemented war upon southern armies.

HARD WAR

In a small way, the North's destructive war against the South began early. The first southern homes and villages were put to the torch in 1861, not 1864. By the same token, Union field armies began to forage for supplies within a few months of the war's outset. But in the war's first year, most northern commanders consciously refrained from such activities, and until mid-summer 1862 Federal forces followed an informal policy of conciliation toward all southern whites. Soldiers were detailed to guard private property and often forbidden to take even fence rails to build campfires. Most significantly, for the war's first year the Lincoln administration disavowed any intention of disturbing slavery. The conciliatory policy had no greater advocate than the North's foremost general of the period, George B. McClellan. "We shall most readily suppress the rebellion and restore the authority of the

Union soldiers systematically wreck the Atlanta roundhouse in November 1864, just prior to the March to the Sea. Sherman did not set out to burn the city, as is often supposed, but he insisted that railroads, factories, and anything that could be used to support the Confederate war effort should be demolished. The effort produced fires that got out of control, however, and although Sherman personally supervised attempts to extinguish the flames, much of Atlanta was destroyed. Even so, few residents were endangered by the conflagration: Sherman had expelled them two months before. (National Archives)

OPPOSITE *Soldiers Plundering a Farmhouse by Sebastian Vrancx (1573–1647), vividly illustrates that marauding and mayhem directed against civilians did not originate with the Civil War. Although it depicts a scene from the 16th-century Dutch Revolt, with minor changes to the soldiers' clothing and equipment it could apply to virtually any European war from the Middle Ages through the mid-18th century. Rape, pillage, torture, and outright murder were common occurrences. The Civil War was remarkably free of such extreme violence directed against civilians – with one important exception: the fierce guerrilla struggle in Missouri and eastern Kansas. The worst single incident took place on August 21, 1863, when pro-Confederate guerrillas sacked Lawrence, Kansas, killing an estimated 150–200 men, though refraining from assaults on women. (Courtesy of Deutsches Historisches Museum)*

Government by religiously respecting the Constitutional rights of all," McClellan told a subordinate in a typical pronouncement.

> Preserve the strictest discipline, among the troops, and while employing the utmost energy in military movements, be careful so to treat the unarmed inhabitants as to contract, not widen, the breach between us & the rebels.[16]

Most "unarmed inhabitants," however, responded not with gratitude but disdain, and soon the common Union soldier became impatient with a policy that often had him standing in the cold to protect the property of a pro-secessionist farmer. Officers began to look the other way as troops stole fence rails, chickens, fruits, and vegetables. When a soldier's sister expressed dismay at a letter in which he reported seizing an Alabama farmer's wheat to feed his horse, the soldier responded:

> The old fellow voted for secession twice... and I would rather have him starve than the horse. My horse is doing all in his power for the Nation and the old man all he can against it.[17]

Lincoln's issuance of the Emancipation Proclamation signaled a decisive turn away from conciliation. Though it was still not unheard-of for Union officers to protect private property, it became increasingly common to seize crops and livestock when needed by the army or in order to deny their use by the enemy. By mid-1863, Grant's army in central Mississippi was employing thousands of troops in the systematic dismantling of Confederate railroads, warehouses, cotton gins, and factories.

It is a tradition zealously held by many southerners that the Yankees destroyed everything in their path. In a few cases, notably South Carolina in February 1865, something not far from that occurred. For the most part, however, Union troops destroyed public, not private, property, and many officers made serious attempts to differentiate between white southerners who were actively secessionist, neutral, or Unionist in sympathy. To deny food and forage to the Confederate army, northern troops might invade a farm and set fire to a barn containing the year's harvest and drive away the livestock. But the farmer's residence would usually

remain unscathed. Indeed, Civil War soldiers rarely destroyed private dwellings if they were occupied. Apparently a moral inhibition against such destruction persisted, though soldiers sometimes broke into southern homes to pilfer silverware and other goods. An Ohio surgeon was sure enough of the strength of this inhibition that he urged his wife, "Should the rebels ever succeed in making a raid into Ohio, you must not run away. It will be better for you and your house to remain at home."[18]

The dominant pattern that emerged was one of both severity *and* restraint. Substantial restraint persisted because the Lincoln administration and its generals recognized that hopes for national reunification would be jeopardized by needlessly harsh treatment. It also persisted – and this may have been crucial – because Union soldiers by and large retained the peacetime values with which they had grown up and, for the most part, recognized southern whites as fellow Americans. They were very different from the soldiers of early modern Europe, long-service veterans divorced from their societies who nakedly preyed upon the civilians in their path. For that matter, they were very different from the volunteer soldiers engaged during the war years in campaigns against the western Indians, who were seen as racially inferior, and on several occasions, massacred.

The severity in the North's war upon the southern economy came about because northern armies proved unable to gain outright victory on the battlefield – though the much-maligned McClellan came close to doing so in June 1862. They turned to

Ohio soldier James E. Taylor made this ink wash drawing of Federal cavalry in northern Virginia, called "Mosby's Confederacy" because it was the haunt of Colonel John S. Mosby and his Partisan Rangers. Unable to locate and destroy Mosby's band in combat, Union forces resorted to cutting off its supply of food and forage. The practice was part of a larger policy of stripping the Confederacy of anything that could support its war effort. The drawing shows this policy in idealized form. Soldiers have torched the barn and are driving away the livestock, but the main residence at right stands unscathed. In practice, the inhabitants might or might not escape acts of theft and vandalism, though outright assaults were rare. (Courtesy of Western Reserve Historical Society, Cleveland)

economic warfare in a bid to weaken the Confederate forces arrayed against them. Even if they had not chosen to attack the southern economy for its own sake, they still were often obliged to draw upon the local countryside for supplies. Generals like Grant and Sherman discovered that this could be done so extensively as to permit their armies to cut loose entirely, for brief periods of time, from orthodox supply lines. Grant did so during the Vicksburg campaign and Sherman did so on a massive scale during the Savannah and Carolinas campaigns. Eventually they came to recognize that such raids could achieve not just economic but political and psychological effects. They became a way of demonstrating to southern whites that the Confederate government could not protect them and that the Federal government was grimly determined to prevail.

It remains only to discuss the Civil War's influence upon future warfare. Actually it exerted much less influence than some readers might suppose. The Civil War occurred at about the same time as the German Wars of Unification. The first of these conflicts, by Prussia against Denmark in 1864, was a walkover whose main significance was to demonstrate the superiority of the breech-loading Dreyse "needle gun." The second, the so-called *Brüderkrieg* between Prussia and Austria in 1866, is tellingly known as the Six Weeks' War. In the third, the Franco–Prussian War of 1870–71, the Prussians wrecked the French Imperial armies within seven weeks and within ten months had inflicted punitive peace terms upon the overmatched Third Republic, which tried to continue the French war effort following the abdication of Napoleon III. In short, the German Wars of Unification appeared to show that decisive victory through battle was possible.

The Civil War, by contrast, offered no such lesson. On the contrary, as historian Brian Bond notes:

> Though great battles were highly relevant to the course of the war, they were only one factor in the attritional process as the Confederacy was drained of manpower, blockaded, divided, and subdivided by the Union advances, and eventually overrun. [T]he costs were great and the wounds slow to heal. No military theorist was likely to take this as a model of 'decisive victory.'[19]

And none was readily going to believe that attrition, not swift triumphs like Moltke's victories, were likely to be the hallmark of future warfare.

American soldiers were no more willing to see this than their European counterparts. Though they studied the campaigns of their own Civil War closely, they emphasized great battles of maneuver, like Second Manassas and Chancellorsville, that most closely resembled the *Hauptschlachten* of the Prussian Army. Only in hindsight would the Civil War come to be seen as a watershed event: the first major conflict that harnessed the passions of mass politics to emergent industrialization.

> *"Nor must Uncle Sam's web-feet be forgotten. At the watery margins they have been present. Not only on the deep sea, the broad bay, and the rapid river, but also up the narrow muddy bayou, and wherever the ground was a little damp, they have been and made their tracks."*

Abraham Lincoln to James C. Conklin, August 26, 1863

Uncle Sam's web-feet
Winning the War at Sea

Craig L. Symonds

The American Civil War was primarily a land war, decided in the end by the nearly 3¼ million men who struggled on battlefields from Pennsylvania to New Mexico, and who gave up their lives profligately for their respective causes. But naval forces – along the Atlantic coast, on the high seas, and especially on the western rivers – played a significant role in determining how that war was fought. Navies in the Civil War fought on five oceans and on dozens of rivers both large and small, and when they were not fighting they were blockading (or blockade running), transporting troops, supplying armies, or acting as floating warehouses and recruiting depots. Moreover, because the American Civil War took place in the midst of a technological revolution, the war also marked a milestone in the way navies looked and the way they fought. Civil War navies reflected the recent shift from sail to steam, from smoothbore guns to rifled artillery, from round shot to explosive shells, and the war introduced new kinds of weapons altogether, including ironclads, mines (then called torpedoes), and even submarines. This technological

The British-built CSS Alabama *was the most successful of all Confederate raiders that practiced economic warfare on the high seas. Commanded by Rear-Admiral Raphael Semmes, the* Alabama *stopped Union merchant ships, evacuated their crews, and then burned the ships in order to devastate Union commerce. (US Naval Historical Center)*

revolution would have come about sooner or later even if the Civil War had never been fought, but the war accelerated the changes, and by the end of it naval warfare itself had been transformed.

The United States Navy found itself in the unfamiliar position of being the dominant sea force in the Civil War. During both the Revolution and the War of 1812 when Americans had confronted the mighty Royal Navy, the United States had avoided fleet engagements, relying instead on a strategy of attacking British commerce, a practice known by its French phrase as *guerre de course*. The British countered by blockading the American coast so that the privateers as well as American merchant ships could not get to sea. In short, the superior navy sought to impose a blockade while the weaker navy relied on commerce raiding, a pattern that repeated itself in the Civil War. In addition, both North and South embraced the new technology, but the superior industrial capacity of the Union states meant that the North was able to take better advantage of it despite the dramatic success of Confederate innovations like the ironclad *Virginia* and the submarine *H.L. Hunley*.

THE BLOCKADE

Any discussion of the naval history of the Civil War must begin with a consideration of grand strategy, and in particular the Union's so-called Anaconda Plan. The brainchild of army general Winfield Scott, the key elements of this plan were for the United States to establish (in Scott's words) "a complete blockade of the Atlantic and Gulf ports" that would cut the rebelling states off from the outside world, and to conduct "a powerful movement down the Mississippi to the Ocean" that would cripple the South's internal transportation and separate the trans-Mississippi states of Texas, Arkansas, and Louisiana from the rest of the Confederacy, as well as to pin down Confederate armies near the capital. Scott, himself a Virginian, hoped that such a program would "envelop the insurgent states and bring them to terms with less bloodshed than by any other plan."[1] Many in the North found these proposals too passive for the current emergency and derisively called it the Anaconda Plan after the South American serpent that strangles its prey. Despite public criticism, however, Scott's plan became the basic blueprint of Union strategy, and two of its three elements – the blockade, and the conquest of the Mississippi – involved the navy.

The most challenging element of this strategic plan was the establishment and maintenance of a coastal blockade, which Lincoln declared on April 19, 1861, only a week after Fort Sumter. Virtually the first strategic decision made by the administration, it immediately involved Lincoln in the nuances of international law since declaring a blockade of the South implied *de facto* recognition of the Confederacy as a belligerent power. Lincoln's solution was to announce that America's southern ports were being temporarily closed to foreign trade because domestic unrest in those cities prevented the collection of duties. But this semantic distinction fooled no one, and eventually the government had to accept the word blockade after all, along with all that it might imply about the Confederacy's belligerent status.

A second legal problem was that international law also held that it was not sufficient simply to declare ports closed or blockaded. According to both law and tradition, the blockading force had to establish naval squadrons offshore powerful enough to enforce the declaration. Otherwise it was simply a "paper blockade" and imposed no responsibility on neutral nations to stay away. In recognition of that, Lincoln declared that "a competent force will be posted to as to prevent entrance and exit of vessels."[2]

This was an extraordinarily ambitious assertion. The Confederate coastline extended for over 3,500 miles from Arlington, Virginia, on the Potomac to Brownsville, Texas, on the Rio Grande, and was pierced by 189 river mouths or navigable inlets that could be used for trade. To blockade that coast, the US Navy possessed a total of only 90 warships, fewer than half of which were on active service, and only eight of which were in home waters and available for blockade duty. Obviously, in order to make the blockade tangible and therefore legal, the US Navy would have expand dramatically.

The first step was to call home all the vessels on overseas duty and activate all the vessels that were laid up in ordinary. In addition the government purchased merchant ships in order to turn them into blockading vessels. In the mid-19th century, all that was necessary to achieve such a conversion was to reinforce the deck so that it could bear the weight of a few naval guns. Blockaders did not need to carry a large battery, for their object was to interdict unarmed merchant ships, not fight battles at sea. The government bought almost anything that could float: passenger ships, cargo vessels, even ferry boats, and in just a few months the navy had doubled in size as the government added 89 ships to the fleet for the bargain price of $3.5 million. By war's end, 418 of the navy's total of 671 vessels were converted merchant ships.[3]

The government also built new warships. Gideon Welles, the Connecticut politician and newspaperman whom Lincoln appointed to be his secretary of the navy, was so eager to get started, he let contracts for the construction of two dozen new warships without a Congressional appropriation. Welles assumed that Congress would approve his actions once it assembled, as indeed it did. Foreshadowing the astonishing shipbuilding programs during both world wars in the 20th century, northern shipyards turned out warships in record time. The initial contracts

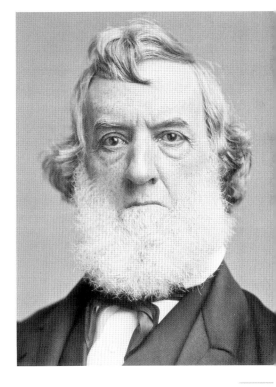

Gideon Welles was a former newspaper publisher from Connecticut who served as secretary of the navy throughout Lincoln's presidency. A strong advocate of the navy, he became a champion of monitors. Indeed, so infatuated was he with those new vessels that some claimed he had succumbed to "monitor fever." (Library of Congress)

specified that the ships were to be built in 90 days, and this first generation of new-construction warships were subsequently known as "ninety day gunboats." Other new-construction vessels were laid down soon afterward, and by the time the war came to an end, the United States had built more than 200 warships in less than four years, more than all the warships constructed in the nation's history up to that time.[4]

Promotions, which had languished in the years of peace, suddenly came thick and fast as officers who had served in subordinate positions for decades suddenly found themselves raised to dizzying heights. Overnight, lieutenants got command assignments, commanders became commodores, and captains became flag officers. Junior officer assignments went to brand new midshipmen with virtually no sea-going experience. Acting Volunteer officers – merchant sailors and even fishermen – came into the service in large numbers to fill out the greatly expanded officer corps.

Like the raw recruits that made up the army's rank and file, the navy's enlisted

The artist of this contemporary cartoon of Scott's "Anaconda Plan" intended to be derisive, but he nevertheless captures the principal elements of Scott's plan: pin down Confederate armies near the capital; blockade the South's entire coastline; and seize control of the Mississippi River. (Library of Congress)

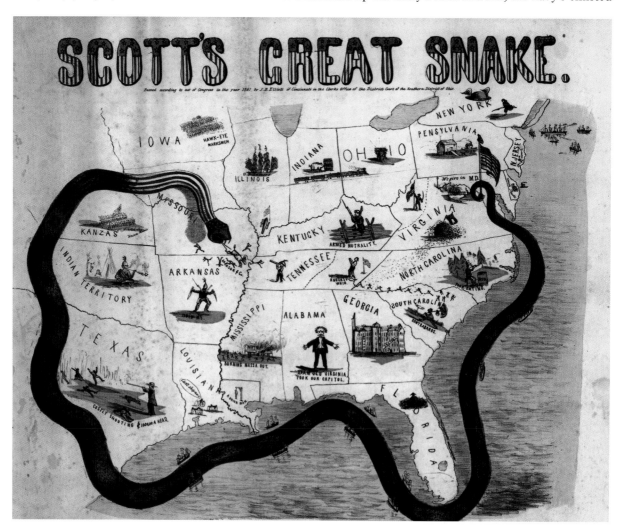

force consisted mainly of volunteers straight from their jobs as farmers, mechanics, and laborers. Michael Bennett, who has made a careful study of these men, concludes that 80 percent of them had never been to sea before. After the institution of a national conscription law in 1863, many men volunteered for naval service in order to avoid service in the army. By the time the Civil War ended, some 118,000 men had served in the wartime US Navy. About 18,000 of these (15 percent) were African Americans, and on some ships, especially those in the Mississippi River Squadron, their presence caused racial friction. Former slaves – called "contrabands" – were initially rated as "boy" regardless of their age, until the Navy Department allowed them to enlist as "landsman" in 1862, which also doubled their pay from $10 to $20 a month. White sailors initially welcomed the contrabands on board, particularly since African Americans often performed the most onerous tasks, especially as coal heavers. But whites sometimes resented it when skilled African American sailors assumed other jobs with greater status. The Navy Department authorized ship captains to segregate blacks and whites at their discretion, but in almost every case the practical realities of working in a small confined place made segregated work crews impractical, and unlike the African American soldiers who served in segregated units in the Union army, ship's crews in the Union navy were generally integrated.[5]

Having assembled the ships and the men, the navy next had to overcome the logistical problem of trying to maintain a steam-powered navy year-round off a

1861
24 May

Butler coins "contraband": Benjamin Butler accepted within his lines three escaped slaves and held them according to rules of war that allow participants to seize contraband that can be used for warfare. Though not adopted universally by US commanders, the policy provided one way for the federals to shift manpower, usually used for the construction of forts, from the South to the North.

THE CONSCRIPT BILL!
HOW TO AVOID IT!!
U. S. NAVY.
1,000 MEN WANTED, FOR 12 MONTHS!

Seamen's Pay, - - - - - - - $18.00 per month.
Ordinary Seamen's Pay, ... 14.00 " "
Landsmen's Pay, ... 12.00 " "
$1.50 extra per month to all, Grog Money.

$50,000,000 PRIZES!

Already captured, a large share of which is awarded to Ships Crews. The laws for the distributing of Prize money carefully
protects the rights of all the captors.

PETTY OFFICERS.—PROMOTION.—Seamen have a chance for promotion to the offices of Master at Arms, Boatswain's
Mates, Quarter Gunners, Captain of Tops, Forecastle, Holds, After-Guard, &c.
Landsmen may be advanced to Armorers, Armorers' Mates, Carpenter's Mates, Sailmakers' Mates, Painters, Coopers, &c.
PAY OF PETTY OFFICERS.—From $20.00 to $45.00 per month.
CHANCES FOR WARRANTS, BOUNTIES AND MEDALS OF HONOR—All those who distinguish themselves in
battle or by extraordinary heroism, may be promoted to forward Warrant Officers or Acting Masters' Mates,—and upon their
promotion receive a guaranty of $100, with a medal of honor from their country.
All who wish may leave HALF PAY with their families, to commence from date of enlistment.
Minors must have a written consent, sworn to before a Justice of the Peace.

For further information apply to U. S. NAVAL RENDEZVOUS,
E. Y. BUTLER, U. S. N. Recruiting Officer,
No. 14 FRONT STREET, SALEM, MASS.

FROM WRIGHT & POTTER'S BOSTON PRINTING ESTABLISHMENT, No. 4 SPRING LANE, CORNER OF DEVONSHIRE STREET.

Fully 80 percent of all recruits in the Civil War US Navy had never been to sea before. Some enlisted for the adventure, some for the promised prize money, some out of patriotism, and some – as suggested in this 1863 recruiting poster – to avoid service in the army. (US Naval Historical Center)

distant and hostile shore. A blockading steamer could not return to Baltimore or Philadelphia every few days to re-coal – doing so would burn up almost a full load of coal in each transit. The only feasible alternative was to obtain coaling stations along the coast of the Confederacy itself. The Union fleet was aided in this object by two factors. One was geographic: the offshore islands along the coast of the Carolinas and Georgia made it possible for naval forces to take and hold naval bases that were relatively secure from enemy land forces. The second factor was technological. In the two decades before the outbreak of war, the adoption of steam power, rifled guns, and explosive shells had given ships a greater relative firepower to shore-based artillery. Whereas in the Mexican War, forts had been relatively secure against a purely naval attack, the new technology had evened the contest so that a naval squadron could now challenge a shore battery of equal strength with a fair chance of success.

That became evident on November 7, 1861, when a squadron of ocean-going screw steamers under Flag Officer Samuel Francis Du Pont entered Port Royal Sound about half way between Charleston and Savannah, and battered the Confederate forts there into submission. After a brief resistance, the Confederate defenders abandoned both Fort Walker on Hilton Head Island and Fort Beauregard on St Helena Island. This allowed US Army forces to occupy both islands as well as the town of Beaufort, and Port Royal Sound became a safe harbor for the South Atlantic Blockading Squadron. Similar bases were established for each of the other three blockading squadrons: the North Atlantic, and the East and West Gulf Squadrons.

An important witness to Du Pont's conquest of Port Royal was Robert E. Lee, who had been sent to the South Carolina coast by Confederate president Jefferson Davis to determine how the South might best defend its Atlantic frontier. Impressed by the domination of Du Pont's squadron over Forts Walker and Beauregard, Lee concluded that an extended defense of the southern coast was impossible. Unable to know where the Union navy might strike next, the South faced the conundrum of scattering its resources in an attempt to defend everywhere or trying to guess where the next blow might fall. It was a losing game, and Lee knew it. He recommended that with the exception of a few key sites – Wilmington, Charleston,

Savannah, Mobile, and New Orleans – the Confederacy should essentially give up its coastline. This gave the Union navy almost complete freedom of movement around the Confederate periphery. It made possible McClellan's Peninsular Campaign and the Union occupation of the North Carolina Sounds, interrupted the coastal trade, and made the blockade more efficient.[6]

Just how efficient the blockade was, is a question that historians still dispute. One school of thought is that the blockade did little to stem the flow of essential goods into the Confederacy and was therefore largely a waste of Union resources. Scholars in this camp note that despite the hundreds of ships and thousands of men that the Union committed to the blockade, most of the ships that tried to run through the blockade did so successfully. In the first year of the war, as many as nine ships out of ten ran the blockade without being caught. Even in 1865, with the blockade fleet greatly expanded and the Confederacy on its last legs, as many as half of all blockade runners that tested the blockade were successful. Over the course of the war, those blockade runners brought in more than a million pairs of shoes, nearly half a million rifles, a thousand tons of gunpowder, hundreds of cannon, as well as medical supplies, canvas, lead, and other essential military goods.[7]

On the other hand, such statistics can be misleading. While most blockade runners that challenged the blockade made it, there are no statistics to show how many vessels never attempted to run the blockade in the first place because they were deterred by the presence of the blockade fleet. The real question is: How many ships, carrying how much cargo, would have entered or left Confederate ports if the blockade had not been there? One way to try to answer this question is

This contemporary painting depicts Flag Officer Samuel Du Pont's attack on Confederate forts guarding Port Royal Sound in November 1861. Du Pont's vessels completed three circles past Fort Walker on Hilton Head Island before the defenders abandoned their works. The attack demonstrated the increased effectiveness of warships against shore fortifications, a result of the Ordnance Revolution of the 1850s. (US Naval Historical Center)

Blockade Running Routes

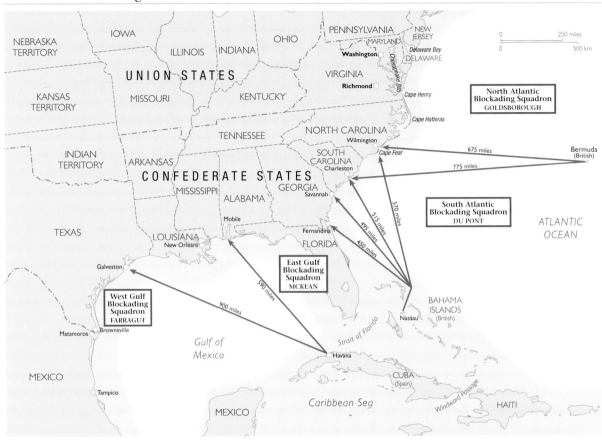

Flush-decked and built for speed, Confederate blockade runners like the Colonel Lamb, *pictured here, made the relatively short dash into Confederate ports from Nassau in the Bahamas. Built expressly for blockade running in Britain in 1864, the* Colonel Lamb *made several successful runs and was never caught. (US Naval Historical Center)*

to note that in the last 12 months of peace, a total of 20,000 ships entered or left southern ports. Though the interruption of the internal trade between North and South should have increased the South's dependency on overseas trade after the war began, the number of ships entering or leaving southern ports averaged only 2,000 ships per year over the four years of war, a reduction of 90 percent. Moreover, most of the ships that ran the blockade were narrow, specially designed packet ships built for speed rather than cargo capacity. Another factor, pointed out by the economic historian David Surdam, was that the Union occupation of much of the intercoastal waterway compelled the Confederacy to shift much of the trade that might otherwise have gone by coastal barge onto the South's already overburdened rail system.

A precise calculation of how much the Confederate economy suffered because of the Union naval blockade is difficult. Although Confederate armies managed to obtain the rifles, gunpowder, and lead that kept its armies active and dangerous, the blockade had a cumulative wearing effect on the overall health of the southern economy and contributed to hardship and war–weariness among soldiers and civilians alike.[8]

THE RIVER WAR

Of even greater importance than the blockade was the effect of Union naval forces on the conduct of the war in the large expanse of territory between the Appalachian Mountains and the Mississippi River, a theater of operations known simply as the West. Unlike the eastern theater where the rivers ran mostly west to east and acted as barriers to a Union advance, the major navigable rivers in the western theater mostly ran north to south (or south to north) and therefore served as potential avenues for a Union advance. In addition to the Mississippi, Union river squadrons also operated on the Tennessee and Cumberland Rivers, and the Union used all three rivers to penetrate Confederate defenses.

The struggle for the western rivers was characterized by a contest between Confederate forts and Union gunboats. The Confederates built forts just below the Tennessee–Kentucky state line on all three rivers: Fort Donelson on the Cumberland, Fort Henry on the Tennessee, and Island Number 10 on the Mississippi. Unlike the stone and brick forts along the coast built by the US Army Corps of Engineers in the 1830s and '40s, these were mostly dirt and log forts thrown up in a matter of months, and all three proved vulnerable, though for different reasons.

This photo of Commander Henry Walke, taken after the war, suggests something of the daredevil character of the man who ran the Carondelet *past Island Number 10 batteries in April 1862. (US Naval Historical Center)*

The USS Carondelet was one of the ironclads designed by Samuel Pook expressly for service on the western rivers. Called "Pook's Turtles" for their appearance or tin-clads due to their relatively thin armor, these vessels made up the backbone of the Union's Mississippi River flotilla. (US Naval Historical Center)

To attack these forts successfully, the Union army and navy had to work together. In the 19th century, however, there was no protocol for such cooperation. The army and navy were entirely independent of one another: each service had its own cabinet secretary, and there was no individual besides the president who had joint command over both. As a result, voluntary cooperation was the key to Union operations in the West. When officers of the army and navy managed to work together effectively, the Union generally found success; when they did not, the result was disappointment and failure.

Like the blockading ships along the coast, many of the early river gunboats were simply refitted commercial vessels. In time, however, the Union's industrial superiority allowed it to produce warships that were specially configured to operate on the shallow and often sluggish waters of the western rivers. Samuel Pook designed and built seven iron-armored, flat-bottomed vessels that carried a heavy battery of guns fore and aft as well as in broadside, and which had a paddlewheel amidships. Despite their armor, they had a relatively shallow draft of only 6ft and could operate even on small tributaries; admirers declared they could navigate on a heavy dew. Nicknamed "Pook's turtles," these vessels became the backbone of the Union riverine flotilla. The Confederates could not match the Union's technological or industrial capability. Lacking the resources to manufacture maritime engines, they had to cannibalize ship engines from existing river steamers; unable to produce iron plate in quantity, they often "armored" their ships with heavy timbers, or even cotton; and lacking a plentiful supply of naval guns, they generally armed their vessels with only one or two pieces of artillery.

The Union struck first at Fort Henry on the Tennessee River. Brigadier-General Ulysses S. Grant planned to assault the fort from the landward side while the armored gunboats of Flag Officer Andrew Hull Foote's river squadron bombarded the fort from the river. In the duel between Foote's gunboats and the fort, one well-aimed shot from Fort Henry went through the thin armor of the *Essex*, penetrated to its boiler, and put it out of action. Nevertheless, the punishing shells from Foote's little flotilla compelled Fort Henry to surrender before Grant's soldiers even arrived. Afterward, Foote's gunboats steamed upriver, past the fort, to destroy a crucial railroad bridge over the Tennessee, thus cutting the principal east–west communications link of the Confederate defenders in Tennessee.

Foote could not duplicate this success in the Union assault on Fort Donelson. Only half a dozen miles east of Fort Henry, Fort Donelson on the Cumberland River was the lynchpin of Confederate defenses in the West. Foote's gunboats proved far less formidable here mainly because Donelson was situated on higher ground and its gunners could fire down onto the vessels. On this occasion, it was Grant's army that surrounded the fort from the landward side and compelled its surrender.

Army–navy cooperation was particularly evident in the Union assault on Island Number 10 on the Mississippi. Once again Foote commanded the squadron of river gunboats, but because Grant had continued up the Tennessee River to a small country church called Shiloh, the Union army contingent at Island Number 10 was under the command of Major-General John Pope. Pope's army occupied New Madrid, Missouri, on the western bank of the Mississippi, but the principal Confederate defenses were on the eastern shore and on the island itself, called Island Number 10 because it was the tenth island in numbered sequence from the confluence of the Ohio and Mississippi Rivers. The Confederate position was protected by an impassable marshland to the east and by the river itself to the west. Both Pope and Foote recognized that they could achieve success only if the navy vessels on the river could somehow join with Pope's army on the western bank of the river, and ferry the soldiers across to attack Confederate defenses from the flank and rear.

On April 4, 1862 (two days before the battle at Shiloh), Commander Henry Walke, the rather piratical-looking captain of the ironclad *Carondelet*, volunteered to run his vessel past the rebel batteries on Island Number 10. Foote was skeptical of his chances, but gave permission. Despite a harrowing journey, Walke and the *Carondelet* made the passage safely, and the next night a second ironclad duplicated his feat. Those vessels then successfully escorted Pope's army across the river to the vulnerable flank and rear of rebel defenses and the result was a spectacular and nearly bloodless Union victory.

David Dixon Porter commanded the Mississippi River flotilla as an Acting Rear-Admiral during the Union's campaign against the Confederate citadel at Vicksburg in the spring and summer of 1863. Porter's ability to work cooperatively with his army counterpart (Ulysses S. Grant) was a key element of Union success. (National Archives)

Island Number 10

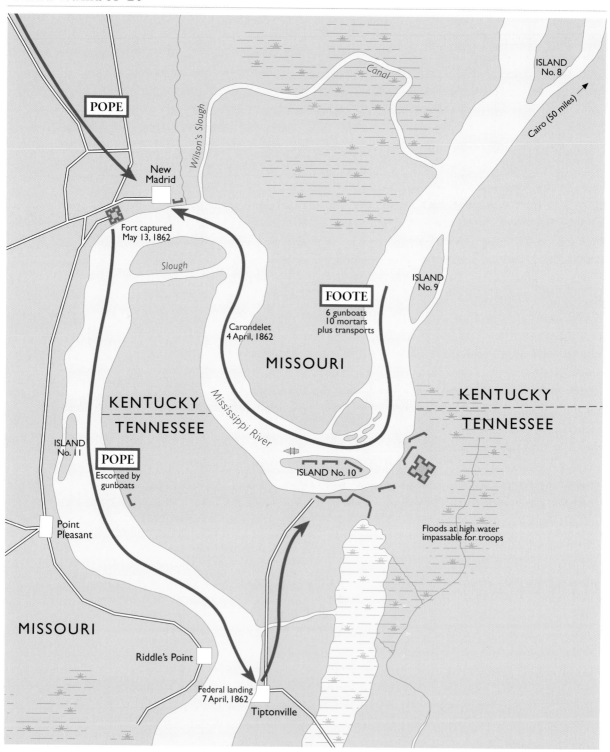

ISLAND
No. 8

Cairo (50 miles)

Canal

POPE

Wilson's Slough

New
Madrid

Fort captured
May 13, 1862

Slough

ISLAND
No. 9

FOOTE

6 gunboats
10 mortars
plus transports

Carondelet
4 April, 1862

MISSOURI

KENTUCKY

TENNESSEE

Mississippi River

ISLAND
No. 11

POPE

Escorted by
gunboats

KENTUCKY

TENNESSEE

Point
Pleasant

ISLAND No. 10

Floods at high water
impassable for troops

MISSOURI

Riddle's Point

Federal landing
7 April, 1862

Tiptonville

Three weeks later, at the other end of the Mississippi, David Glasgow Farragut repeated Walke's feat on a much larger scale by running his ocean-going warships past the forts south of New Orleans, steaming up to the Crescent City and demanding its surrender. Because most of the Confederate troops had been withdrawn from New Orleans to concentrate against Grant at Shiloh, New Orleans had little choice but to submit. The Confederacy thus lost its largest and most important city to a purely naval force, an event of enormous strategic significance.

The success of Union squadrons at both the northern and southern ends of the Mississippi left the Confederacy in control of only a 120-mile stretch of the river between Vicksburg, Mississippi and Port Hudson, Louisiana. The key to this last bit of the river was the rebel bastion at Vicksburg. Situated high on a bluff that overlooked a hairpin turn in the river, Vicksburg was the Confederate Gibraltar. Union success there could not have been achieved without the cooperation of the navy's river flotilla, by then under the command of Acting Rear-Admiral David Dixon Porter. Indeed, the triumvirate of Grant, Sherman, and Porter was a model of effective joint command, especially when compared to the non-cooperative bickering that characterized the Confederate command hierarchy. When in early April, 1863, Grant asked Porter to run his squadron past the Vicksburg batteries, Porter agreed to make the attempt even though he was under no obligation to do so. Grant was not his reporting senior, and if the campaign failed it would have been Porter who took the blame for accepting so risky a move. In effect, Porter bet his career on Grant's success. And Grant did not let him down. After a series of complicated maneuvers, much hard fighting, and a 47-day siege, Vicksburg capitulated on July 4, 1863 – the day after Pickett's Charge in far-away Pennsylvania. Port Hudson capitulated soon afterward, and Lincoln was able to write that "The Father of Waters again goes unvexed to the sea." The second element of Scott's Anaconda Plan had been fulfilled.[9]

1863

4 July

Surrender of Vicksburg: The seizure of this last major river fort on the Mississippi was a long-sought objective of the Union. In addition to capturing 30,000 troops in the city, by gaining control of the river, the North effectively cut the Confederacy in half.

TECHNOLOGICAL INNOVATION

While the Union navy blockaded the coast and seized the major rivers, the Confederate navy sought to moderate the impact of Union naval superiority in two ways: first by relying on cutting-edge experimental weapons, and second by employing the traditional tactic of weaker naval powers, that of attacking enemy commerce. Confederate navy secretary Stephen Mallory, who had chaired the Senate Naval Affairs Committee in the prewar years, knew that the South could not match the industrial capacity of the Union states. As he wrote to his wife:

Knowing that the enemy could build one hundred ships to one of our own, my policy has been to make ships so strong and invulnerable as would compensate for the inequality of numbers.[10]

In particular, Mallory focused on the construction of a few ironclads to defend southern ports and to break the blockade. At the same time, he sought to obtain a handful of specially designed steam-powered commerce raiders to harass Union trade on the high seas.

There is a certain irony in the fact that the Confederacy, which honored the traditional values of individual courage and honor and disdained Yankee machinery, helped to usher in the kind of impersonalized and mechanized warfare that would characterize future wars. For the CSS *Virginia*, built atop the hull of the partially burned USS *Merrimack*, was nothing less than a machine of war, and the duel between the *Virginia* and the USS *Monitor*, created in just over three months specifically to counter the *Virginia*, was less a battle between men at war than a duel between engines of war.

Mallory and the Confederacy staked a lot on the transformation of the *Merrimack* into the *Virginia*. It required 800 tons of iron, scavenged from all across the State of Virginia, to construct the massive 2in-thick iron plates bolted in two layers onto the *Virginia*'s 2ft-thick frame. When the dramatically reconstructed CSS *Virginia* eased gingerly down the Elizabeth River into Hampton Roads on March 8, 1862, it represented a disproportionate amount of the Confederacy's assets as well as its hopes. Under the command of Flag Officer Franklin Buchanan, the *Virginia* wasted no time in sea trials. On its maiden voyage it steamed across Hampton Roads and plunged its 1500lb ram into the starboard side of the USS *Cumberland*. After dispatching that ship, it pounded the nearby USS *Congress* into a wreck, then set it afire with hot shot. For a brief moment it seemed that the *Virginia*, by itself, might wrest control of the sea from the Union navy. The arrival in Hampton Roads that night of the John Ericsson-designed *Monitor* set the stage for the first ever duel between armored ships.

The fight on March 9 was one of the great set-piece dramas of the Civil War. The two ironclad vessels circled one another, firing as fast as they could, for most of the morning and into the afternoon. Tactically the battle was indecisive, and historians have often called it a draw. But the *Monitor*'s timely arrival in Hampton Roads had

Stephen Mallory served as Confederate secretary of the navy and sought to compensate for Union numerical superiority by relying on cutting-edge technology such as ironclads and on commerce raiding. Mallory was a knowledgable and competent secretary, but he faced impossible odds trying to compete with Union industrial superiority. (Library of Congress)

effectively neutralized the *Virginia's* offensive potential and its continued presence in Hampton Roads allowed the Union to retain command of the sea.

Welles, elated at the news of the *Monitor's* survival against the larger and more heavily armed *Virginia*, became an enthusiastic champion of monitors – a victim of what some both then and since have called "monitor fever." Over the ensuing months and years, the Union built scores of ironclad monitors and sent them down the coast to join the growing blockading squadrons. Mallory, whose strategy of innovation had initiated the ironclad arms race, found that the South could not match the Union's industrial juggernaut. Though the Confederacy initiated construction of a total of 52 ironclads, and managed to complete almost 30 of them, most of them languished for the lack of an engine or sufficient iron plate, and more than a few had to be destroyed when Union forces threatened to seize the ports and harbors where they were under construction. Only one other rebel ironclad, the CSS *Albemarle*, which was built in a cornfield on the Neuse River in North

The duel between the Confederate ironclad Virginia *and the Union* Monitor *was the most famous naval engagement of the war. Though the battle was a tactical draw, the* Monitor's *timely arrival and continued presence allowed the Union navy to retain possession of Hampton Roads and hold it throughout the duration of the war. (US Naval Historical Center)*

Carolina, experienced the kind of spectacular, if temporary, success as the *Virginia* when it sank the Union gunboat *Southfield* in April 1864.[11]

The South had more success with torpedoes, which the Federals called "infernal machines" and which today would be called mines. Early in the war, some northerners looked upon these silent, deadly, and impersonal weapons as immoral, even unmanly. When a Confederate officer planted an artillery shell in the ground in front of McClellan's advancing horde on the Virginia Peninsula in 1862, both sides were horrified at the use of such weaponry. But wars create a momentum of their own, and at sea the South sowed hundreds of mines in its waterways and rivers in the hope of evening the odds against the superior US Navy.

The most spectacular use of mines came in the battle for Mobile Bay in August 1864. One of the few seaports not yet closed by the Union, Mobile was a prime target of the Union high command in 1864, and Rear-Admiral David Glasgow Farragut knew that the rebels had sown mines in the ship channel. To enter Mobile Bay, he would not only have to run the gauntlet of Confederate forts (as he had in his approach to New Orleans two years earlier), but also thread his way through the

This painting by J.O. Davidson depicts the critical moment in the battle of Mobile Bay when the Union monitor Tecumseh *struck a Confederate mine and went down. Soon afterward, Farragut led his column of wooden warships through the minefield and into the bay to defeat the small Confederate flotilla that included the CSS* Tennessee *(left foreground). (US Naval Historical Center)*

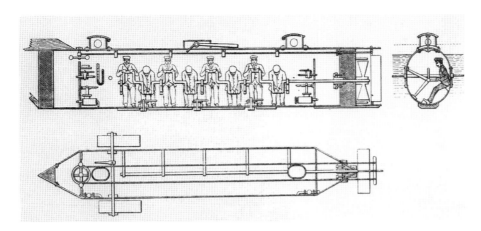

This sketch of the interior of the Confederate submarine H.L. Hunley *suggests something about the cramped quarters on board. Despite that, and despite the fact that two previous crews went to their deaths in this experimental vessel, the* Hunley *succeeded in sinking a US Navy warship, the* Housatonic, *off Charleston in 1864. (US Naval Historical Center)*

minefield in the narrow channel. Farragut arranged his squadron in two columns with the monitors to starboard and his wooden vessels to port. As Farragut's twin columns steamed toward the channel entrance, his lead monitor, USS *Tecumseh,* was all but lifted out of the water by the explosion of a submerged mine. It turned onto its starboard side, then plunged bow-first into the water, going down in a matter of seconds taking 93 men with her. Witnessing this startling event, and seeing a row of buoys in front of him that marked the presence of more mines, James Alden, the captain of Farragut's lead wooden vessel *Brooklyn,* ordered his ship to stop, an order that threatened to throw the whole squadron into chaos. Farragut therefore ordered his flagship, the *Hartford,* to swing out around the stalled *Brooklyn.* When Alden called over to him that there were torpedoes in the water ahead, Farragut is supposed to have shouted back: "Damn the torpedoes!" As it happened, the Union fleet made it safely into the bay without detonating any more mines. Once there, it dispatched the Confederate squadron, including the ironclad CSS *Tennessee,* commanded by Franklin Buchanan, the same man who had commanded the CSS *Virginia* in its initial sortie back in 1862.

The South also experimented with submarines, though this was less a product of Mallory's strategic plan than of individual initiative. The most famous submarine of the war was the ill-fated *H.L. Hunley,* built originally in Mobile from a boiler and transported to Charleston by rail. The *Hunley* had no engine; to propel the vessel through the water, a crew of eight men, hunched over in pitch darkness, turned a hand-cranked propeller while the commanding officer manipulated diving planes that caused it to submerge or ascend. After sinking twice during trial runs, each time killing most of the crew on board, the *Hunley* succeeded in sinking the USS *Housatonic* outside Charleston on February 17, 1864, though the *Hunley* herself sunk a third and final time en route back to port.[12]

Despite Confederate efforts to seize the technological initiative with ironclads, mines, and submarines, significantly greater Union industrial capability allowed the North to counter Confederate innovation with superior productivity.

COMMERCE RAIDING

In addition to seizing on cutting-edge technology, the Confederacy sought to influence the outcome of the war at sea by adopting a strategy of *guerre de course*. Just as the Union blockade was designed to cripple the southern economy, Confederate commerce raiding was supposed to weaken the Union economy and thereby weaken popular support for Lincoln's war. Though the Davis administration issued a number of Letters of Marque that authorized individuals to send out privately owned raiders called privateers, the most effective commerce raiders of the war were government-owned warships purchased in England by Confederate naval agent James D. Bulloch and commanded by officers of the Confederate navy.

The most famous of these was the cruiser *Alabama*, built in the Birkenhead shipyard at Liverpool where it was known simply as Hull No. 290. Though its paperwork indicated that it was being constructed for the Turkish Navy, everyone, including US Ambassador Charles Francis Adams, knew its actual intended destination. Adams protested vehemently to the British government, but despite his protests, No. 290 went to sea on July 30, 1862, on what was supposed to be a trial run and never returned. Instead it went to the Portuguese Azores where it took on an international crew of volunteers and a dozen Confederate naval officers, and then embarked on a two-year cruise that resulted in the destruction of 64 Union merchant vessels and one US Navy warship, USS *Hatteras*, before it was finally defeated in a classic ship-to-ship duel off Cherbourg, France, by USS *Kearsarge*. Even then the *Alabama*'s skipper, the flamboyant Raphael Semmes, refused to accept defeat, hurling his sword into the sea and swimming to a nearby British yacht. Eventually he made his way back to Richmond where he served briefly with Lee's army before its capitulation at Appomattox.

It was a Confederate commerce raider, the CSS *Shenandoah* under the command of James I. Waddell, that had the distinction of being the last organized element of the Confederate military to surrender. In the spring of 1865, the *Shenandoah* was in the North Pacific wreaking havoc on the US whaling ships, when its commander learned that Lee had surrendered. Not until Waddell spoke to the crew of the British bark *Baracouta* in August, 1865 – four months after Appomattox – did he accept the fact of southern defeat. Even then, he decided to take his vessel back to Britain where it had been purchased rather than to surrender to the Union. He arrived in Liverpool in November 1865, and only then hauled down the Confederate flag.[13]

Like the historical debate about the impact of the blockade, the impact of Confederate commerce raiding is disputed. The handful of Confederate raiders kept perhaps four times their number of Union warships busy looking for them, which

1865

9 April

Lee surrenders at Appomattox: Lee's surrender was an event which marked an end to the war for many, although James I. Waddell, captain of the Confederate raider *Shenandoah*, did not haul down his flag until November 6, 1865.

marginally weakened the Union blockade force, though not enough to make a substantive difference. Then, too, in addition to the nearly 100 Union merchant ships that were captured and burned by Confederate raiders, the very threat of being seized by one of these raiders led some northern merchants to re-flag their ships under foreign registry. This "flight from the flag" continued even after the war was over, and some scholars trace the decline of the American merchant marine to the rampage of the *Alabama*.[14] In the end, however, Confederate depredations on Union commerce were not enough to turn the northern public against the war.

Overall, the naval war was an important element of Union victory in the Civil War. The blockade created shortages and hardships within the Confederacy that were only partly ameliorated by blockade runners, and the navy was an essential partner in the Union's successful conquest of the western rivers. Despite innovations such as ironclads, mines, and submarines, the Confederacy found itself overmatched in its effort to produce and sustain a naval force that could contest the seas and the rivers with the US Navy, and the handful of rebel raiders was simply not enough to break, or even seriously threaten, Union control of Neptune's element.

> *"They came here to butcher our people
> and got butchered themselves."*

Missouri surgeon William McPheeters, 1864

They came to butcher our people
The Civil War in the West

Jeffery S. Prushankin

THE TRANS-MISSISSIPPI

Civil war in America started and ended in the states west of the Mississippi River. In 1854, violence in Kansas ushered in a period of conflict that ended 11 years later with Confederate surrender in Indian Territory. Bereft of battles such as Gettysburg and Chickamauga, the Civil War in the West was every bit as destructive and heart-wrenching as the war in the East. Further, Trans-Mississippi operations affected the outlook of the warring nations. Often dismissed as a backwater, the Trans-Mississippi influenced the prosecution of the war and helped shape its outcome.

Union and Confederate governments approached the Trans-Mississippi with similar objectives but different expectations. For both, territorial security was important, but to Washington, political control was essential. To Richmond, the Trans-Mississippi provided a source of manpower and raw materials. Sending

Often considered "the Gettysburg of the West," the battle of Pea Ridge, Arkansas, was the high-water mark of the Confederacy's attempt to wrest control of Missouri from the Union. Confederate defeat in the two-day battle, March 7 and 8, 1862, paved the way for Federal conquest of Arkansas. (Library of Congress)

Trans-Mississippi recruits to fight in the East, however, left the department vulnerable. Consequently, Washington seized the strategic offensive and waged a war of occupation, forcing the Confederates to extend their military resources beyond the limits of their defensive capacity. Moreover, inadequate communications with Richmond, particularly after the loss of Vicksburg, forced Trans-Mississippi Confederates to operate independently. This ultimately contributed to numerous departmental breakdowns. The Union's integrated command structure kept their military focus closely aligned with Washington's war aims.

Trans-Mississippi America stretched west from the Mississippi River to California and south from Minnesota to the Rio Grande. Missouri, Arkansas, Texas, and western Louisiana covered 600,000 square miles and counted 2.7 million inhabitants, amounting to over 20 percent of the Confederacy's population. Of these, some 2 million were free whites, 9,000 free African Americans, and 658,000 slaves. New Mexico Territory accounted for another 100,000 people including 65,000 Indians, while Indian Territory had at least 60,000, made up predominantly of members from the Five Civilized Tribes plus 7,000 slaves.

Early in 1861, Abraham Lincoln established Trans-Mississippi military departments to pacify western border states and to put Federal armies in position to invade Confederate territory. Although Lincoln modified these departments according to changing circumstances, his centralized approach remained constant. Jefferson Davis believed that the states should handle internal matters and he designed a departmental system based loosely along state lines. This arrangement left military organization up to each state and required cooperation between civil and military leaders. Cooperation was not always forthcoming and, in January 1862, Davis created the Trans-Mississippi District consisting of northwestern Louisiana, most of Arkansas and Missouri, and Indian Territory. In 1863, he established the Trans-Mississippi Department to encompass territory west of the river. By this time, the Federals held key areas of Confederate territory, particularly along the border.

Among the Trans-Mississippi states in antebellum America, Missouri was the most volatile. The border state boasted a population of over one-half of the region's free whites, one-third of the free blacks, and one-fifth of the slaves. The number of Missouri slaveholders had declined steadily, and with less capital tied up in slaves, Missourians diversified their investments. As a result, Missouri moved closer to the industrialized North. Ideologically, however, Missouri remained allied with the agrarian South.

Internal dissent reflected this trend and discord spilled into neighboring Kansas territory. Clashes between antislavery Kansans and proslavery Missouri Border Ruffians sparked a series of skirmishes along the Kansas–Missouri border dubbed the Wakarusa War. In May 1856, a band of Border Ruffians sacked Lawrence, the center of antislavery activity. In retaliation, John Brown, a migrant from New England, murdered five Missourians at Pottawatomie Creek. The escalating violence earned Kansas the nickname "Bleeding Kansas" and newspapers declared a state of civil war in the territory.

Although Lincoln failed to carry a single district within the Trans-Mississippi's slave states, his election did not make their secession a certainty. In Louisiana, enthusiasm for secession was mild, particularly around New Orleans, an area tied to commerce. Nevertheless, secessionist governor Thomas Moore gained control of his state's secession convention and on January 26 Louisiana left the Union. Delegate Richard Taylor "marveled at the joyous and careless temper" of those who consummated the act of secession. In Texas, Unionist governor Sam Houston refused to call a convention. The legislature, however, put the issue to the voters and Texas seceded on February 23. Arkansas rejected immediate secession and called for a statewide referendum. Fort Sumter and Lincoln's call for troops prompted governor Henry Rector to reconvene the convention. On May 6, Arkansas passed an ordinance of secession.[1]

Many Missourians supported secession, but the state's infrastructure tied Missouri to points north and east. Furthermore, Illinois, Iowa, Kansas, and Nebraska bordered Missouri on three sides. Except for a tip of southeastern land across the river from Tennessee and Kentucky, the Arkansas line was Missouri's only boundary with the Confederacy. Despite pressure from secessionist governor Claiborne Jackson, Missouri's convention voted to remain in the Union and await further developments. Former governor Sterling Price attempted to serve as peacemaker between opposing factions but his efforts proved futile. Congressman Francis Blair raised a Unionist Home Guard while Jackson called up the militia. Jackson condemned Lincoln's appeal for troops as "illegal, unconstitutional, and revolutionary in its object." Blair offered his Home Guard to Nathaniel Lyon, the Federal commander in St Louis. Lyon mustered the men into service.[2]

MISSOURI AND KANSAS

Lyon feared that secessionists would seize the St Louis arsenal. In fact, that was precisely what Jackson had planned, but Lyon struck first and secured the armory's 60,000 muskets. Then, disguised as a woman, he personally scouted the militia encampment. Despite learning that the militia was about to disband, Lyon surrounded the camp and arrested 600 Missourians. As Lyon paraded his prisoners through town, spectators gathered along the roadside. Some began to taunt the soldiers and, when the crowd turned violent, Lyon's men opened fire killing 28. For these actions, Lyon received a promotion to brigadier and command of 10,000 troops. He had provoked the violence and, to many, fears of coercion were no longer an abstraction. Jackson received aid from the Confederacy and appointed Price to command Missouri troops. Efforts to avoid further bloodshed failed when a

Trans-Mississippi Theater

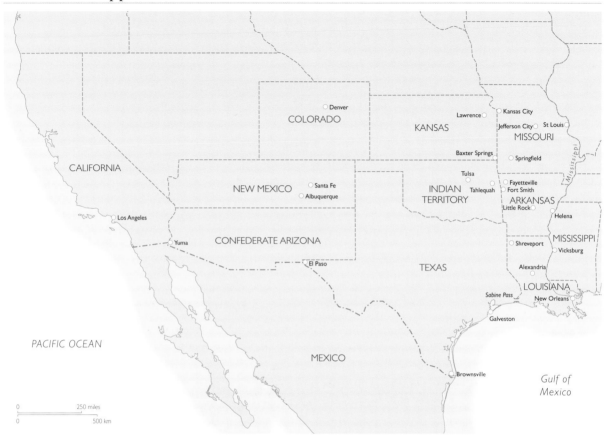

meeting between Price and Lyon resulted in the latter issuing a threat to kill his counterpart along with "every man, woman, and child in Missouri."[3]

Lyon had issued a declaration of war. In mid-June he seized Jefferson City, forcing Jackson and pro-Confederate legislators to flee to southwest Missouri. With the rebels on the run, remnants of the secession convention reconvened under Lyon's bayonets and declared themselves the new legislature. They appointed a Unionist governor and proclaimed their loyalty to the United States. Jackson and the fugitive legislators voted to secede and Missouri became a star on the Confederate flag.

By August, Lyon had moved 6,000 troops to southwest Missouri. Ten miles below Springfield he discovered Price with a rebel army twice his number, encamped along Wilson's Creek. On August 10, the Federals launched a surprise attack, but the Confederates won the day and Lyon paid for the gamble with his life. With each side suffering 1,200 casualties, the Federals retreated to Rolla while Price advanced to Lexington. When John C. Frémont, commander of the Federal Western Department, pushed 38,000 Federals west from St Louis, Price fell back to the Arkansas line.

Since Frémont's arrival in July, and his decision to declare martial law, he had made powerful political enemies. Most damaging was his decision to confiscate the property of Confederate sympathizers including their slaves. This *de facto* emancipation was too much for most Missourians and Lincoln would let neither the order nor the officer remain in place. On November 2, he relieved Frémont and appointed Henry W. Halleck to head the Department of Missouri. The Federals withdrew to central Missouri and the Confederates moved into Springfield.

The ensuing guerrilla war that engulfed the Kansas–Missouri border made Bleeding Kansas seem like a skirmish. Kansas senator James Lane directed a series of raids into Missouri and murdered anyone who stood in his way regardless of age or gender. Missourians branded him "The Grim Chieftain." In Kansas City, Doctor Charles Jennison organized his own gang of marauders, drawing on a pool of manpower from local jails. Jennison carved out a sadistic reputation by adding rape and mutilation to his repertoire of terror. Lane, Jennison, and other Unionist guerrillas, known as Red-Legs, did much to drive Missourians to the Confederate cause. Yet, Kansas governor James Ingalls considered them "a band of destroying angels."[4]

In March 1862, the Confederates responded in kind as William J. Quantrill, a transplanted Ohio schoolteacher, led a band of Missourians into Kansas. A skilled horseman with a flair for leadership, Quantrill soon acquired a fearful reputation, and his Bushwhackers became the best known Confederate guerrillas in the Trans-Mississippi. Quantrill did not merely attack civilians but also targeted Union patrols and installations, thereby drawing Federal troops away from other duties.

In 1863, the Federals created the District of the Border and appointed former Kansas judge Thomas Ewing to secure the Missouri–Kansas line. Ewing recently served with Lane and one of his first acts as commander was to imprison southern sympathizers. On August 13, five women died and dozens more were maimed when a jail collapsed. Already incensed by Ewing's policy, the debacle further inflamed Quantrill's men and on August 21 they thundered into Lawrence to extract revenge. Quantrill slaughtered 150 Unionists and fired the town before escaping across the state line. Ewing sought retribution and implemented General Order 11, deporting 20,000 Missourians from counties along the border. After sending these civilians into exile, the Federals laid waste to their farms and homes.

Ewing's measures escalated the bloodletting along the border. In October, Quantrill butchered Union troops at Baxter

Bold, often to the point of rashness, Nathaniel Lyon developed a reputation for his nasty temper and his hatred of southerners. He believed himself an instrument of God and maintained that slaveholders should be put to the sword. Lyon hoped to wage a war of annihilation against secessionists and his antagonism precipitated bloodshed in Missouri. His decisions on the battlefield cost him his life at Wilson's Creek. Lyon was the first Federal general killed in the Civil War and became a martyr to the Union cause. (Courtesy of Robert K. Krick)

Springs, Kansas, and in 1864 one of his lieutenants, William Anderson, wiped out an enemy force at Kingsville, Missouri. For Anderson, the conflict had become personal. He lost his father to Jayhawkers and a sister in the prison collapse, and consequently harbored a hatred of Unionists. His guerrillas reflected their leader's attitude by employing a savage brand of warfare. Anderson recorded each kill with a knot tied into his sash and hung Yankee scalps from his bridle. The raids earned him the nickname "Bloody Bill" and his attack at Centralia, Missouri, in September 1864, ranked among the most gruesome of the war. A Kansas Federal labeled the atrocities at Centralia "the most extensive and barbarous" of the war while a Confederate recalled "The Centralia fight reminds me of Macbeth in 'Never shake thy gory locks at me.' "[5]

When the war ended, many Confederate guerrilla units simply disbanded rather than surrender. While Quantrill and Anderson did not live to see the war's conclusion, some who served with them, like Frank and Jesse James, continued their violent ways as postwar outlaws. Some Jayhawkers, like William (Buffalo Bill) Cody, parlayed their service into more legitimate postwar ventures. Guerrilla warfare in the Trans-Mississippi did not influence the outcome of the Civil War. Guerrilla raids, however, did force both sides to divert military resources to contain partisan activities. Moreover, much of the hatred stirred by guerrillas continued throughout Reconstruction.

NEW MEXICO, CALIFORNIA, AND COLORADO

Like Missouri, divided loyalties in the far west left much to chance for both the Union and Confederacy. In New Mexico, the population around Santa Fe was predominantly neutral, while settlers farther south called themselves Arizonians and harbored pro-Confederate sentiments. In 1861, southern sympathizers decreed Arizona a territory and the Confederacy sent Texan John Baylor to secure the region. Baylor declared himself governor and began to wage war against local Indians. This ended his tenure and prompted Richmond to explore other options.

Davis saw an opportunity to extend Confederate influence across the southwest to the Pacific. Nearly half of California's 400,000 citizens had emigrated from slave states and although the legislature trumpeted its allegiance to the Union, there was strong pro-Confederate sentiment around Los Angeles. Furthermore, in Colorado, some 7,500 secessionists were "ably and secretly organized" and with their assistance the Confederacy could gain a foothold in the territory. Richmond looked to capitalize on this friction to secure a Pacific port and to cash in on western gold and silver mines.[6]

Henry Hopkins Sibley was a West Pointer with antebellum frontier service and seemed a logical choice for command. In December, Sibley led his 3,700-man Army of New Mexico north from El Paso along the Rio Grande toward Fort Craig and

Albuquerque. Sibley reached the fort in mid-February but could not draw Federal commander Edward R.S. Canby into battle. Sibley decided to bypass Fort Craig and continue along the high bluffs to the east. On February 20, Canby moved to intercept the rebels. The next day, the armies clashed at Valverde and Sibley emerged victorious. Afterward, things began to go wrong for the Confederates. Sibley was apparently drunk during recent operations and his intemperance unsettled southern troops. In addition, Canby still held Fort Craig and refused to surrender, thus depriving the Confederates of supplies. Sibley reduced his men to half-rations and ordered the army to press on to Santa Fe. "Starvation seems to stare us in the face," a Texan groaned.[7]

While Sibley's force grew weaker, Colorado volunteers rushed to contest the advance. John P. Slough led nearly 1,000 men on a forced march from Denver across mountains and through snowstorms. On March 26, the "Pikes Peakers" confronted a portion of Sibley's force at Apache Canyon. Both sides concentrated around Glorieta Pass and, on March 28, skirmishing near Pigeon's Ranch erupted into a pitched battle. Although Sibley drove the Federals from the field, Colorado major Thomas Chivington, a fiery prewar preacher, turned the Confederate rear and destroyed rebel trains. Chivington's feat rendered Sibley's tactical victory meaningless and forced him to abandon the campaign. Without provisions, southern soldiers endured a punishing retreat to San Antonio. The Confederates lost 1,000 men and accusations of incompetence haunted Sibley for the rest of his career. For years to come, a trail of bleached bones marked the track of Sibley's army.[8]

Meanwhile, in the weeks preceding Fort Sumter, Lincoln sent Edwin Sumner to California to relieve Texan Albert Sidney Johnston, commander of the Department of the Pacific. Sumner deployed troops across California, and in a crackdown on southern sympathizers, tried to arrest Johnston who escaped to Texas. In March 1862, California recruits under James Carleton drove Sherod Hunter's Arizonians from Tucson to Texas. The firefight at Stanwix Station, 80 miles east of Yuma, marked the westernmost combat of the war. The power of the Union in California, combined with Sibley's defeat, dashed Confederate hopes in the southwest.

ARKANSAS

In January 1862, Davis chose Earl Van Dorn to command Trans-Mississippi forces. Van Dorn believed in taking swift action and set his sights on St Louis. To Price, he suggested "rapid marches and assault" and to his wife he insisted "I must have St Louis – then huzza!" By March, however, a Federal army under Samuel Curtis had already pushed Price into Arkansas. Curtis had orders to clear the Confederates from southwest Missouri and he had done just that.[9]

Van Dorn arrived in early March, exhausted from his journey and suffering with the flu. He assessed Curtis's position and decided against a frontal assault, instead ordering a turning movement around the Federal right. The march took all night and by dawn only Price had reached the objective, deep in the Federal rear, east of Big Mountain, known locally as Pea Ridge. In the interest of time, Van Dorn ordered General Ben McCulloch (McCulloch was the Confederate commander in western Arkansas and Indian Territory) to march east through Leetown and join Price near Elkhorn Tavern. Despite the risks involved in dividing the army, the gamble would, if successful, win acclaim for Van Dorn.

During the night of March 6, Curtis suspected something was afoot and the Federals reoriented their front 180 degrees. Accordingly, McCulloch's march carried him across the new line of Federal fire. The armies battled fiercely at Leetown, but Federal sharpshooters killed McCulloch, leaving the rebels in disarray. Meanwhile, Price held at Elkhorn Tavern and Curtis fell back to the fields south of Pea Ridge. The following day, Curtis launched a furious counterattack and the Confederates withdrew. Before the battle Van Dorn boasted of taking St Louis.

Flamboyant and daring, Earl Van Dorn suffered two wounds and earned two brevets in his ante-bellum military career on the frontier. At the outbreak of the Civil War he served in Texas until promoted to command in the Trans-Mississippi. His tenure ended in failure but Van Dorn later excelled as a cavalry leader, particularly in operations against Grant in Mississippi. His fondness for women led to Van Dorn's demise when a jealous husband murdered the general in 1863. (Courtesy of Mississippi State Archives)

Afterward he explained, "I was not defeated, but only foiled in my intentions." Nevertheless, Pea Ridge was a Union victory. Van Dorn suffered 2,000 casualties and Curtis 1,000, including scores of Iowans "scalped, tomahawked, or otherwise mutilated" by Confederate Cherokees. The significance of the battle lay in the strategic victory for the Federals. Pea Ridge secured Missouri as Union territory and slammed the door on the Confederates.[10]

After Pea Ridge, the Federals moved east to protect the Missouri line. When the Richmond government ordered Van Dorn across the Mississippi, Curtis turned toward Little Rock. The removal of Confederate forces from Arkansas seemed to signal Richmond's intention to abandon the state. Without troops for protection Arkansans turned to partisan warfare and attacks on Federal supply lines derailed Curtis's plans for Little Rock. Curtis promptly shifted his attention to Helena. In a campaign that foreshadowed things to come, he employed a rudimentary brand of total war and Federal troops stormed down the White River, bringing ruin to everything in their path. Helena fell on July 12.

Tennessean Thomas C. Hindman settled in Arkansas after the Mexican War and won election to the US Congress in 1858. An ardent secessionist, he joined the Confederacy and rose to command at the brigade, division, corps, and district levels. A fierce fighter, Hindman sported a colorful personality, often wearing elegant clothing and pink kid-skin gloves into battle. After the war he remained an unreconstructed rebel and died at the hands of an assassin in 1868 at his home in Helena. (Library of Congress)

Six weeks earlier, Richmond elevated parts of the Trans-Mississippi to department status and selected Thomas Hindman for command. An Arkansas political general, Hindman pledged "to drive out the invader or perish in the attempt." He believed that cavalry and partisans were efficient ways to wage war, and among the mounted units Hindman mustered, Missourian Joseph Shelby's "Iron Brigade" became one of the most effective fighting forces in the Confederacy. In September 1863, Shelby led his men on the longest cavalry raid of the war, covering 1,500 miles in 41 days through Arkansas and Missouri. Afterwards, one Confederate crowed, "You've heard of... Jeb Stuart's Ride around McClellan? Hell, brother, Jo Shelby rode around Missouri!"[11]

While Hindman proved himself a skilled organizer, his austere methods alienated many and, by August, Richmond demoted him to Arkansas district command. In his place, aging veteran Theophilus Holmes took control of the Trans-Mississippi. Called "Old Granny" by his men, Holmes was cautious to a fault. He dismissed Hindman's proposal to invade southwest Missouri, but after conferring with his subordinate, sanctioned a movement into northwest Arkansas.[12]

Curtis anticipated such a move and having succeeded Halleck to command of the Department of Missouri, ordered John Schofield to take the Army of the Frontier and secure northwest Arkansas. Schofield scattered his forces across the region and thus gave Hindman an opportunity. In early December, Hindman marched the 11,000-man Army of the Trans-Mississippi north from Fort Smith toward an isolated Federal force at Cane Hill. Union commander James Blunt chose to confront the threat with just 5,000 troops and called for help from Francis Herron in Springfield.

Blunt's decision was foolhardy. Rather than fall back to meet reinforcements, he demanded Herron undertake a forced march of over 120 miles. Herron's march was one of the greatest feats of the war. His 7,000 men covered 35 miles per day, reaching Fayetteville before dawn on December 7.

When Hindman learned of Herron's approach, he established a position at Prairie Grove, 10 miles west of Fayetteville on the hills overlooking the Illinois River. Although outnumbered, Herron's men were better trained and better equipped than Hindman's recruits and the armies fought to a standstill. As the fighting died down, Blunt arrived and fell on Hindman's left. The day was cold and wounded men crawled into haystacks for shelter, but bursting shells set fire to the hay and many were burned alive. As the sun set, the fighting sputtered to a halt with neither side achieving victory. That night, wild hogs "gorged themselves upon the unholy banquet" of charred human flesh left smoldering on the field. A battle-hardened veteran described the macabre scene as the most "sickening and appalling" of the war.[13]

Hindman requested a truce to gather his casualties but the cease-fire was a ploy and, after midnight, the Confederates withdrew. As the men trudged toward Little Rock hundreds fell from the ranks, disillusioned with the war, with Hindman, and with the Confederacy. Like Pea Ridge, Prairie Grove was a strategic Union victory. Pea Ridge had slammed the door on the Confederates, and Prairie Grove nailed it shut. The Federals controlled the area above the Arkansas River from Indian Territory to the Mississippi. By September, Little Rock and Pine Bluff had fallen and the shadow of the Union closed in on southwest Arkansas.[14]

Defeat led to a shakeup for Trans-Mississippi Confederates and Richmond appointed Edmund Kirby Smith to department command. A West Pointer who achieved fame at First Manassas and in the Kentucky campaign, Smith owed his promotion to politicians from Missouri and Arkansas who pressured Davis for his appointment. Accordingly, Smith focused on these states often at the expense of the rest of the department.[15]

With the secession of his native Florida, Edmund Kirby Smith resigned from the US Army and joined the Confederacy. Wounded at Manassas, Smith became one of the South's first heroes and his new wife was known as "The Bride of the Confederacy." Smith failed to find glory in the Kentucky campaign and in the Trans-Mississippi, but, as commander of the last department to surrender, he acquired a measure of fame after the war. Smith died in 1893, the last of the full-Confederate generals. (Courtesy of Robert K. Krick)

LOUISIANA AND TEXAS

More than any other Trans-Mississippi state, Louisiana suffered under Smith's leadership. When he arrived there in February 1863, district commander Richard Taylor had begun an attempt to relieve Vicksburg by threatening New Orleans. Taylor, a Louisiana political general and Jefferson Davis's brother-in-law, had confidential orders from secretary of war George Wythe Randolph to liberate New Orleans. Yet, by the time Smith received his assignment, Randolph was gone and plans for New Orleans forgotten. Unaware of Taylor's instructions, Smith did not consider New Orleans part of his mission. Richmond's failure to reconcile conflicting orders undermined Smith and Taylor's relationship.[16]

In April, the Federals pushed Taylor along Bayou Teche, past the mouth of the Red River to Alexandria. Union troops occupied Alexandria for a short time before marching east to Port Hudson. To Taylor's dismay, Smith then ordered him to northeastern Louisiana with instructions to attack Federal depots opposite

Vicksburg. During one such action at Milliken's Bend, John Walker's Texans battled a brigade of US Colored Troops and northern reports charged the rebels with murdering African American soldiers. In addition, a Confederate deserter accused Taylor of executing captured white officers. Although both allegations were false, a perception emerged that the rules of civilized warfare did not apply in the Trans-Mississippi.

Smith was the first Confederate department commander to confront the "disagreeable dilemma" surrounding African American Federals. At first, he instituted a policy of no quarter but revised the order to conform to a Confederate directive ordering "all negro slaves captured in arms," turned over to state officials. Richmond instructed him to consider captured black Federals "deluded victims" of Yankee treachery, to be "treated with mercy."[17]

In September 1863, as the number of African American Federals increased, Smith considered training slaves for Confederate service. Although his plan never came to fruition, warfare in the Trans-Mississippi propelled Smith's thinking ahead of those in Richmond. Nevertheless, for Trans-Mississippi soldiers in the field, combat took on ghastly dimensions. In 1864, at Poison Spring Arkansas, Texas troops reportedly massacred African American prisoners and Confederate Choctaws mutilated the corpses. Days later at Jenkins Ferry, African American Federals took their revenge and slit the throats of wounded Confederates.

Beyond racial issues, tensions between Smith and Taylor continued to worsen. Cut off from Richmond by the loss of Vicksburg, Smith exercised control over civilian agencies. While Davis endorsed this expansion of powers, many state and military officials believed that Smith had exceeded his authority. His creation and administration of the Trans-Mississippi Cotton Bureau turned into a bureaucratic nightmare, rife with corruption and scandal. Taylor insisted that Smith considered the Trans-Mississippi a "lost empire" and cynical Confederates called the Trans-Mississippi "Kirby-Smithdom."[18]

After winning Vicksburg, the Federals looked to Texas. Texas was vulnerable along its coastline and Union ships prowled the Gulf. In September, a flotilla carrying 6,000 Federals ascended the Sabine Pass. Confederate lieutenant Dick Dowling, a 25-year-old Irish immigrant, held the Pass with 42 men and 12 guns. Dowling turned back the invasion, inflicting 375 casualties without losing a single man. District commander John Magruder called the victory "the most extraordinary feat of the war."[19]

In November the Federals captured Brownsville, just across the Rio Grande from Matamoras. Brownsville was the Confederacy's gateway to international trade and Union troops occupied the Rio Grande Valley up to Laredo. Still, the Federals failed to shut down commerce or pacify civilians. In 1864, John "Rip" Ford

1863

28 November

Proclamation of Amnesty and Reconstruction: Called Lincoln's "10 Percent" plan because it required only 10 percent of the participants in the 1860 presidential election to reorganize a loyal state government, the policy was Lincoln's way of beginning the process of Reconstruction. It offered pardons to any Confederate willing to take an oath of allegiance.

unleashed his Cavalry of the West against Union outposts and the Federals relinquished their position.

The architect of these failed missions was Nathaniel Banks, a Massachusetts political general in command of the Department of the Gulf. Banks received his commission more for his political skill than his military prowess. Conquest of Texas was vital to Lincoln's domestic and foreign policy. Seizure of Texas cotton fields would yield thousands of bales for starving New England textile mills and improved economic conditions, combined with a "reconstructed" Texas under the "10 Percent" plan, would bolster Lincoln's reelection bid. Moreover, French Emperor Napoleon III had established a regime in Mexico and favored Confederate independence. A Union presence in Texas would preclude the French from aiding the rebels.

Banks decided that Louisiana provided the best staging ground for a Texas campaign. He planned to take the 20,000-man Army of the Gulf, along with 10,000 troops on loan from William T. Sherman, up the Red River to Shreveport, the Trans-Mississippi capital. A naval squadron under David Dixon Porter would accompany Banks's columns. En route, the Federals planned to procure cotton and upon reaching Shreveport destroy the rebel military-industrial complex. From Arkansas, Frederick Steele's army would join Banks in Shreveport. Once united, they would conquer Texas.

Two essential factors undermined the Union's Red River campaign. First, the objectives were more political than military. This influenced the selection of Banks to lead the mission. Banks's leadership, however, fostered the second problem: the Federals lacked unity of command. Inter-service squabbling between army and navy marred the occupation of Alexandria, and Sherman's rugged midwesterners, under command of A.J. Smith, loathed Banks's prim easterners. Meanwhile, Smith, William Franklin, and Banks's other lieutenants considered the commanding general incompetent.

Once the Federals reached Natchitoches, 60 miles below Shreveport, Banks turned away from the river and abandoned Porter's fleet. Taylor was under orders to retreat, but saw an opportunity in Banks's blunder. Disobeying orders, he attacked the Federals at Mansfield on April 8, and chased Banks to Pleasant Hill. The next day Taylor struck again and Banks tumbled back to the river, abandoning the campaign.

Taylor out-generaled Banks at Mansfield, bringing to bear his force of 9,000 against one-quarter of Banks's army. At Pleasant Hill, he followed up his victory, a rarity in the Civil War. Taylor also turned Banks into a commissary, capturing hundreds of supply wagons, some designated "Austin, San Antonio, Houston, Galveston" by the overconfident Federals. The battles were costly to both sides with Taylor losing 2,500 and Banks 4,400. After days of tending the wounded, Missouri surgeon William McPheeters reflected the sentiment in Taylor's army. He confided to his diary, "They came here to butcher our people and got butchered themselves."[20]

Outraged at the order to retreat, A.J. Smith summoned Franklin and demanded Banks's arrest. "Don't you know this is mutiny?" growled Franklin, and Smith backed down. Once the army reached the river, Porter found Banks studying a book on military tactics. The admiral suggested that the general should have read the book before the campaign.[21]

Although the army and navy reunited at Alexandria, the falling water level stranded the fleet above the rapids. Earlier, Porter boasted that he could take his fleet "wherever the sand was damp." Now, he was stuck and forced to rely on his rival for help. Porter allegedly threatened to fire on the infantry if Banks withdrew, and so the Federals dug in at Alexandria, a force of 30,000 surrounded by a few thousand Confederates. Taylor hoped to take advantage of the opportunity and snare both the fleet and the army. He might have been successful, but Smith detached two-thirds of Taylor's infantry to campaign in Arkansas.[22] Upon learning of Banks's defeat, Steele began a retreat to Little Rock. On April 30, Smith caught Steele along the Saline River at Jenkins Ferry and scored a costly victory. Meanwhile, at Alexandria, Joseph Bailey, a Wisconsin colonel, insisted that he could construct a series of dams to free the fleet. Skeptical but desperate, Banks and Porter approved the project. Bailey's dams were the most innovative engineering feat of the war and on May 13 the fleet made good its escape. Afterward, the army burned Alexandria and pillaged its way out of western Louisiana.

The Red River campaign was a disaster for the Federals. Derisively, Banks's men referred to him as "Napoleon" and Halleck removed him from command. Taylor also considered the campaign a failure and blamed Smith for taking his infantry and allowing the enemy to escape. He argued that the destruction of Banks and Porter would have prevented thousands of Federals from joining campaigns in the East and influenced the outcome of the war. Taylor launched a scathing attack on Smith's leadership and Smith arrested him for insubordination. When news of the campaign reached Richmond, however, the Confederate Congress issued a congratulatory message to Taylor for his "brilliant successes," and Davis summoned him east of the river with a promotion.[23]

In September, Smith sent Price and 12,000 cavalrymen on a raid through Arkansas and Missouri. He hoped Price could seize St Louis, gather recruits, and sway the November elections. Price encountered stiff resistance below St Louis at Pilot Knob and turned west, racing across Missouri with the Federals in pursuit. On October

Cherokee Indian Stand Watie was born in Georgia in 1806 and educated at a missionary school. He wielded influence among the Cherokee and served on the Tribal Court and Council. In 1835, he supported removal to Indian Territory as the Cherokee split into violent factions. Watie accepted a Confederate commission in 1861 and his Cherokee Mounted Rifles fought in Indian Territory and along adjacent borders. Watie was the only Native American to become a Civil War general. (Courtesy of Robert K. Krick)

23, near Kansas City, Price narrowly averted disaster at Westport before escaping into Indian Territory. He returned to Arkansas having covered over 1,400 miles but with 4,000 casualties and few recruits. Publicly, Smith called the raid a success; privately, he condemned Price.

Smith's disputes with Taylor and Price soon crossed into the political realm. In Richmond, Louisiana congressmen opened an investigation into charges of corruption in the Cotton Bureau and Missouri representatives proposed that Joseph Johnston relieve Smith. The southern press joined in the chorus of criticism and after receiving an unsympathetic letter from Davis, Smith considered resigning.

In 1865, Camille Polignac, a French general serving in Louisiana, met with Smith to discuss a diplomatic mission to France. Polignac would carry a letter from Smith offering a "system of gradual emancipation" in exchange for diplomatic considerations. Polignac left for France in January, but Smith's statesmanship did not have time to develop. With news of Lee's surrender, discipline in the Trans-Mississippi dissolved. Smith fled to Texas upon hearing rumors of a coup by Price and other disgruntled officers to remove him from command. "I am left a commander without an army" he declared and on June 2, at Galveston, Smith surrendered the Trans-Mississippi to Edward Canby.[24]

The war's last battle between ground troops took place on May 13 at Palmito Ranch. There, along the Rio Grande east of Brownsville, Rip Ford's cavalry defeated Theodore Barrett and the 62nd Colored Infantry, only to learn from prisoners that Lee had surrendered. The Confederates disbanded and went home. Six weeks later in Indian Territory, Stand Watie became the last Confederate general to surrender.

INDIAN TERRITORY

The war in Indian Territory had been particularly venomous. In 1861, the Confederate Congress established a Bureau of Indian Affairs and commissioned Albert Pike to secure treaties with the Five Civilized Tribes. Pike was an antebellum attorney who had argued and won several cases on behalf of Indian claimants before the Arkansas Supreme Court. His message to the Tribes was that Lincoln would open Indian Territory to free-white settlement and, thus, Indians and Confederates were "natural allies" in the war against "northern aggressions." Pike obtained treaties with the Chickasaws, Choctaws, and Seminoles, but found the Cherokees and Creeks more difficult. John Ross, the Cherokee principal-chief, opted for neutrality, but the influential Stand Watie endorsed Pike. After Wilson's Creek, Ross acquiesced and accepted Pike's offer to recognize Cherokee autonomy in exchange for an alliance with the Confederacy.[25]

Factions within the Creeks proved even more troublesome. Pike obtained a treaty with the Lower Creeks, but the Upper Creeks, under Chief Opothleyahola, repudiated the agreement and marched toward Kansas for protection. Douglas Cooper led a 1,400-man army of Texans and Indians to stop the exodus and, on November 19, Opothleyahola confronted him with 1,500 braves at Round Mountain. The battle was indecisive and the forces met again on December 9 along Bird Creek at Chustenahlah. There too, Cooper could not destroy his quarry. In fact, some Confederate Cherokees refused to fight while others defected to the Union side.[26]

Cooper feared losing control over his Indian troops and retired to Fort Gibson, near Tahlequah, the Cherokee capital. He then petitioned Wilson's Creek veteran James McIntosh to bring his command to Indian Territory explaining, "The true men among the Cherokees must be supported." McIntosh complied, and on December 26, the Confederates routed Opothleyahola at Shoal Creek. The following day, Watie's men overtook Opothleyahola and annihilated Creek resistance. Those who escaped reached Kansas and sought shelter from the Union

army, but none was forthcoming. Many starved while others froze to death. Noted one Kansasan, "The destitution, misery, and suffering amongst them is beyond the power of any pen to portray."[27]

In 1862, the Federals organized two Indian regiments, including Opothleyahola's survivors. They became part of William Weer's 6,000-man force that invaded Indian Territory and captured John Ross. James Blunt, in command of the Department of Kansas, shipped Ross to Washington where he renounced the Cherokee–Confederate alliance. Meanwhile, a mutiny among Weer's lieutenants led to his arrest on charges of intoxication. Frederick Salomon, a German immigrant, assumed command claiming that whiskey had driven Weer mad. Much to Blunt's chagrin, Salomon withdrew to Kansas and Watie's Cherokees reasserted control over Indian Territory.

Nearly three weeks after the battle along Bull Run Creek, Virginia, Union and Confederate forces clashed at Wilson's Creek, Missouri. Called Oak Hill by the victorious rebels, the war's second major battle was particularly vicious as green troops on both sides engaged in a bloody struggle that helped convince Cherokee Indians to support the Confederate cause. (Library of Congress)

Born in Maine, James G. Blunt settled in Kansas where he fought as a Jayhawker. At the start of the Civil War, Blunt served as one of James Lane's guerrillas and soon received a commission as a brigadier. His aggressiveness led to several promotions although he often took imprudent risks. After the war he practiced medicine and later worked as a claims agent in Washington. Blunt was committed to a mental asylum and died destitute in 1881. (National Archives)

Blunt renewed operations in 1863 and in April the Federals captured Fort Gibson. In July, Blunt routed a Confederate force at Honey Spring and drove many Cherokee south, into Choctaw lands. William Phillips led the Union Indian Brigade into Choctaw territory and the campaign resembled guerrilla warfare in Kansas and Missouri with strikes against non-military targets. The Federals destroyed dozens of Choctaw villages and slaughtered hundreds.

Watie proclaimed himself Cherokee principal-chief and launched counterattacks behind Union lines. In June 1864, he netted $100,000 in supplies with the capture of the USS *J.R. Williams*, on the Arkansas River, and in September, near Cabin

Creek, he seized a Federal supply train valued at $1.5 million. These exploits earned Watie a promotion to brigadier.

Upon learning of Lee's surrender, Watie called for a council of Tribes. Representatives met at Boggy Depot and agreed that each Tribe should pursue "friendly relations with the United States government." Watie granted furloughs to most of his men keeping only a skeleton force under arms. He met Federal representatives on June 23 near Doaksville and signed papers surrendering both the Cherokee Nation and his Confederate command.[28]

THE LOST CAUSE

By 1865, the Federals had achieved significant territorial gains in the Trans-Mississippi, but did not destroy rebel armies. As the Confederacy collapsed in the East, much of western Louisiana and Texas remained beyond Union control. For southerners learning of Lee's surrender, the Trans-Mississippi embodied the last hope for their cause. Many Confederate soldiers, politicians, and civilians tried to reach the Kirby-Smithdom where they hoped to "carry on the war forever." By then, it was too late. Richmond did not appreciate the strategic importance of military operations west of the river until after the fall of Vicksburg. In contrast, the Union tied the Trans-Mississippi to their grand strategy from the beginning. This made the difference between victory and defeat.[29] Moreover, the Federal successes in Missouri and Arkansas riveted Union fetters on those states early in the war. Later, along the Red River, the Confederates failed to exploit an opportunity to impact the war in the East. On both sides there were commanders whose visions of glory took precedence over grand strategy and others who took foolish chances and paid with the blood of their men. The Union's command structure, however, enabled the Federals to overcome strategic blunders and tactical defeats. During the war, General Samuel Curtis wrote "While we carry death and destruction to the enemy the real union men, [carry] the benign influence of a fostering and affectionate government." In the postwar Trans-Mississippi, these hopes were lost in a legacy of violence. Guerrilla warfare left scars across Missouri and Kansas that would not heal for decades. In Louisiana, Arkansas, and Texas, Reconstruction was brutally repressive for whites and some fled to California or Latin America. Across the Trans-Mississippi, many Republicans exploited the freedmen, including those who served in Union ranks, and Redeemers reacted violently to notions of equality for former slaves. Indians suffered more than any group as the United States waged a series of Indian wars, in part to punish those who had supported the Confederacy. Pike's prediction that Indian Territory would be open to white settlement came true less than 25 years after the end of the Civil War.[30]

That great essential of success
Espionage, Covert Action, and Military Intelligence

William B. Feis

In his final report at the end of the Civil War, Major-General Philip H. Sheridan thanked his scouts for risking their lives and for "cheerfully going wherever ordered, to obtain that great essential of success, information."[1] During the Civil War, the quest for that "great essential" involved a wide array of clandestine activities called "secret service." Cloistered in the war's shadows, these pursuits ranged from detecting government fraud and smashing smuggling rings to conducting espionage, military intelligence, and counterintelligence operations, encoding and decoding signal messages, and undertaking covert actions. And since all these involved the collection, analysis, or use of intelligence (whether political, military, diplomatic, or economic) or perhaps the spreading of propaganda, disinformation, or fear behind enemy lines, they were essential components of the broader "intelligence war" waged within the Civil War.

This "intelligence war," however, remains shrouded in mystery and misunderstanding. "In the secret service," noted one observer, "the novelist can find

Illustrating the dangers inherent in intelligence work, this painting shows Union scout James A. Hensal, disguised in a Confederate uniform, escaping under fire from an enemy camp in Mississippi sometime in 1863. Painted by John H.G. Hood, a comrade of Hensal's from the 7th Kansas Cavalry, the scene is based on an actual event during Hensal's remarkable covert career. (From the Neil Davis Collection)

truth certainly stranger than fiction."[2] But confusing truth and fiction poses significant challenges to understanding this war. For many, the totality of Civil War "secret service" is contained in the image of a beautiful damsel in a hoop skirt delivering a crucial message – often concealed in her flowing locks – that changes the course of a battle and perhaps the war. The dashing Belle Boyd and defiant Rose O'Neal Greenhow immediately come to mind as preeminent examples of what one historian called the "magnolia blossom school" of Civil War intelligence history.[3] While it does not detract from their very real contributions, these marquee spies were merely the tallest trees obscuring a lush forest below. Postwar literature often focused on small parts of the story, but this essay will show that the history of the "intelligence war" was not all Belles and Roses.

CONFEDERATE COVERT ACTIONS

Covert action, a term unknown in the Civil War, falls under the rubric of "secret service" and includes a broad range of clandestine activities – from espionage to sabotage – undertaken by both governments for political, diplomatic, or military ends. The opposing governments possessed a variety of secret service organizations with multiple missions, but neither side created a centralized, national-level agency (akin to the Central Intelligence Agency) to direct and coordinate all diplomatic, political, and military intelligence operations and covert actions. Thus, to understand the covert war means grappling with the ad hoc, haphazard, and often disorganized nature of these pursuits.

In 1861, secretary of the navy Stephen Mallory dispatched agent James D. Bulloch, a former naval officer, on a covert mission to England and later to France to purchase ships (including ironclad vessels) for the resource-poor Confederate navy and to acquire other much-needed supplies. He also contracted with English shipyards to build several commerce raiders, including the famed CSS *Alabama*. Though the Confederacy's *guerre de course* inflicted significant damage on Union commerce, Bulloch's clandestine efforts failed to have a major impact on the war's outcome.[4]

In early 1864, Confederate authorities targeted sagging northern home front morale in the run up to the November presidential election. The Confederate Congress authorized $5 million for covert actions and President Jefferson Davis dispatched commissioners Jacob Thompson and Clement C. Clay to Canada with instructions to undermine the northern war effort by spreading antiwar sentiment and supporting northern Democrats (known as "Copperheads") in their quest to defeat Lincoln. To accomplish this, the commissioners and Thomas Hines, a former cavalry officer with ties to pro-Confederate secret societies in several northwestern states, hatched an ambitious scheme to liberate Confederate prisoners at Chicago's Camp Douglas, spark a Copperhead uprising, overthrow the governments of

Illinois, Ohio, and Indiana, and make a separate peace with the Confederacy. Though the so-called "Northwest Conspiracy" failed, the Confederates in Canada orchestrated less ambitious covert operations aimed at inciting fear and panic in the North, including hijacking Union ships on Lake Erie and using incendiary devices called "Greek fire" to damage several New York hotels. In October 1864, Confederate raiders from Canada robbed several banks in St Albans, Vermont, escaping with over $200,000. These efforts, however, could not offset Union victories in Georgia and in the Shenandoah Valley in late 1864, which helped catapult Lincoln to reelection and mortally wounded the Confederacy.[5]

The Confederate War Department also created agencies for covert action, including the Torpedo Bureau, an explosives unit responsible for blowing up the Union supply depot at City Point, Virginia, in 1864, and several small field units formed for "secret service against the enemy."[6] They also authorized Thomas E. Courtenay to undertake sabotage operations against Union supply trains and river steamships in the West. Using "coal torpedoes," which were devices disguised as lumps of coal that exploded when placed in the boiler of a steamer or a locomotive, operatives sank a number of Union ships and may have even destroyed the *Sultana*, a Union ship carrying thousands of liberated Union prisoners home at war's end.[7] The most prominent War Department organization, however, was Major William Norris's Signal and Secret Service Bureau. Though not a centralized, government-wide establishment, Norris's bureau maintained the Confederacy's covert communication network between Richmond and agents in Canada, Washington, and elsewhere in the North. Over this "Secret Line," an underground network of safe houses scattered across northern Virginia and southern Maryland, traveled couriers bearing official correspondence, northern newspapers, and medicine, as well as agents on covert missions.[8]

The bureau also had ties to the attempted kidnapping of Abraham Lincoln in March 1865. In 1864, bureau agent Thomas Nelson Conrad tried and failed to seize the president but the concept attracted John Wilkes Booth, who planned to kidnap Lincoln and exchange him for Confederate prisoners of war. The famous actor met with Confederate authorities in Canada and John H. Surratt, a courier on the Secret Line whose mother Mary operated a Maryland safe house. The abduction failed, but in early April Booth decided on his own to kill the president and directed co-conspirators to assassinate the vice-president and the secretary of state. Only Booth succeeded.

John Surratt was implicated in the assassination plot and fled the country. He was captured and tried for conspiracy in 1867, but a jury failed to return a verdict and he eventually went free. Mary Surratt, whose boarding house was a meeting place for the conspirators, was hanged with three of Booth's other accomplices. Some historians have made much of these connections to argue that the Confederate Secret Service – with Jefferson Davis's approval – conspired with Booth to murder Lincoln. Though some of Norris's men dabbled in abduction schemes and Booth was familiar with Secret Line safe houses and agents in southern Maryland, little convincing evidence suggests the bureau or the Confederate government knew about Booth's assassination plans let alone conspired with him. Even at the time, Joseph Holt, who as judge advocate general prosecuted the assassination conspirators, tried valiantly to implicate Davis and the Confederate government in the conspiracy but ultimately failed due to evidence problems.[9]

UNION COVERT ACTIONS

When war erupted in 1861, the Federal government lacked secret service organizations and personnel to meet both its intelligence and counterintelligence needs. By 1862 that void was partially filled by Lafayette C. Baker, chief of the War Department's so-called "National Detective Bureau," which he later claimed was actually called the "United States Secret Service," even though no official department by that name existed until after the war. Baker's unit performed counterintelligence missions by ferreting out Confederate spies and subversives, but also hunted deserters and bounty jumpers and investigated government fraud and

Allan Pinkerton (center, background, smoking a pipe) and his scouts during the Peninsula campaign, 1862. Though proficient at counterintelligence, the famous detective found catching spies much easier than becoming one. (Library of Congress)

corruption. His most famous acts were the capture of Confederate spy Belle Boyd and helping track John Wilkes Booth after the Lincoln assassination. Charges of bribery, corruption, abuse of power, and especially lying forever tainted his reputation. "It is doubtful," remarked one official, "whether he has in any one thing told the truth, even by accident."[10]

When Major-General George B. McClellan took command of the Union army after the disaster at First Bull Run in 1861, he hired Allan Pinkerton, head of a nationally renowned detective agency, to head the army intelligence service. Before taking the field, however, Pinkerton chased spies in the city and eventually netted Rose O'Neal Greenhow, who had alerted Confederate officials about Union troop movements prior to First Bull Run. More importantly, Greenhow's arrest shattered a major spy ring and severely curtailed Confederate espionage efforts in the Federal capital.[11]

As Union authorities pursued subversives in the capital, they also dispatched covert agents to counter southern efforts at courting European nations for recognition and aid. Henry Sanford, the US minister to Belgium, and Thomas Haines Dudley, a US consul in Britain, established a network of undercover agents to thwart attempts by James Bulloch to procure ships and supplies for the South. Though the Confederates had nominal success in building commerce raiders, in the end, both Sanford and Dudley successfully frustrated Confederate efforts to cultivate foreign allies.[12]

MILITARY INTELLIGENCE: COMMON CHARACTERISTICS

Like the name "secret service," in the mid-19th century the terms information and intelligence were also imprecise. In the modern definition, *information* is defined as raw, undigested bits of news not yet analyzed, which is compared with other evidence, and evaluated for its importance. *Intelligence* is the end product of the evaluation, corroboration, and interpretation of information. In the Civil War, however, military and political leaders used both terms synonymously. When someone claimed to have received *intelligence*, they most likely referred to unprocessed *information* that had yet to be examined. But there were no professional intelligence analysts to systematically study and interpret information and produce a final product. This task was done mostly in the head of the decision-maker. Moreover, neither side created a centralized army-wide intelligence organization to systematize the collection, analysis, and distribution of information to field commanders. Left to the discretion of individual military officers and government officials, intelligence operations were often initiated without much supervision, systematization, and coordination of efforts, or incentive to share information or intelligence assets. In essence, intelligence operations were mostly improvised, often uncoordinated affairs as varied in their scope, character, and effectiveness as the personalities and experience of the individuals directing and undertaking them.

In the end, neither superior intelligence nor profound military genius, however, could overcome basic human nature. "[I]ntelligence problems are human problems," wrote one intelligence scholar, "and thus are not likely to disappear."[13] Essentially, excellent information did not guarantee correct decisions but neither did bad intelligence always lead to erroneous conclusions. Regardless of the era or technological advances in collection methods and communications, the decision-maker – buffeted about by fear, overconfidence, timidity, past experience, fixed beliefs, paranoia, wishful thinking, physical and mental exhaustion, illness, uncertainty, and self-delusion – always plays the pivotal role in the intelligence cycle. After all, intelligence does not make decisions, commanders do.

MILITARY INTELLIGENCE: COMMON SOURCES

Both Federal and Confederate officers mined a number of different sources for information. As noted, spies (individuals living behind enemy lines who reported via secret messenger) have received the lion's share of the attention even though they were far less consistent as intelligence producers and the reliable ones were few in number. However, because they often lived in the midst of the enemy and had the ability to see and hear much more, they possessed the potential to bring in information far superior to anything divulged by other sources. But finding reliable spies – all of whom had no training whatsoever in this covert art – posed significant difficulties.

Whether a resident in hostile territory or a civilian or soldier recruited to cross enemy lines on a mission, to be effective a spy had to know something about military organization, understand the importance of vigilance, possess a keen eye for detail, be able to ask questions and observe activities without raising suspicion, report only substantive news, and find secure ways of getting messages to his or her employer across the lines. Discretion was also a *sine qua non* of espionage. Interestingly, some of the most famous spies of the war earned their fame because they violated this imperative by openly professing their allegiances and barely concealing their activities, which garnered them celebrity status during and after the war but severely limited their effectiveness as spies. On the other hand, many southerners who spied for the Union never received any recognition both for security reasons and for their safety. "There are citizens living in the South who give me the most valuable information," wrote one Federal officer, but they "will not sign a voucher for fear of consequences in the future." Even long after the war, that same officer refused publicly to divulge their identities to protect them from vengeful southern

Allan Pinkerton's "agreement" with Major-General McClellan to artificially inflate enemy force estimates sometimes undermined the hard work of the scouts of the Army of the Potomac, pictured here in October 1862. (National Archives)

neighbors.[14] Some former spies came in from the cold after the war applied for Federal pensions but were rejected because, as one pension official noted, they had "[abandoned] the ways of open and manly warfare and... [adopted] the devious methods of personal misrepresentation, trickery, and deceit" and were therefore

Signal towers, like this Union station at Bermuda Hundred, Virginia, in 1864, provided a platform for both visual observation and faster communication. Since both sides routinely broke each other's signal codes, however, signalmen sometimes transmitted false information in hopes of deceiving the enemy. (Library of Congress)

Balloons like the Union's Intrepid *operated by Prof. Thaddeus S.C. Lowe, pictured here in Virginia in 1862, provided commanders with aerial reconnaissance capability. Both armies experimented with balloons early on – the Union at one time had a fleet of seven – but by midwar logistical problems, financial troubles, and the fortunes of war eventually grounded both air arms. (Library of Congress)*

deemed dishonorable, morally flawed, and unworthy of the same privileges given uniformed veterans.[15]

Mostly volunteers from the ranks, scouts performed a variety of missions. Typically, a scout patrolled along enemy lines but at times, either in civilian garb or a Confederate uniform, penetrated hostile territory to get a better look. Operating alone or in organized units, scouts sought information on enemy movements, deployments, order of battle, and terrain but at times they also hunted guerrillas. In all of these pursuits, operatives flirted with extreme danger. Perhaps reflecting the thoughts of many fellow scouts, James Hensal, who survived at least seven missions behind enemy lines, wrote later that when ordered to carry a dispatch into enemy territory, he always knew that "if I got through it would bee [sic] a merical [sic]."[16] Though all soldiers faced death, wrote Union scout William Callender, "the army scout, occupying as he does a position outside of the general military system, literally takes his life into his own hands." If captured, "he may expect no quarter."[17] The number of those executed remains unknown, but for every documented instance there are likely dozens of cases like that of Oliver Smith Rankin, a scout executed for spying in Tennessee, whose wartime deeds and sacrifices remain lost to history.[18]

By far the most prolific and steady source of information came from interrogations, especially of prisoners and deserters who had first-hand knowledge of the enemy situation. Even if they offered little more than their regimental affiliation, that information provided valuable insights into the enemy's order of battle (organization and composition), recent movements, deployments, and morale in the ranks. Though often unable to distinguish between a regiment and a division, refugees, local citizens, and, for the North, escaped slaves, could still provide skillful interrogators with insights into terrain features, road systems, and recent enemy activity.

The use of balloons and signal towers for visual observations also gave some commanders an advantage in surveying terrain and perhaps glimpsing the enemy on the move. Early in the war, both sides experimented with aerial reconnaissance using balloons. In the North, Professor Thaddeus S.C. Lowe, a civilian balloonist, joined McClellan's army during the 1862 Peninsula campaign and, using portable generators for inflation, his aeronauts logged hundreds of missions. By 1863, army disinterest and poor health led to Lowe's resignation, effectively terminating the Union's brief romance with the balloon. Suffering from scarce resources, the South's attempts at balloon reconnaissance were less ambitious. The so-called "Silk Dress Balloon," allegedly made from the gowns of numerous southern belles in Savannah, went aloft a number of times during the Seven Days battles, but its capture by Union forces ended its service. Aside from another balloon that saw limited service in Charleston, the Confederacy invested little of its scarce resources in this form of visual reconnaissance.

Signal towers and elevated terrain features provided platforms for viewing enemy movements, and also for sending messages using a visual signaling system – transmitted by flags or torches – developed by Major Albert Myer, head of the Union Signal Corps. His chief assistant, Edward P. Alexander, left the service to fight for the South and brought with him Myer's system, which the Confederates adopted. However, the secret codes – or ciphers – employed by both sides to protect signal messages were easily broken, making it possible to intercept and read enemy transmissions. Aware that their ciphers were compromised, however, Union and Confederate commanders sometimes turned this to their advantage by sending messages with false information knowing the enemy would read it. One such fake message, transmitted by a Union signal station and read by Confederates in northern Virginia in 1862, led Robert E. Lee to redeploy his cavalry, leaving a gap in his lines. Major-General Joseph Hooker used that gap to get in the rear of the Confederate army at Fredericksburg. But the advantage was

A new innovation in warfare, the mobile telegraph, housed in wagons like this one operated by the US Military Telegraph in 1864, allowed commanders to communicate quickly during a campaign. Both sides developed complex codes to secure transmissions but only Union cipher operators succeeded in breaking their counterpart's cipher system. (Library of Congress)

temporary. Lee responded with a brilliant campaign that culminated in a stunning victory at Chancellorsville.[19]

The use of the telegraph, which made communication between theaters as well as in an area of operations nearly instantaneous, also impacted on the intelligence war and led to the creation of the US Military Telegraph (USMT), headed by Anson Stager, and the Confederate Signal and Secret Service Bureau under Major William Norris. Telegraph lines proved vulnerable targets to cavalry raiders, but also to operatives tapping into them to intercept message traffic. To prevent this, both sides developed cipher systems – the Confederates used the 400-year-old "Vigenère" system while the Union chose the more secure Route Transportation Cipher – to encode messages. The North apparently won the war of the ciphers since they broke Confederate codes while stymieing their counterparts. By 1864 the task of enciphering and deciphering dispatches became so crucial that Ulysses S. Grant never traveled without his cipher clerk.[20]

Correspondence from behind enemy lines and newspapers were also possible sources of information. At times, army officers found themselves in possession of both military and civilian mail, which they perused for tidbits on everything from troop movements to the price of bread in the Confederacy. Though notoriously prone to embellishment and the perpetuation of falsehoods, newspapers also became a popular information source, especially due to lax censorship. For example, during the siege of Richmond in 1864–65, Grant monitored daily newspapers from within the Confederate capital for news of troop movements, the arrival of supplies, food and clothing shortages, and the price of civilian goods. Robert E. Lee found much useful news in newspapers, especially in reports from war correspondents notorious for divulging military information. A main mission for both the Confederate Signal and Secret Service Bureau and various Union intelligence organizations was to procure enemy dailies and smuggle them across the lines. One southern sympathizer in Union-occupied Kentucky subscribed to several northern papers at the request of General Braxton Bragg and secretly delivered them to his headquarters. Aware that Union authorities in Tennessee relied on the *Chattanooga Daily Rebel* for information, Bragg even planted several fake stories in that paper.[21]

Overall, these diverse sources provided Union and Confederate commanders and government officials with information they needed to formulate strategy and to conduct campaigns and battles. How they went about obtaining "that great essential of success" and, more importantly, how they used (or did not use) what they found remains the key to understanding the true impact of the intelligence war.

MILITARY INTELLIGENCE: UNION ESPIONAGE, ORGANIZATIONS, AND OPERATIONS

Lacking any formal intelligence organization when the war erupted, President Abraham Lincoln was forced to hire his own personal spy to gather information from the South. Not until Major-General George B. McClellan took command of the Union army after First Bull Run would formal military intelligence operations emerge. The general outsourced the army's intelligence needs to a civilian contractor, Allan Pinkerton, who created the first organized intelligence bureau in American military history. During the Peninsula campaign, Pinkerton – relying primarily on interrogations of refugees, prisoners, and deserters – identified all 178 Confederate regiments protecting Richmond. However, he also feared many more regiments remained undetected, which led him to double Confederate strength estimates as a precaution. This did not mean McClellan, who also believed the enemy outnumbered him, was deceived by his intelligence chief. Both men had privately agreed to pad estimates just to be safe. But even when Pinkerton increased the number, it was never high enough for McClellan, who often inflated the figure even more in order to justify his legendary caution. This game continued until Pinkerton either came to believe McClellan's higher estimates or, tired of disappointing his boss, bought into his self-deception.[22]

By late 1864, Col George H. Sharpe and his Bureau of Military Information staff (l to r: Sharpe, John C. Babcock, Lt Paul Oliver, Capt John McEntee) had created the war's most sophisticated "all source" intelligence unit and, through systematic interrogations of prisoners and deserters, developed an accurate order of battle for Confederate forces in Virginia. (Library of Congress)

McClellan's subsequent defeat on the Peninsula could have been redeemed had he smashed Robert E. Lee's Army of Northern Virginia during the Maryland campaign that fall. And luck seemed to be on his side. A group of Union soldiers resting in a field found a copy of Lee's Special Orders No. 191, which revealed that the Confederate army was divided into four segments and dangerously dispersed. This information gave McClellan an opportunity afforded few generals in military history; he had the chance to destroy Lee's army in detail. His great caution, however, allowed Lee to recover and the advantage quickly vanished. After the subsequent inconclusive battle at Antietam in September, the Union commander allowed Lee to escape to Virginia to fight another day. When Lincoln fired McClellan in November, Pinkerton's contract expired as well, leaving Major-General Ambrose P. Burnside, the new commander, lacking an intelligence arm.[23]

That void was filled in early 1863 when Major-General Joseph Hooker, who gained command after Burnside's disaster at Fredericksburg, created the Bureau of

Military Information (BMI) within the Army of the Potomac. Headed by Colonel George H. Sharpe, the bureau worked diligently to access numerous information sources, making it an "all source" intelligence service far ahead of its time and one of the significant innovations of the war. However, the BMI worked *only* for the Army of the Potomac, leaving other Union commanders – especially in the West – to fend for themselves with regard to intelligence procurement. But collecting information was only part of the bureau's mission. The BMI's permanent staff, consisting of Sharpe, civilian John C. Babcock, and Captain John McEntee, also collated the information, assessed the veracity of the sources, compared reports, analyzed contents, and then composed an "intelligence brief" for the commanding officer. By early 1865, the BMI had also established branch offices with other major commands in Virginia.[24]

Pinkerton had great difficulty consistently penetrating Richmond, but Sharpe established solid contacts with the "Union underground" within the Confederate capital, most notably with Samuel Ruth, the superintendent of the Richmond, Fredericksburg & Potomac Railroad and wealthy spinster Elizabeth Van Lew. Ruth used his position as head of a major railroad serving Richmond to inform Union authorities about timetables, supply shipments, and troop movements over the rails. In March 1865, his information led to a raid on Fredericksburg, Virginia, that netted scores of Confederate prisoners and the capture of black-market tobacco being exchanged for food by southern agents. Though arrested on suspicion of espionage, after his release the unshakeable Ruth continued spying despite the lingering suspicions of Confederate authorities.[25]

Sharpe depended most upon Van Lew's organization, crediting her with establishing a vital communication network between Grant's headquarters and Richmond using a system of couriers and "depots" established by the BMI.[26] Using that network, Federal scouts delivered US and Confederate currency and supplies and brought out information. One legend states that Van Lew even placed one of her African American servants, Mary Elizabeth Bowser, in the Confederate White House, where she allegedly eavesdropped on top-secret conversations and then relayed them to Van Lew. Though a fascinating tale, and enough to win Bowser a place in the US Army Intelligence Hall of Fame, the evidence supporting the claim that Bowser worked for Jefferson Davis or passed along the sort of high-level intelligence she would have overheard remains fairly unpersuasive.[27]

During the siege of Richmond in 1864–65, Van Lew used a homemade cipher to report on troop movements, living conditions, and the state of morale within the city and, on occasion, sent Grant copies of Richmond newspapers. On occasion, Federal authorities requested specific information, sending their queries using invisible ink. In March 1864, they asked: "Will there be an attack in North Carolina? How many troops are there? Will Richmond be evacuated?"[28] Van Lew's pleas to rescue Federal prisoners languishing in Richmond's prisons in early 1864 led to an ill-fated cavalry

Prisoners such as these Confederates captured in the Shenandoah Valley in May 1862 could, if interrogated properly, provide significant information on the enemy's order of battle and morale. (National Archives)

raid that ended in the death of Union colonel Ulric Dahlgren. In a bizarre twist, her agents stole Dahlgren's body, hidden by Confederate authorities, and returned it to his father, Union admiral John Dahlgren. Unlike more famous spies, Van Lew penned no reminiscences and even destroyed some of her papers, thus gaining neither fame nor fortune from her efforts. After the war, she became an outcast in Richmond society and even received death threats when her wartime activities became public. She died in 1900 vilified by her fellow citizens and unheralded in the annals of the war even though, according to Sharpe, most of the information collected and spirited out of Richmond was due to "the intelligence and devotion of Miss E.L. Van Lew."[29]

The BMI routinely dispatched scouts to penetrate the Confederate army. For example, when Union commanders "lost" Lee's army across the Blue Ridge Mountains early in the Gettysburg campaign, Sharpe sent four scouts disguised as Confederates fleeing into enemy lines with Union cavalrymen on their heels. They later returned with positive news that the Army of Northern Virginia was near the Potomac River.[30]

Though the BMI was an "all-source" intelligence organization, their primary focus was on the systematic interrogations of refugees, "contrabands" (former slaves), and enemy prisoners and deserters. From these interviews, the BMI assembled a comprehensive order of battle for the Army of Northern Virginia, allowing them effectively to monitor enemy movements. By late 1863, Sharpe bragged that "We are entirely familiar with the organization of the rebel forces in Virginia and North Carolina."[31]

This familiarity paid off during the battle of Gettysburg. On the night of July 2, 1863, following two days of Confederate assaults on his position, Major-General George Meade considered retreating. At a council of war, however, Sharpe reported that BMI prisoner interrogations revealed that all of Lee's brigades had been heavily engaged over the past two days except for those under Major-General George Pickett, whose division had not yet arrived. This information convinced Meade and his subordinates that the Army of the Potomac held a decisive edge in fresh troops and they voted to remain and fight, which led to Lee's defeat the next day. These routine sources and the information they produced, though not as flashy as a spy adventure, not only played an essential role in Meade's victory over Lee, but would also significantly impact Grant's success against the "Gray Fox" in 1865.[32]

Given the BMI's innovations and successes, one would have expected the army to carefully document their operations to learn lessons for the future. However, neither Sharpe nor his subordinates wrote about their experiences and the army never pursued the issue, thereby letting that practical expertise and hard-earned knowledge slip away to be re-learned in later wars.

In the Shenandoah Valley in 1864, Major-General Philip H. Sheridan recruited 50 volunteers from the ranks and organized them into a special battalion of scouts commanded by Major Henry K. Young. Known as "Sheridan's Scouts," these men, often disguised as Confederates, scouted enemy positions, watched for movements, and frequently operated behind enemy lines. They soon became an integral part of an intelligence system linking Sheridan's command with Grant's forces battering Richmond.

Sheridan also contacted Unionists behind enemy lines, most notably Rebecca Wright, a schoolteacher in Winchester. In early September, she told Sheridan about the return of a Confederate division to Richmond and that no new reinforcements were expected in the valley. Confident that the valley Confederates were now weak and isolated, Sheridan attacked and defeated Lieutenant-General Jubal Early at Winchester on September 19 and, three days later, crushed him again at Fisher's Hill. The twin victories brought the lower Shenandoah Valley under Union control and, combined with the fall of Atlanta earlier that month, gave war-weary northerners – and the Lincoln administration – a much-needed boost prior to the November presidential elections.[33]

In the western theater, at least three major intelligence organizations emerged. In late 1862, Grant, in command of the Army of the Tennessee, ordered Brigadier-General Grenville M. Dodge to procure information on Confederate forces in northern Mississippi and western Tennessee. In Corinth, Mississippi, Dodge constructed an intelligence organization that stretched to Atlanta and into Mississippi, Alabama, and Tennessee. By late 1863, Dodge had assembled a corps of scouts and spies numbering over 130 operatives, some culled from the ranks of the 1st Alabama Cavalry (Union), comprised primarily of northern Alabama Unionists. In a famous episode, Dodge's scouts captured Confederate scout Sam Davis, whose steadfast loyalty to his comrades as he faced execution became legendary. Between November 1862 and July 1863, Dodge's operatives completed over 200 missions, logged thousands of miles, and provided important information for Grant's operations in the region.[34]

Major-General William S. Rosecrans created another key intelligence organization while his army occupied Nashville in late 1863. He ordered each corps to organize a company of scouts whose reports were compiled in a concise information digest called "Summaries of the News" and instituted the use of "information maps," which were detailed topographical sketches regularly updated with current information and distributed to all field commanders. Rosecrans also used Colonel William Truesdail's Army Police in Nashville to chase smugglers, arrest spies and subversives, hunt Union deserters, and detect fraud within the army. In addition, Truesdail established a "spy department" that employed around 130 scouts and spies between November 1862 and June 1863. Pauline Cushman, his most famous spy and an actress, used her talents to gather information, but in 1863 Confederate authorities saw through the act and arrested her. Facing execution for espionage, she was spared when Union troops liberated her.

Truesdail's "spy department" contributed most to the Tullahoma campaign in early 1863 by providing Rosecrans with information used in planning a carefully orchestrated thrust against Confederate forces deployed southeast of Murfreesboro, Tennessee. In late June, five months of preparation and good intelligence paid off as Rosecrans, in a near-bloodless campaign, drove the enemy from Middle Tennessee and opened the way to Chattanooga. With "information maps," Truesdail's operatives, and daily summaries of the information crossing his desk, Rosecrans was, for a time, perhaps the best informed commander of the war.[35]

During the Atlanta campaign in 1864, Major-General William T. Sherman utilized a smaller-scale intelligence network run by Major-General George H. Thomas. One of Thomas's most accomplished spies was James G. Brown, a native Georgian, who made numerous trips to Atlanta and elsewhere monitoring Confederate troop movements and making connections with the Unionist underground in northern Georgia. Other Union agents in Georgia – Carrie King,

Émile Bourlier, Mary Summerlin, and Henry Cole – penetrated Atlanta and found many Unionists in the city, loosely organized into the so-called "Union Circle," willing to provide intelligence.[36]

One of the most intrepid Union scouts spent much of the war in the West. Charles S. Bell completed at least 37 missions behind enemy lines and traveled hundreds of miles in Missouri, Mississippi, Arkansas, Louisiana, and Virginia. Often disguised as a Confederate staff officer, he worked for Dodge, Sherman, Thomas, and Grant, and made a signal contribution to the Vicksburg campaign in 1863. He also infiltrated pro-southern secret societies in St Louis and Richmond and spied on Confederate government officials in Canada.[37]

Though the true extent of Union intelligence operations in Georgia and, for that matter, in the rest of the Confederacy, may never be known, it is clear that the few agents and their exploits that caught the eye of the reading public after the war are merely "vague glimpses… [just] as one sees an ever receding figure at the turn of a winding road."[38]

Confederate spy Rose O'Neal Greenhow was a key member of an espionage network in Washington, DC. Though she had high-level connections and alerted Confederate authorities at Manassas, Virginia, to the approach of Union forces prior to First Bull Run, Greenhow's lack of discretion led to her arrest and eventual exile from the North. (Public domain)

MILITARY INTELLIGENCE: CONFEDERATE ESPIONAGE, ORGANIZATIONS, AND OPERATIONS

Of all facets of Confederate military intelligence, espionage remains the most well known thanks to the fame of a few female spies. If southerners possessed an advantage in espionage, it was because thousands of Confederate loyalists – and potential spies – remained in Washington after the war commenced. Moreover, as Union armies advanced, every southern civilian behind them became a prospective source. The penetration of the Federal bureaucracy by southern sympathizers, however, became the most pressing internal security problem early in the war.

In early 1861, Captain Thomas Jordan, a US Army officer stationed in Washington who resigned to fight for the Confederacy, recruited Rose O'Neal Greenhow, a pro-southern socialite with connections in the government, to become a spy. Jordan's choice proved propitious because she knew many government officials and was supposedly intimate with Senator Henry D. Wilson, chair of the powerful Committee on Military Affairs. Greenhow's covert career ended with her arrest in August 1861, though not before she had informed Confederate general P.G.T. Beauregard that Union troops were on the move toward his position along Bull Run Creek in northern Virginia. The news, according to Beauregard, proved critical in formulating the battle plan that led to victory at First Bull Run in July 1861, though historians disagree on the actual significance of the information she provided. Her memoirs, written in 1863, and her heroic death while running the Union blockade cemented her fame in southern lore.[39]

Described by one historian as the "Civil War's most overrated spy," Belle Boyd won acclaim for bringing information that supposedly convinced Major-General Thomas J. "Stonewall" Jackson to attack Union forces at Front Royal, Virginia, during his masterful 1862 Shenandoah Valley campaign. Jackson nearly destroyed the garrison and then threatened the Union line of communications, forcing the Federal commander to withdraw northward. Though Boyd and others claimed her information was critical, some historians argue that it merely corroborated what Jackson already knew. In any event, Boyd won instant fame that she cashed in on for the rest of her life. But, like Greenhow, the discretion so important for espionage eluded her, thereby compromising her future effectiveness. Skilled at self-promotion, she penned reminiscences in 1865 and after the war toured with her one-woman show reliving her exploits, all of which entrenched her celebrity status.[40]

In the West, Confederate operatives penetrated Union armies and worked behind the lines in occupied cities. Sam Davis, a scout for General Braxton Bragg who was captured by Dodge in Tennessee and executed for espionage in 1863, and Clara Judd, who worked for General John Hunt Morgan in Nashville, are but two of

Scouts of the Army of the Potomac's Bureau of Military Information, pictured here in Virginia in 1864, risked their lives searching for information on enemy movements and dispositions as well as maintaining contact with Union agents in Richmond. (Library of Congress)

perhaps dozens of agents employed by various commanders. Within Union-occupied Nashville, Federal authorities constantly battled smugglers and spies, or what they called the "Petticoat System" due to the number of women who hid medicine and secret correspondence in their voluminous dresses.[41]

Within Confederate armies, commanders never created formal intelligence units like the Army of the Potomac's BMI or Grenville Dodge's corps of scouts. Many officers, including Robert E. Lee, employed spies and scouts, but apparently not on a systematic basis. On occasion, however, they earned their pay. Lieutenant-General James Longstreet's scout Henry T. Harrison provided crucial information on the location of the Union army during the Gettysburg campaign and Franklin Stringfellow, an agent in Norris's bureau, brought news that initiated a raid on Union general John Pope's headquarters prior to Second Bull Run. Brigadier-General J.E.B. Stuart employed individual scouts to augment his cavalry while others used scouting companies like "Coleman's Scouts" in Tennessee and Major John Richardson's battalion of scouts in Virginia.[42]

For information procurement, however, Confederate commanders depended far more on cavalry, especially given the superiority of their mounted arm early in the war. Perhaps the best example is Stuart's horsemen, who proved adept at information collection through reconnaissance, relying on mobility and speed not only to scout enemy positions and deliver their findings in real time, but to perform the counterintelligence mission of screening Confederate movements.

Two episodes involving Stuart's cavalry reveal that the reliance on reconnaissance was decidedly a double-edged sword. First, with McClellan's army on the outskirts of Richmond in June 1862, Lee ordered Stuart to locate McClellan's right wing. The dashing cavalrymen discovered that one Federal corps remained north of the Chickahominy River while the rest of McClellan's army remained south of it. Knowing the value of this news, Stuart decided that, instead of returning the way he had come and fighting through Union cavalry, he would continue on and ride completely around McClellan's army. When he reached Lee, the information he brought led to an attack on the Union right at Mechanicsville, which resulted in a tactical defeat for the Confederates but forced McClellan abandon his planned siege of the capital and retreat to the James River.[43]

The Gettysburg campaign, however, revealed the dangers of Lee's heavy reliance on Stuart. As the Army of Northern Virginia moved north into Maryland and Pennsylvania in late June 1863, Stuart rode ahead to raid supplies but, most importantly, to watch for and report the whereabouts of the Union Army of the Potomac, now commanded by Major-General George Meade. But Stuart decided to ride once again around the Union army, which severed his contact with the Confederate main body and, with no intelligence unit to fill the void, left Lee blind to Union movements. The Confederates learned the enemy's position only on June 28 when Longstreet's scout Harrison returned with positive news. Stuart returned on July 2, but only after Lee had been forced to fight an entire day without much knowledge of the enemy's strength or dispositions, a disadvantage he never quite overcame.[44]

Whereas the BMI had an all-source capacity in which cavalry reconnaissance comprised only one of many information sources, Confederate commanders in both theaters never created anything approaching the sophistication of Sharpe's unit, relying instead upon their mounted arm and leaders like Stuart, John Singleton Mosby, Nathan Bedford Forrest, and Joseph Wheeler to scout the enemy. Beyond that, many officers improvised by assigning intelligence duties to a staff officer or handling it themselves, making information procurement and analysis a truly extemporized affair. As a result, neither Lee nor his subordinates systematically interrogated Union prisoners or deserters for order of battle intelligence, a critical element in determining enemy strength and, as evidenced by the BMI, information that could be used with impressive results. For the most part, however, Lee made the best of his limited resources. Whenever he received critical information, he usually knew what to do with it, which contrasts sharply with the image of McClellan cautiously weighing his options while clutching Special Orders No. 191.[45]

THE IMPACT OF THE "INTELLIGENCE WAR"

Assessing the impact of the "intelligence war" remains largely uncharted territory. Though romanticized and heavily unreliable spy memoirs and other episodic treatments still dominate Civil War intelligence literature, more recent studies – some inspired by the reassessment of World War II following the discovery of the ULTRA secret – discovered that significant revelations still remained buried beneath the Civil War's well-plowed furrows. Though intelligence or covert actions were not by themselves decisive in the war's outcome, at some critical moments they provided "that great essential of success" and became part of a grand web of contingencies that, when complete, determined the final result. Moreover, diving into the war's shadows has the potential to provide new perspectives from which to view the struggles both on the battlefield and behind the lines and to forge new understandings of how and why events transpired as they did. As with any historical study, however, the whole story will probably elude us. What archaeologist Howard Carter once wrote about the difficulties of penetrating the mysteries of King Tutankhamen sums up well the basic problem confronting modern-day intelligence scholars who study the Civil War. "The shadows move," Carter observed, "but the dark is never quite uplifted."[46]

OUR HEARTS
ARE WITH OUR BROTHERS
IN THE FIELD.

"We never yielded in the struggle until we were bound hand &
foot & the heel of the despot was on our throats."

Sarah L. Hine, of Savannah, Georgia, to Charlotte Branch, 1866

We never yielded in the struggle
The Home Front

Victoria E. Bynum

Commenting in 1866 on the recent Civil War, Sarah L. Hine, of Savannah, Georgia, assured her friend, Charlotte Branch, that "we never yielded in the struggle."[1] The "we" Sarah referred to was white southerners like herself and Charlotte, who on the home front remained true to the Confederate cause. Yet her words might have been spoken by any member of society, North or South. Struggle was the central fact of the American Civil War, although what one struggled for often differed radically, both outside and within the Union and the Confederacy.

As America's Civil War ripped at the fabric of society, it created a home front of uncertainty, deprivation, and grief, forcing people to draw on their deepest psychological and material resources to sustain themselves and each other. When we look back, it is comforting to think of people "pulling together" during a time of such intense stress, and to imagine that their suffering led to a deeper appreciation of fellow human beings, but the Civil War home front was far too complicated for glib characterizations. True, there were many touching instances of kindnesses shared

"Our hearts are with our brothers in the field." Leaders of both the Union and the Confederacy drew on conventional images of the true woman's "place" as outside the realm of politics to discourage women from questioning the cause of war. Loyalty to kin and community and absorption by domestic concerns assured that most women would endure their losses with patient martyrdom. As increasing numbers of women entered the public sphere during the war, so also did their criticism of male leaders increase. (Courtesy of New York Historical Society)

between strangers and some unexpected alliances between groups separated by barriers of class, race, and gender. Yet, home front conditions also remind us of how rigid those barriers were. As the war exacerbated old tensions and created new ones, fear, mistrust, and hatred flourished alongside patriotism, altruism, and courage.

The very phrase "home front" evokes images of women, children, and old folks struggling to perform the daily routines of life amid disruptions brought by war. As the opposite of war fronts, home fronts are commonly imagined as places where people react to rather than participate in war. In reality, the boundaries between Civil War battlefields and home fronts were quite fluid. Home fronts presented a complex arena of interactions between civilians, soldiers, and governments that directly impacted on the course of war. For the Confederacy, that impact was especially important, if not decisive, in determining the war's outcome.

Initially, the vast majority of citizens' commitment to the cause of war was strong. Just as white northerners believed that their boys in blue would save the Union from the folly and treason of secession, so also did white southerners fervently believe that their boys in gray defended the South against an all-too-powerful Yankee government that threatened their liberties and their honor. Political leaders and newspaper editors continuously trumpeted these "truths," while ministers from northern and southern wings of the same churches appropriated God for their side's cause. As a result, political ideals, notions of honor, and religious faith sustained a dogged loyalty and grim stoicism for the majority of people, even as levels of deprivation increased and death tolls mounted.

Civilians responded to the war in widely disparate ways in large part because there was no single home front. Some regions of North America were barely touched by war, while others were devastated by internal conflicts or occupations by enemy forces.

"RICH MAN'S WAR AND POOR MAN'S FIGHT"

Wealth and race had a major impact on one's experience of the Civil War. Wealthier civilians did without many daily comforts while poor people struggled simply to keep body and soul together. White men's wartime experiences were most directly affected by their conscript status, which in turn was affected by age and economic status. African Americans' home front experiences were most obviously shaped by whether they lived in the North or South. From the North, many young black men fought for the Union, while some black women formed soldiers' aid societies and lobbied for equal treatment of their sons and husbands who served in the Union army. In the South, proximity to Yankee soldiers or the ability to form alliances with disaffected whites greatly influenced African Americans' experiences during the

Civil War. The South's free people of color were especially active in underground networks of trade that flourished during the war. Archibald Kearsey, a prosperous free African American of Granville County, North Carolina, developed an interracial trade network in illegal goods that stretched all the way to the state's eastern coast. Arrested in mid-1863 for theft, he was sprung from prison by two white men who valued his connections.

Many of the South's plain yeoman farmers resented members of the planter elite such as Samuel Andrew Agnew of Lee County, Mississippi, a Presbyterian minister and the son of a slaveholding physician who in 1852 had transplanted his family from South Carolina to northeastern Mississippi. Agnew supported the Confederate cause, but as a minister obtained an exemption from military service. A diarist and scrupulous chronicler of local and national events during the war, he spent much of his time preparing and delivering sermons, but also reading newspapers, novels, and books on Roman history. By his own account, he frequently spent days "lolling" or "lying" about the home he shared with his parents. By 1863, men such as Agnew would personify for many farmers the Civil War as a "rich man's war and poor man's fight."[2]

THE "TRUE WOMAN"

Gender, like region, race, and class, profoundly impacted men and women's experiences of the war. Civil War chroniclers typically depicted battlefields as male domains of honor and glory and home fronts as domestic retreats where women endured the hardships of war with courage and resolve. Consigned to the feminine sphere of domesticity and motherhood, the "true woman" sacrificed her husband and sons for the greater good of her nation, providing moral sanction for male leaders' decision to make war.

The division of war into distinctly male and female spheres was embodied by the endless stream of letters that flowed between women on the home front and men in uniform. These letters and diaries are telling about the female experience of war. The letters of Rachel Cormany, who lived just outside Gettysburg, and the diary of Judith McGuire, a Confederate nurse in Richmond, provide eyewitness accounts of historic battles and events. Others, such as those of Mollie Houser, of Augusta County, Virginia, provide insights into the day-to-day adjustment of ordinary people to war. Mollie's letters expose the angst of a young single woman who wondered whether she was destined to be an old maid on account of war. Raised to view marriage as their one true vocation, women such as Mollie had good reason to be anxious. Some southern women responded to the shortage of young males by marrying men considerably older than themselves, or even Yankees. As Mollie's cousin, Kit, put it, "girls has come to the conclusion that... they had better get married wen they can." But not Mollie, who swore to her soldier cousin Jim that she would never marry an "old bachelor," not even a rich one, as a "good many" young ladies were doing. Pronouncing herself a devout "Cecess," Mollie vowed she would never marry a Yankee, either. She did offer to play matchmaker for Jim, however, if *he* wished to marry. "If you want a wife," Mollie wrote, she knew a young woman who "wants to marry." Mollie offered to "court her for you & you Can Marry one [another] as soon as the war is over." Mollie's letters attest to her determination to enjoy life and maintain a spirit of hope, despite the travails of war.[3]

Other women left behind not letters but court records, which alongside manuscript censuses illuminate the lives of ordinary women. In 1861, Malinda Cranford Beaman was a typical farm wife who lived in the North Carolina Piedmont. She and her husband, John, lived among a wide network of kin near the Randolph and Montgomery County line, where they raised corn, wheat, and hogs. Region, class, and religion combined to make the Beamans and their kinfolk less than enthusiastic about the Confederacy. Not only did they live outside the plantation belt, but they also lived among large populations of Quakers, Moravians, and Wesleyan Methodists. Court records reveal that several of Malinda and John's relatives were Wesleyan Methodists who had publicly questioned the morality of slavery shortly before the outbreak of war. But despite their political and religious convictions, the men of these families were conscripted into the Confederate army, thus forcing their wives to assume responsibility for farms and children in their absence. Making a living was hard for these farm wives, despite numerous kinfolk, but at least they did not face their struggles alone.

In contrast, Rachel Cormany, of Chambersburg, Pennsylvania, had no close kin to rely on during her husband's absence, although comfortable financial circumstances helped alleviate the ravages of war. Originally from Canada, Rachel said goodbye to her husband Samuel in September, 1862, when he joined the Union army. She and the couple's young daughter, Cora, lived briefly with Samuel's parents, but Rachel decided to live in town, although it meant lodging with non-kin Jonathan Plough and his adult daughter, Annie. She was soon to witness one of the Civil War's most famous battles. In June 1863, the town of Chambersburg served as the staging ground for General Lee's invasion of Gettysburg, forcing Rachel to endure the dangers of warfare without the comforts of family, and under the roof of a landlord she concluded was "the meanest pile of dirt I have seen for some time," after he considered fleeing his home and leaving his tenant alone for the duration of the siege.[4]

Although northerners experienced far fewer invasions than did southerners, the siege of Gettysburg demonstrated how battleground and home front might merge into one. Faith in God was particularly important to women such as Rachel. After witnessing "Greybacks" flying by on horseback from her front window, she slept well, she claimed, only because her "Heavenly Parent" watched over her. As the fighting worsened, her fears escalated, causing her to wish "Oh, for more religion." Many Confederate women wished for the same. Somehow, the same heavenly parent comforted them, too, during their worse moments. Sue Carter, of Augusta County, Virginia, assured her cousin Mary that God had willed it that "our once prosperous & happy nation must be divided" and "devastated" by civil war. The end result, she wrote, would be "for our good & his own glory."[5]

"WAR WORK"

Many women felt compelled to act on their patriotic and religious principles. As they joined the war effort as nurses, clerks, teachers, and charity workers, the walls between the private and public spheres of society collapsed. Women driven by need found employment as laundresses and cooks for the military, necessitating life in camp alongside soldiers. Female camp followers inevitably included prostitutes as well. A few women, we will never know how many, even disguised themselves as men and served as soldiers on the battlefield. But it was women's voluntary work in soldiers' aid societies and their employment as nurses in hospitals throughout the North and South that brought the greatest number into the public sphere of "war work."

Early on during the Civil War, women were a visible presence in hospitals where they volunteered their services as nurses. This illustration thus suggests the war-time merging of the feminine domestic sphere of care with the masculine sphere of battlefields, demonstrating the fluid boundaries between home front and war front. (Library of Congress)

A long history of organized benevolent work, the abolitionist movement, and institutionalized charity accelerated women into work in the North. Within weeks of the war's outbreak, Dr. Elizabeth Blackwell, the first woman to obtain a medical degree in the United States, and "Ninety-Two Respected Ladies," created the Women's Central Relief Association (WCRA). Likewise, the Republican government centralized northern recruitment of nurses by appointing humanitarian reformer Dorothea Dix as Superintendent of Women Nurses for the Army Nursing Corps. The ultimate centralization of women's war work was achieved by the independent but government-sanctioned United States Sanitary Commission (USSC). Ostensibly designed to work side-by-side with the WCRA, the male-dominated USSC soon converted the WCRA into a branch of its own organization.

The leading light of the USSC was Henry Whitney Bellows, a Unitarian minister, conservative social reformer, and wealthy Whig nationalist drawn to Republican politics during the 1850s. Bellows personified the economic nationalism, religious reform, and antislavery views that drove Republican efforts to build a modern industrial state based on middle-class, Protestant moral principles. Neither a radical abolitionist nor a women's rights advocate, he sought a victorious, stable, Union. To this end, he reasoned, the leadership of the USSC could not be left to the "zeal of women," although women would play a major role in its success by donating their unpaid labor and household products to that end.[6]

Like most social and political leaders of the day, Bellows viewed benevolent activity as the perfect expression of female patriotism and defined voluntarism as feminine self-sacrifice writ large to meet the needs of the nation. Sewing uniforms, preparing food, and nursing fallen soldiers for the Union were extensions of women's "natural" domestic role, and constituted the essence of female citizenship, much as military service and political enfranchisement represented the core of male citizenship. Of course, this left political leadership firmly in the hands of men.

The USSC's sentimentalized image of women's public work completely ignored the vision of female citizenship articulated at the Women's Rights Seneca Falls Convention of 1848. Activists such as Elizabeth Cady Stanton and Lucy Stone deferred the cause of women's rights and joined in the patriotic work, hoping their efforts would convince Republicans to include women in the body politic once the war was won. Mary Livermore, a Chicago nurse, agreed. Throughout the war, she visited camps and hospitals and organized sanitary aid societies. Surely, Livermore reasoned, political leaders would recognize women's abilities and contributions by granting them suffrage. Leaders of the USSC were not moved, however. They viewed women's voluntarism as a noble but temporary expedient to winning the war.

Never questioning the wisdom of their leadership, Henry Bellows and his associates expected women dutifully to follow their instructions for production and distribution of goods at the local level. Instead, a contest emerged over whether the USSC or local women's organizations would distribute goods to soldiers. Charges of profiteering and speculation in women's handmade goods dogged the USSC throughout the war. Many women resented the condescending behavior of the commission, while others simply did not trust a national bureaucracy to work for the public good.

The USSC provides a particularly vivid example of the interplay between gender and class on the Civil War home front. Its close ties with the Republican Party only increased suspicions of corruption among rural farm and urban working-class women from Democratic families. Many of them reminded the commission that home fronts, not just battlefields, were scenes of deprivation, thanks to the war. It was hard enough to find time and resources to produce goods for the Sanitary Commission, but then to trust the commission to transfer those goods to suffering soldiers was just too much to ask. Analogous to working men's protests against the draft, poor women's protests against the USSC reflected a female class perspective. The Republican government had already taken their fathers and husbands, leaving them to fend for themselves; now it expected those same women to feed and clothe the soldiers en masse.

During the Civil War, the US Sanitary Commission (USSC) provided vital food and medical care to war-ravaged soldiers. Although the USSC presented the work of women (several of whom are visible in this photograph) as merely an extension of their traditional domestic duties of cooking, sewing, and nursing, in fact, war work accelerated women's movement into the public sphere of politics and professional employment. (Library of Congress)

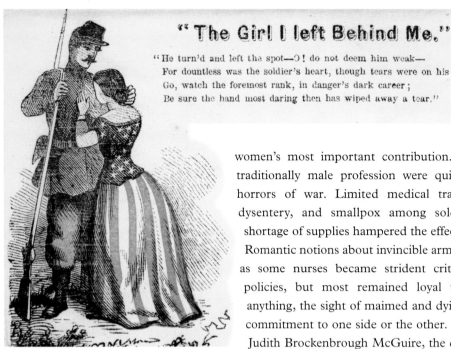

"The Girl I left Behind Me."

"He turn'd and left the spot—O! do not deem him weak—
For dauntless was the soldier's heart, though tears were on his
Go, watch the foremost rank, in danger's dark career;
Be sure the hand most daring then has wiped away a tear."

"The Girl I left Behind Me." This sentimentalized image of a woman's goodbye to her soldier sweetheart depicts the "true woman" as naturally altruistic, patriotic, and self-sacrificing. Building on middle-class notions that men and women occupied "separate spheres" of society, it reinforces the popular belief that women's contribution to the war effort consisted of domestic sacrifice. (Courtesy of New York Historical Society)

Despite northern women's mistrust of the USSC, they did contribute vast amounts of goods and unpaid labor to the war effort, as did southern women. On both sides, nursing was arguably women's most important contribution. Thousands who entered this traditionally male profession were quickly confronted by the worst horrors of war. Limited medical training, epidemics of typhoid, dysentery, and smallpox among soldiers, and hospitals' chronic shortage of supplies hampered the effectiveness of nurses and doctors. Romantic notions about invincible armies and quick victories vanished as some nurses became strident critics of war and governmental policies, but most remained loyal to their respective causes. If anything, the sight of maimed and dying soldiers reinforced women's commitment to one side or the other.

Judith Brockenbrough McGuire, the daughter of a Virginia Supreme Court judge, was a staunch Confederate with two sons in the army when she and her husband moved to Richmond, Virginia, in November, 1863. There, she served as a nurse in several hospitals during that city's occupation by Yankee forces. During the war's earliest stages, McGuire expressed "utter scorn" for "old men" who doubted the South's ability to prevail over the North. "We must not admit weakness," she wrote in her diary.[7] Though often critical of the war, her support for the Confederacy never wavered. Two years into the war, and just months before her relocation to Richmond, she learned of General Lee's attack on Gettysburg. Delighted by the news, she declared, "So may it be! We [southerners] are harassed to death with their ruinous raids, and why should not the North feel it in its homes?" She quickly added that "I don't want their women and children to suffer,… but I do want our men and horses to be fed on the good things of Pennsylvania."[8]

McGuire's wishes were fulfilled, although it was impossible (as she surely knew) that the women and children of Gettysburg would not suffer from an invasion by 65,000 rebel troops. Elizabeth Plank attested to that suffering when she described Major-General John Bell Hood's conversion of her family's farmhouse into a hospital for wounded Confederate soldiers. The shocking sight of family beds "filled with the wounded" caused the Plank family to abandon their home for the duration of its occupation. When they returned, five or six weeks later, their home was in ruins. Many of the 1,542 soldiers treated there had died and been buried in shallow graves in the orchard; mud roads replaced their flower and garden beds; all the family's poultry, hogs, and cattle had been eaten. Inside, they found floors strewn with blood-soaked straw and rooms infested by "flies and vermin."[9]

From nearby Chambersburg, Rachel Cormany feared for her and daughter Cora's safety as the battle for Gettysburg raged on. On June 15, Rachel watched as "contraband" raced by on horses, "their eyes fairly protruding with fear" of the rebel soldiers in hot pursuit. Having to care for herself and Cora without the protection of a husband made Rachel particularly sensitive to the plight of slave women liberated by the Union army, now left behind by the fleeing men. "O! How it grated on our hearts to have to sit quietly & look at such brutal deeds," wrote Rachel after watching rebels gather up African American women and children and drive them off like cattle. Mothers, she noted, naturally grabbed their children when told to "march on," but what, she wondered, would the rebels do with all those babies?[10]

Even more so than Cormany, Cornelia Hancock viewed at first hand slaves' experience of the war. A New Jersey Quaker with abolitionist sympathies, Hancock was 23 years old and single when she decided to serve her country as a military

On December 13, 1862, Fredericksburg was the site of one of the bloodiest battles, and Confederate victories, of the Civil War. During and after the battle, the US Sanitary Commission was present, dispensing clothing and bandages to wounded Union soldiers donated by women on the northern home front. (Library of Congress)

nurse. Her first nursing position was in Gettysburg, where the sights and smells inside military hospitals threatened to unnerve her. Perseverance inured her to the sight of blood, however, for she soon declared to her family that she would "never feel horrified at anything that may happen to me hereafter."[11]

Hancock's time at the Contraband hospital of Washington, DC, exposed her to the worst effects of slavery and white racism, which in turn contributed to her growing hatred of white southerners and northern Copperheads. In November, 1863, she estimated to her sister that 40 or 50 African Americans arrived each day at the hospital, freed by Yankees and on the run from rebels. Beginning her letter with "If I were to describe this hospital it would not be believed," she portrayed a vivid picture of her patients: two children with limbs broken from falling off trains (they were not allowed by white conductors to ride inside the cars); a man and a woman with frozen feet that had to be amputated; a driver "pounded nearly to death" by white soldiers; several escaped slaves exhibiting the worst effects of torture from masters. Refugee slave women especially concerned Cornelia because motherhood so complicated their plight. One mother arrived at the hospital with three children at her side, the "most worn out looking creature" Cornelia had ever seen.[12] Four of the woman's children were still held in slavery, her husband was dead.

Hancock's wartime experiences exposed her to scenes of life and death considered too grisly for the gaze of respectable ladies. Whereas patriotism motivated her to become a nurse, witnessing the agonizing deaths of so many young men quickly "robbed the battlefield of its glory." So also did her respect for those in authority dwindle. She "detested" both war and military officers, whom she condemned for their drunkenness and arrogance. By 1864, Hancock respected only the common foot soldier, "faithfully plodding through the dust protecting me."[13]

Cornelia Hancock's ordeal altered forever her view of humanity, future goals, and self-identity. Like so many women who entered the public sphere in response to national crisis, she never returned full time to the domestic sphere. In 1866, she opened a school for free African American children in Mt Pleasant, South Carolina; in 1878, she helped found the Society for Organizing Charity in Philadelphia. Anticipating the Social Gospel Movement, she worked throughout the 1880s to improve the lives of children and indigent people. Marriage was not in the picture for Cornelia. Explaining this to her mother, she wrote in 1866 that "men, as the generality of them appear in public life, have few charms for me."[14]

Women's entry into the public sphere undermined the image of the war front as a distinctly male sphere. Nor were home fronts devoid of young men, particularly in the South, where many of those men were slaves. In addition, many communities regularly endured or entertained soldiers who camped nearby. Also present were disabled soldiers and men who had obtained exemptions or furloughs from military service or paid substitutes to serve in their place. Especially in the South, "home guard" units enabled many men to fulfill their military duty by offering protection

to their own communities. Thus, home fronts were not only places where families privately waited out the war, but were also sites of ongoing political debates and various conflicts, many of which derived from the presence of so many men of soldiering age, in and out of uniform.

Although the war impoverished or displaced many civilians, it was a watershed for increased agricultural and industrial production in the North. Wartime demands for farm products created an economic boom for northern farmers, while longstanding class and ethnic divisions generated by industrialization and immigration were exacerbated. Among the urban working class of northern society, disillusionment with the war was rooted in class cleavages forged during a half-century of economic development. Throughout the 1850s, this working class consolidated its power to counter the burgeoning influence of white Protestant middle-class reformers, businessmen, and politicians. Then came the war. The Conscript Act of March 1863, which increased the number of white men drafted, but allowed wealthier men to hire substitutes and exempted African American men altogether (who legally

Although the Civil War home front was commonly portrayed as the province of women and children, this romantic portrayal of a soldier's homecoming realistically depicts several men present for the event. Enslaved men and white men exempted on account of age, occupation, and physical condition comprised the majority of civilian men, but so also did many wealthy men hire substitutes to serve in their place. (Library of Congress)

were not citizens), symbolized to working-class Democrats the sweeping powers assumed by a Republican-dominated national government. Working-class men supplied the greatest number of soldiers to the Union army, and suffered the greatest casualties.

RIOTS RAGE

Despite widespread resentment of conscription, most workers did not participate in the draft riots that convulsed New York City for five days in July 1863. Neighborhoods most vulnerable to the spirit of protest were those knit together by kinship, ethnicity, and deeply held attitudes about work and politics. In many such neighborhoods, the fact that employers of working people were Republicans personalized their resentment of Republican politicians who shaped national policies that had a profound impact on their lives. Democratic leaders eagerly capitalized on working men's resentment of Republican policies by launching a virulent white supremacy campaign that equated Republican policy with radical abolitionism. Coming on the heels of the Emancipation Act of 1862, the Conscript Act of 1863 would complete the degradation of white working men, according to northern Democrats. The emancipation of southern slaves, they predicted, would send "hordes" of impoverished freedmen to the North, where they would provide cheap labor for northern industrialists and further displace white working men.

1863

13–17 July

New York City Draft Riots: Over five days in New York City, frenzied mobs of mostly immigrant workers rioted in opposition to conscription, killing or wounding hundreds of victims, many of them African American citizens resented as a visible cause of the war and the draft.

The rioters' efforts to disrupt the draft began on Monday, July 13, 1863, when hundreds of men gathered in Central Park and proceeded to the Ninth District Provost Marshal's office, where the draft lottery was to be held that day. Protestors burned buildings and disrupted street cars, aided by Irish women who pulled up railway tracks with crowbars, while police officers and wealthy Republicans were attacked. As the riots gathered momentum, thousands of men, women, and children gathered on the streets of New York City to watch or participate in the pandemonium. When the carnage ended, over 100 people were estimated to have died as a result of the violence. Rioters launched their most vicious attacks on African American men and boys, especially in the waterfront area. At least 18 African Americans were hanged; five others drowned. Interracial couples were also targeted, highlighting fears that cultural amalgamation as well as economic displacement threatened the integrity of the white working class. Most shocking was rioters' burning of the Fifth Avenue Colored Orphan Society. These pointed attacks on African Americans reflected the deeply ingrained racism of northern society, as well as workers' own precarious class standing. One black leader condemned the rioters, but also criticized city

leaders, pointing out that "the language addressed to colored men" had long been "the common language of the street, and even some of the fashionable avenues" of New York City.[15]

Home front violence also ripped through the Confederate South in mid-1863. White women were clearly in the forefront of disorders as they protested high prices, hoarding of food, and speculation in commodities. During the famous April 2nd riot in Richmond, "Agnes," the wife of a Confederate army colonel, wrote to her equally well-placed friend, Sara Rice Pryor, expressing shame for having complained about the absence of "petty comforts" such as "hats, bonnets, gowns, stationery, books, magazines, [and] dainty foods" after meeting a young woman rioter two days earlier. "We celebrate our right to live. We are starving," the emaciated young woman proclaimed to Agnes. "This is a frightful state of things," wrote Agnes, who was particularly incensed that the newspapers had published not a word about the riots, but instead focused on Confederate efforts to reassert control over railroads. "Your General has been magnificent," Agnes commented to Sara. "He has fed Lee's army all winter – I wish he could feed our starving women and children."[16]

For five days in mid-July, 1863, thousands of people engaged in armed warfare against New York City's ruling elite. Entire neighborhoods, including women and children, participated in what began as a protest against the Conscription Act of 1863. Rioters especially targeted Republican elites, whom they blamed for the war, and black workers, who they believed threatened their economic and social integrity. (Courtesy of Illustrated London News Gallery)

As in the North, conscript laws, combined with the desperate condition of many people's lives, generated social upheaval on the southern home front. In the North Carolina Piedmont, many farmers such as John Beaman refused to fight any longer. As Beaman explained in a letter to governor Zebulon Vance, farmers produced vast quantities of corn and beef for the nation, yet it was planters and manufacturers who received exemptions from the army. How could his family be forced to "fight for such men as thes [sic]?" he asked. The plain farmers, he warned Vance, would be forced to "revolutionize unles this roten conscript exemption law is put down, for they air laws we don't intend to obey."[17]

Wealthy speculators in scarce goods were the scourge of society to farmers like the Beamans. For many such farmers, textile entrepreneur Edwin M. Holt of nearby Alamance County exemplified the ill-begotten profits of war. Although Confederate laws established price controls during the war, and although the Holts occasionally donated goods to hospitals and Ladies Aid societies, they nevertheless profited handsomely by charging high prices to customers (who often paid in wheat, corn, or meat), and by denying credit to poor people who sought cloth, thread, and yarn from their Alamance Factory at a time of dire shortages. Holt also took advantage of conscript laws that favored manufacturers and planters by obtaining exemptions for at least 11 men who worked for him. Although three of his sons served as Confederate soldiers, two others received exemptions on account of the family business. Not surprisingly, Edwin Holt and his Alamance Factory became a favorite target for the discontented.

OPPOSITE *In 1863, women in several southern cities launched bread riots against bakeries, groceries, and government facilities. The most famous occurred in cities such as Richmond but throughout the rural South smaller groups of women also raided plantations and mills. The breakdown of the South's gender and race hierarchy is depicted here by gaunt white women wielding weapons on a public street, joined by a black child who has also seized a loaf of bread. (Courtesy of Gary Gallagher)*

BELOW *This home front scene depicts the disruption and deprivation suffered by the southern plain folk during the war. Non-slaveholding households bore the brunt of food shortages, and starvation threatened the lives of many civilians by 1863. That suffering contributed to many soldiers' decisions to desert the army. (Library of Congress)*

Rising desertion rates and bread riots convinced many Confederate politicians that the war must become a rich as well as poor man's fight. Beginning in early 1864, the Confederate Congress passed legislation that addressed the needs of ordinary people. The criteria for class-based exemptions, such as the "Twenty-Negro" law, were tightened, the hiring of substitutes was ended, and price controls were established. Although poverty continued to plague the land, such efforts helped convince many white southerners that the Confederacy was doing the best it could.

Such assurances worked best in those regions where the Union army wreaked havoc on men and women. Despite the Confederate government's inability to truly alleviate suffering, Yankee incursions stimulated greater support for the Confederate cause among suffering people, particularly in Virginia. Even those who had lost heart with the Confederate government often expressed support for the "Holy Cause" as their hatred for Yankees grew. Ironically, in the throes of defeat, an elusive Confederate identity emerged, one based on images of Union soldiers as the barbaric henchmen of a despotic government. Indeed, in the desperate final year of war, an image of the Confederate "Lost Cause" as a defense of liberty and honor against greedy, invading Yankees, and only incidentally about slavery, gained strength.

However, such beliefs did not triumph throughout the whole South. In non-plantation regions where desertion and disaffection were common, Confederate tax-in-kind collectors, home guard soldiers, and special militia forces were the enemy of many plain folk. These men seized precious food and animals, forced sons and husbands into the army, occasionally tortured women who hid their men in the woods, and summarily executed deserters.

An unlikely defender of common people against such abuses was physician Samuel L. Holt, a first cousin to Edwin M. Holt. Moved by his conversation with a poor man of Randolph County whose only plow horse had been seized by a Confederate "press gang," Holt fired off a letter to governor Vance on May 24, 1863, charging that "this county has sent many & true men to this piratical war," while the "coxcombs, cowards, & puppies," of the planter class manage "to screen their own carcasses from yankee bullets."[18]

A year and a half after the Richmond bread riots, "Agnes" had equally harsh words for the Confederate government. Still haunted by "the pale, thin woman with the wan smile" she had encountered, she blamed the starvation that drove women to riot on politicians' rants. "Ah!" she wrote to Sara:

1863

2 April

Richmond Bread Riots: Desperate with the high price and scarcity of flour, several hundred women took to the streets of Richmond, breaking into public warehouses and private bakeries in search of food. Calm was restored only when Jefferson Davis ordered a regiment of soldiers to disperse the protesters at gunpoint.

1863

24 April

Tax-in-Kind Law: Passed by the Confederate Congress, this highly unpopular measure required agricultural producers to give 10 percent of various crops to the national government. Though onerous for most producers, the act ensured a regular supply of food that was distributed to both soldiers and needy families.

These are the people who suffer the consequence of all that talk about slavery in the territories you and I used to hear in the House and Senate Chamber… I am so shocked and disturbed I am hysterical. It is all so awful.[19]

By 1864, communities of dissent had emerged throughout the South, comprised of evaders or deserters of the Confederate army and civilian populations willing to harbor and defend them. Inadequate food and shelter had made unlikely associates, even allies, of slaves, free African Americans and non-slaveholding whites, who organized underground networks of pillaging and mutual defense. One of the most notorious hotbeds of anti-Confederate dissent was the "Free State of Jones," so-called because Jones County, Mississippi, allegedly seceded from the Confederacy. There, between 50 and 100 men linked by bonds of kinship and neighborhood organized an ad hoc military band dedicated to fighting the Confederacy. Their leader was Newt Knight, the non-slaveholding grandson of a Jones County slaveholder. So powerful and well known was the "Knight Company" that Confederate officials dispatched numerous troops to the area and launched two major raids in efforts to quell them. A raid led by Colonel Robert Lowry in April 1864 resulted in the execution of ten suspected deserters and the flight of numerous others to the Union army in New Orleans. But about 20 of the band's members, including Newt, eluded capture and remained in the woods for the duration of the war.

Newt Knight was the leader of the "Knight Company," Mississippi's most notorious band of deserters. By 1864, many organized bands of men were armed and hiding in woods to avoid military Confederate service in regions throughout the South. Such men relied on home front civilians (especially women) and slaves for food and protection. (Author's collection)

Women were vital to the Free State of Jones, and most of those who sheltered and fed the men were their wives, sisters, and daughters. Newt's slave accomplice, Rachel, was credited with using red pepper and ground glass to confound and kill militia hounds on the trail of deserters. Her alliance with Newt Knight bound them to one another for the rest of their lives, creating a mixed-race community in the Jones County region that endures to this day.

In North Carolina, a similar civil war erupted on the Montgomery–Randolph County line between the Beaman, Cranford, Hulin, and Moore families, who openly defied the Confederacy, and their pro-Confederate neighbors. Like the men of Jones County, Mississippi, many of the anti-Confederate men of this rural Piedmont community hid in the woods rather than serve the Confederacy, relying on female kin to feed and shelter them. This put the women in danger of harassment and torture, the men in danger of execution. Between September and November 1864, two wives of "outliers," Caroline Hulin and Malinda Beaman, were harassed by pro-Confederate men: Caroline was assaulted by local home guard soldier Martin Overton; two months later, Malinda accused Romulus F. Sanders, the 20-year-old son of Montgomery County sheriff Aaron H. Sanders, of stealing her mare.

By January 1865, Caroline and Malinda's cousin, Martha Cranford Sheets, could no longer contain her anger over the war. Several of her male relatives had died serving the Confederacy, while many others risked execution by hiding in the woods. Yet many slaveholders' sons were exempted from service. Martha took the law into her own hands by openly threatening the life of Sheriff Sanders. Accusing Sanders of having urged local citizens to support the Confederacy while obtaining exemptions for his own sons, she directed him to send her "too bushels of wheat and too bushels and a peck of corn in the corse of tenn days," or "I will send anuf of Deserters to mak you sufer," she wrote, "And send me good grain if you want to live." The fact that her husband had previously worked for the sheriff made his actions all the more personal: "Ther you have got all of your suns at home and when my husband is gone and he has dun work for you," she wrote.[20]

During the final year of war, groups of deserters roamed the region at night, raiding pro-Confederate homes to obtain provisions. Confederate home guard and pro-Confederate vigilantes likewise raided the homes of deserters' families and piloted the woods in search of disloyal men. Two weeks after Martha Sheets was arrested for threatening the sheriff, home guard soldiers captured three of her kinsmen, John, Jesse, and William Hulin, and shot them dead. No doubt in retaliation, and apparently emboldened by the defeat of the Confederacy, several women of Montgomery County, including a sister of the executed Hulin brothers, took one last crack at the Confederacy – and the Sanders family – when they armed themselves and rioted for a half hour at Sanders' Mill on May 1, 1865.

The behavior displayed during the war by the interrelated Cranford, Beaman, Hulin, and Moore families demonstrated the merging of personal and political issues in opposition to the Confederate government. Elsewhere, kinship, economic interdependence, and racial solidarity bound white southerners together, creating a "Confederate identity" that would survive long after the Civil War ended. But in places like Montgomery County, North Carolina, and Jones County, Mississippi, the war bred conflict rather than unity on the home front.

THE "CRUEL WAR"

Suffering and social chaos eventually sapped the morale of even the wealthiest and most committed citizens, many of whom had despaired of the "cruel war" by 1864. Mollie Houser, the avid "Cecess," confessed to her cousin Jim that she had developed a growing fondness for homemade brandy, joking that "I expect I will kill myself drinking," and promising to save some "that I may get drunk when this Cruel war is over." By late 1864, Mollie doubted God's command to be "content with our lot." "I don't think I will ever be contented with war," she lamented.[21] From North Carolina, "a poor woman" described God's will in far blunter terms to Governor

Vance: "Slavery is doomed to dy out; god is agoing to liberate neggars and fighting any longer is against God."[22]

Civilians responded to the Civil War in ways that reflected boundaries of geography, wealth, race, and gender. Too often, these boundaries prevented them from empathizing with those who lived on the "other side." Many white slaveholders were enraged by the sight of African American men in Yankee uniforms and disgusted by white women in ragged dresses who raised their fists at mill owners. Likewise, many among the North's white Protestant middle and upper classes considered wage-earning people, particularly if Irish or German, nothing more than ignorant rabble. And, while many white northerners viewed slavery as a sign of the South's barbarity, most by no means favored racial equality in a reconstructed nation.

Even within the two warring nations, common suffering rarely united disparate groups of people for more than a moment. Despite an occasional Samuel L. Holt, or the anonymous "Agnes," most people remained true to the interests of their region, class, or race. Sarah L. Hine, like many of the defeated planter class, remained "unreconstructed" in the wake of North–South reconciliation. Openly declaring her hatred for the United States in February, 1866, she assured Charlotte Branch that she would "cheerfully" endure all the suffering of the previous five years "to live once more under the [Confederate] government of my choice." Union nurse Cornelia Hancock just as fiercely condemned white southerners, whom she lumped together as "Secesh." "I hate them very badly, indeed," she wrote from South Carolina in 1866. With undisguised approval, she described the ragged clothes, burned homes and bridges, and gaunt faces of white southerners in defeat. "I talk to them all I can," she wrote to folks back home, "I like to hear them speak of their ruin."[23]

The opposing perspectives of Sarah Hine and Cornelia Hancock were those of competing cultural elites, but the perspectives of slaves, workers, and farmers remind us that race and class also divided people. Thus, it is perhaps the struggle at the home front that most sharply illuminated the tensions and passions that underpinned the war and rocked the nation for generations to come.

EMANCIPATION
PROCLAMATION.

WHEREAS, On the 22nd day of September, A.D. 1862, a proclamation was issued by the President of the UNITED STATES, containing, among other things, the following, to wit:

"That on the 1st day of January, in the year of our Lord one thousand eight hundred and sixty three, all persons held as slaves within any State, or designated part of a State, the people whereof shall then be in rebellion against the UNITED STATES, shall be henceforth and forever FREE; and the Executive Government of the United States, including the Military and Naval authorities thereof, will recognize and maintain the freedom of such persons, and will do no act or acts to repress such persons, or any of them in any effort they may make for their actual freedom; that the Executive will, on the first day of January aforesaid, issue a proclamation designating the States and parts of States, if any, in which the people therein, respectively, shall then be in rebellion against the United States; and the fact that any State, or the people thereof, shall on that day be, in good faith, represented in the Congress of the United States by members chosen thereto, at elections wherein a majority of the qualified voters of such States shall have participated, shall, in the absence of strong countervailing testimony, be deemed conclusive evidence that such State and the people thereof, are not in rebellion against the United States."

Now, THEREFORE, I, ABRAHAM LINCOLN, PRESIDENT of the UNITED STATES, by virtue of the power in me vested as Commander-in-Chief of the Army and Navy, in a time of actual armed rebellion against the authority of the Government of the United States, as a fit and necessary war measure for suppressing said rebellion, do, on this FIRST DAY of JANUARY, in the year of our Lord ONE THOUSAND EIGHT HUNDRED and SIXTY-THREE, and in accordance with my purpose so to do, publicly proclaimed for the full period of one hundred days from the date of the first above mentioned order, designate as the States and parts of States therein, the people whereof respectively are this day in rebellion against the United States, the following, to-wit: ARKANSAS, TEXAS, LOUISIANA, except the Parishes of St. Bernard, Plaquemine, Jefferson, St. John, St. Charles, St. James, Ascension, Assumption, Terrebonne, La Fourche, St. Mary, St. Martin, and Orleans, including the city of New Orleans; MISSISSIPPI, ALABAMA, FLORIDA, GEORGIA, SOUTH CAROLINA, NORTH CAROLINA, and VIRGINIA, except the forty-eight counties designated as West Virginia, and also the counties of Berkley, Accomac, Northampton, Elizabeth City, York, Princess Anne, and Norfolk, including the cities of Norfolk and Portsmouth; which excepted parts are for the present left precisely as if this proclamation were not issued. And by virtue of the power and for the purpose aforesaid, I DO ORDER and DECLARE, that ALL PERSONS HELD AS SLAVES within designated States, and parts of States, are, and henceforward SHALL BE FREE, and that the Executive Government of the United States, including the military and naval authorities thereof, will recognize and maintain the freedom of the said persons; and I hereby enjoin upon the people so declared to be free to abstain from all violence, unless in necessary self-defence, and I recommend to them that, in all cases where allowed, they LABOR FAITHFULLY for REASONABLE WAGES; and I further declare and make known that such persons of suitable condition will be received into the armed service of the UNITED STATES, to GARRISON FORTS, POSITIONS, STATIONS, and other places, and to man VESSELS, of all sorts in said service.

And upon this, sincerely believed to be an AN ACT OF JUSTICE, WARRANTED by the CONSTITUTION, upon military necessity, I invoke the CONSIDERATE judgment of MANKIND and the GRACIOUS FAVOR of ALMIGHTY GOD.

In witness whereof, I have hereunto set my hand and caused the seal of the United States, to be affixed.
Done at the CITY OF WASHINGTON this FIRST DAY of JANUARY, in the year of our Lord ONE THOUSAND EIGHT HUNDRED and SIXTY-THREE, and of the INDEPENDENCE of the UNITED STATES of AMERICA the EIGHTY-SEVENTH.

(Signed)

ABRAHAM LINCOLN.

By the President:
WM. H. SEWARD, Secretary of State.

THIS PROCLAMATION is an incalculable element of strength to the Union cause. It makes an alliance between the Rebels and Foreign States as impossible as it is for millions of Bondsmen to love Slavery better than Freedom. They loving our Government in proportion as it becomes a free land of promise and shelter from oppression, thus saving thousands of precious lives and millions of treasure from being lost in foreign wars. It perfects the purposes of the DECLARATION OF INDEPENDENCE and imputes no constitutional rights, those whom it would affect, having forfeited those rights by proving false to their country, to humanity and religion. No real support to the Union cause will be lost by this Proclamation, while time-serving traitors, who always covertly opposed the war, will be exposed. It will be a powerful incentive to the slave to fight for the Union instead of his rebel master, and when it becomes executed and Freedom reigns throughout the land, the colored man will leave the Northern regions, whither he has fled from slavery, and join his kindred beneath those sunny skies where nature invites him. Labor will be rewarded, justice fulfilled, and the Old Ship of State will again sail majestic o'er the unrippled waters of Liberty and Peace. Confusion and shame rest upon those who fight against a free Government, and songs of thankfulness and love glorify its defenders.
RUFUS BLANCHARD, Publisher, 52 La Salle St. Chicago, Ill.

> *"We shall nobly save, or meanly lose, the last best hope of earth. Other means may succeed; this could not fail. The way is plain, peaceful, generous, just — a way which, if followed, the world will forever applaud, and God must forever bless."*

Abraham Lincoln message to Congress, December 1862

The world will forever applaud

Emancipation

Michael Vorenberg

"Without shedding of blood there is no remission of sin." So went the favorite biblical passage (Hebrews 9:22) of John Brown, the abolitionist who attempted to foment a slave uprising in western Virginia by attacking the federal armory at Harpers Ferry.[1] Brown's bloody work represented the first *national* war against slavery: just before the raid on Harpers Ferry, he helped found a new nation – in theory only – fully committed to abolition as well as equal rights for all. Although the nation had a constitution and a president (Brown himself), it did not have a name or any land. Brown was caught and tried rather than hailed as the leader of a new republic, and he was executed before he could see the nation he envisioned realized on earth. But within two years of Brown's death, a new nation did exist on American soil, the Confederate States of America. Brown would not have been surprised to hear the vice-president of the Confederacy, Alexander H. Stephens, declare that slavery was the "cornerstone" of the new nation. However, Brown might have been surprised to learn that, only four years after his raid on

A memorial copy, in color, of the Emancipation Proclamation. Soon after Lincoln issued the order, abolition societies began to produce commemorative copies. These became more and more elaborate after the end of the war and the assassination of Lincoln. The original proclamation, an unassuming document written in Lincoln's hand, was destroyed in a fire after the war. (GLC 05508.272 The Gilder Lehrman Collection, courtesy of the Gilder Lehrman Institute of American History, New York)

Harpers Ferry, the United States, now engaged in a bloody conflict with the Confederacy, embraced emancipation as a war aim. Within six years of the raid, in Abraham Lincoln's Second Inaugural Address of March 1865, the president went so far as to suggest that the war should go on "until every drop of blood drawn with the lash, shall be paid by another drawn with the sword."[2] The address echoed Brown's "shedding of blood," though Lincoln, like most Union leaders, had regarded Brown as a dangerous lunatic. Two months after Lincoln's Second Inaugural, the war that Brown had helped to start was over, and the cause of universal emancipation that Brown had championed was victorious.

How had emancipation, once considered a cause of only a tiny minority of Americans, become so quickly a policy of the United States? The answer, quite simply, was the Civil War.

EMANCIPATION AND THE ROAD TO CIVIL WAR

Brown himself had understood that only a violent conflict would bring a sure end of slavery in the United States. By contrast, emancipation in most other slave societies of the western hemisphere had occurred with relative peace, though the revolution in Santo Domingo beginning in 1791 was a notable exception, one dear to the hearts of Brown and other militant abolitionists. In an Atlantic world in which slavery was crumbling, slavery in the United States did not wither but instead became vibrant and profitable.

The abolition of the Atlantic slave trade in 1808 did little to halt the vitality of slavery in the United States. Northern states began to abolish slavery during the American Revolution, though in most of these states emancipation was gradual and slavery lingered on well into the 1800s. A few African Americans in New Jersey were still enslaved on the eve of the Civil War, for example. In the South, however, slavery thrived. The cotton boom of the early 19th century, propelled by the new technology of the cotton gin, infected white southerners with the promise of riches from harvesting cotton and raising slaves. Encouraged and at times even forced by their masters to bear children (some of them fathered by masters), southern slave women reproduced at a high enough rate to make this slave society the only one in the western world that was able to sustain itself without the importation of slaves. In fact, the population grew exponentially.

Prized as high-return investments as well as cheap laborers, slaves found that masters attempted to monitor and regulate their lives with scientific efficiency and paternalistic intrusion. On cotton plantations, slaves usually worked from sunup to sundown every day but Sunday, when the master or a white preacher would deliver sermons extolling the Christian virtue of obedience and promising freedom and glory in the heaven that awaited them. Slaves secretly and subversively held their own religious services and community meetings. Here they talked about the freedom that God would bestow upon them in *this* lifetime. Only in the deepest, fearful recesses of imagination did whites foresee a convulsive event bringing universal emancipation. But slaves thought about a revolutionary "day of jubilee" all the time. They knew that their moment had come when Abraham Lincoln was elected and the states of the Deep South began to secede. Most lingering doubts within the African American community were dispersed after the firing on Fort Sumter on April 14, 1861. Three weeks later, Jefferson Davis, the president of the newly formed Confederate States of America, received a letter from a poor white man in Alabama warning that:

A photograph of John Brown before he became famous, and infamous, for his activities in the Kansas "wars" between antislavery and proslavery settlers in the late 1850s. A militant abolitionist, Brown and his sons murdered five men near Pottawatomie Creek, Kansas, in 1856 and then, in 1859, he led a group of 20 men to seize the federal armory at Harpers Ferry, in western Virginia. The raid failed to spark the widespread slave rebellion that Brown had hoped it would, and Brown was eventually caught, tried, and executed. He became a martyr to the abolitionist cause, and his raid on Harpers Ferry helped bring the country to the brink of the Civil War. (National Archives)

> the Negroes is very Hiley Hope up that they will soon Be free so I think that you Had Better order out All the Negroe felers [fellows] from 17 years oald up. Either fort them up or put them in the army and Make them fite like good fell[ow]s for wee ar in danger of our lives hear among them.[3]

Yet Abraham Lincoln and most others of his antislavery Republican Party were committed not to interfering with slavery where it already existed. They conceded that the original Constitution gave protection to slavery in the South, and, for the most part, they condoned fugitive slave laws that placed increasing responsibility on northerners to deliver up slaves who had escaped to freedom. Republicans demanded only that slavery be excluded from the western territories. Had a war not begun between the Confederacy and the Union in April 1861, the institution might have survived well into the late 19th century and perhaps into the 20th century. Soon after the Confederates fired on Fort Sumter, the abolitionist Frederick Douglass admitted that the war had revived the wilting cause of abolition. "Thank God!" wrote the African American leader. "The slaveholders themselves have saved our cause from ruin! They have exposed the throat of slavery to the keen knife of liberty."[4]

Historical precedent supported the position of Frederick Douglass – and John Brown before him – that emancipation in the United States required an armed conflict. During the American Revolution, Lord Dunmore, the royal governor of Virginia, had promised freedom to slaves who joined the British cause. General George Washington responded with his own promise of emancipation to slaves who served in colonial forces. Slavery survived the Revolution, of course, but so did the notion of slavery ending either as an incident or as a cause of a war. Enslaved and free African Americans, from Gabriel Prosser to Denmark Vesey and Nat Turner, conspired to start an armed black rebellion, and David Walker, the most widely read

IN THE COTTON FIELD.

THE CHRISTMAS WEEK.

THE SALE.

THE PARTING. "Buy us"

THE LASH.

BLOW FOR BLOW.

IN THE SWAMP.

FREE!

"STAND UP A MAN!"

"MAKE WAY FOR LIBERTY!"

VICTORY!

"HE DIED FOR ME"

African American writer prior to Frederick Douglass, called on slaves to rise up against their white masters. No massive slave uprising occurred, but the notion of emancipation by war never faded. In 1842, for example, the Massachusetts congressman and former president John Quincy Adams declared that the Constitution gave Congress a "war power" to abolish slavery if wartime necessity required it (though as secretary of state in 1820 Adams had denied the existence of such a power).

For southern whites, Adams's statement confirmed what they suspected of all northerners: they would fight a war for emancipation. John Brown's raid on Harpers Ferry, then, was regarded by southerners not as anomalous but as the logical fulfillment of wicked northern designs. The election in 1860 of Abraham Lincoln, the candidate of a purely northern party, signaled to southern whites that the deadliest war against them on behalf of southern blacks would soon be upon them.

OPPOSITE *This is a reproduction of a chromolithograph created by James Fuller Queen in 1863 representing the dynamic transition of an African American from a slave on a plantation to a Union soldier struggling on the battlefield for liberty, for which he gives his life. (Library of Congress)*

FROM A WAR FOR UNION TO A WAR FOR EMANCIPATION

Even before Lincoln's election, and certainly after it, southern blacks began to confirm southern white fears. A month before the firing on Fort Sumter, eight runaway slaves arrived to seek asylum at Fort Pickens in Florida, another of the US forts in the Deep South. They were, in the words of a colonel at the fort, "entertaining the idea that we [the army] were placed here to protect them and grant them their freedom."[5] Commanders were reluctant to antagonize their southern hosts in the midst of the secession crisis. The colonel at Fort Pickens delivered the slaves to the marshal at Pensacola, asking him to return them to their owners.

Despite African Americans' hopes that Lincoln's election heralded the awaited moment of freedom, the incoming administration continued to take the line that slavery would not be touched where it already existed. As president-elect, Lincoln opposed the compromise package of senator John J. Crittenden of Kentucky because it allowed slavery into some of the western territories, but he supported Ohio senator Thomas Corwin's proposed constitutional amendment that said nothing about slavery in the West and prohibited federal interference with slavery in the South. Lincoln's promise of non-interference with slavery was aimed mainly at the border states, slave states that had not seceded and that Lincoln was determined to keep in the Union. The new Congress, dominated by Republicans, also adopted an appeasing strategy toward emancipation. Soon after the war began, it approved a resolution proposed by Senator Crittenden declaring that the war was to be fought

1831

Nat Turner: A slave preacher, Nat Turner, organized a rebellion in Southampton County, Virginia that claimed the lives of over 50 local whites before being dispersed by the militia. Turner and his followers were executed, but the event laid bare the anxiety of white southerners regarding their security among African Americans.

for union only, not emancipation. Meanwhile, political and military leaders rebuffed the efforts by northern white and African American abolitionists to raise regiments of African American soldiers.

With federal lawmakers publicly opposing emancipation and black enlistment, some African Americans were inclined to think that their interests might not be aligned with those of the Union. Slaves were left in the lurch: was it worth the risk of running to Union lines if they might simply be returned to their masters to face certain punishment? One Maryland slave named John Boston in early 1862 decided to take the risk, even as his wife Elizabeth (a *de facto* marriage, as southern laws prohibited slave marriage) opted to stay and trust her future to fate. Boston found his way to a New York regiment camped in northeastern Virginia. "This Day I can Adress you thank god as a free man," he wrote to his wife:

> Dear you must make your Self content i am free from al the Slavers Lash and as you have chose the Wise plan Of Serving the lord i hope you Will pray Much and I Will try by the help of god To Serv him With all my hart.

Boston knew that even if his escape was successful, it was likely to come at the price of his former master exacting retribution on his family. So he told his wife to send his good wishes to her mistress as well as the message "that i trust that She Will Continue Her kindness to you and that god Will Bless her on earth and Save her In grate eternity." Elizabeth may never have received the letter. It was eventually presented to a Union commander by Maryland legislators who demanded Boston's return to his owner. We do not know if Boston was ever in fact remanded back to slavery.[6]

While some African Americans like Boston continued to run for Union lines and others bided their time, waiting for the war to become an avowed fight for black liberation, still others decided that they might fare better if they supported the Confederacy. Some free African Americans in Louisiana, for example, fielded a regiment of "Native Guards" to fight for the South. That African Americans would support a nation resting on slavery as its "cornerstone" might seem strange, but their action speaks to the confusion created by the Union's official, initial policies against emancipation and against black enlistment. If the Union would not reward African Americans for the actions that they took on their own behalf, perhaps the Confederacy would. But cases of African Americans fighting for the Confederacy were rare. Most African Americans who supported the southern war effort did so by compulsion, not volition, and they almost always served as drudge workers – fort builders, water carriers, grave diggers – instead of soldiers.

Union commanders grew increasingly frustrated that they were required to return runaways while the Confederacy used slaves in the war effort. Every slave returned, reasoned Union officers, was one more potential worker for the Confederacy. Using

such logic, General Benjamin F. Butler, stationed at Fortress Monroe in Virginia, had refused to return three slaves who arrived at his post in May 1861. He declared that the slaves were "contraband," like any other property seized in war. If the masters pledged loyalty to the Union, he would return their property to them; if they instead continued to support the rebellion, as Butler knew they would, he would free the slaves. Eventually, other Union officers began adopting Butler's "contraband" policy. The flow of former slaves to Union lines increased dramatically, and impromptu contraband villages began to appear in Union-occupied areas across the South, though the largest was in Washington, DC. From the White House, Lincoln could see men, women, and children who, according to federal policy, were supposed to be returned to their owners. He took his first wartime action against slavery (a willful non-action, really) by saying nothing about the military's contraband policy, giving his silent consent to slaves' efforts to seize their own freedom.

Congress took the further step of turning the contraband policy into actual law through a series of confiscation acts. Republican congressmen in August 1861 easily carried the First Confiscation Act, which allowed Federal authorities to confiscate slaves used by Confederates for military purposes. Yet the measure was clearly

This reproduction of a photograph taken in 1862 shows former slaves fording the Rappahannock River in Virginia. As Union armies marched into the South, recently freed African Americans, or "contrabands," often joined them. (Library of Congress)

This is a reproduction of an 1862 photograph of an ex-slave family on Smith's Plantation, Beaufort, South Carolina. Under the direction of the Union army, which occupied Beaufort in early 1862, African Americans continued to work the land but as free, paid laborers. (Library of Congress)

designed to harm the slaveholder more than help the slave. The law treated emancipation as nothing more than the seizure of a traitor's property. Not only did it fail to spell out any rights due to freed people, it even omitted any legal mechanism for assuring the slaves' freedom once the war was over. The Second Confiscation Act, adopted in July 1862, was much more influential than the first, but it, too, tried to conform to the prewar principle of non-interference with slavery where it existed. Rather than limiting freedom to slaves in the service of the Confederacy, the act granted emancipation to all slaves owned by rebel masters.

Once again, Federal authorities were to leave untouched the slaves of a "lawful owner" who had not aided the rebellion. In early congressional policy toward the slave states, African American freedom appeared mainly as a weapon against the Confederacy rather than as an objective in itself.

Matters were different outside of the slave states. In the District of Columbia, where the Constitution gave Congress exclusive jurisdiction, the Republican majority did not need to use military necessity to justify emancipation. Antislavery politicians had long been rankled by the presence of slavery in the District, but conciliatory northern congressmen had joined with southern colleagues to check emancipation initiatives. In April 1862, three months before passing the Second Confiscation Act, Congress approved and Lincoln signed the measure freeing the District's 3,000 slaves. Unlike the confiscation acts, this legislation freed slaves of disloyal *and* loyal owners. After establishing freedom in the District, Republicans carried a bill prohibiting slavery in the territories.

Although these blows against slavery in Union-controlled areas declared that emancipation would be immediate, they contained two vestiges of programs of gradual emancipation common in the northern states and in other one-time slave societies of the early 19th century. First, in conformity with the principle that the government had to compensate owners for any property taken by the government, which was enshrined in the "takings" clause of the Fifth Amendment, the treasury paid loyal masters for the loss of their human property. In Washington, DC, for example, government agents compensated masters according to a schedule of the market value of varying types of slaves (a young adult male might fetch twice as much as an elderly woman). Second, Congress promoted the voluntary colonization of freed people abroad. Between the act emancipating slaves in the District and the Second Confiscation Act, Congress appropriated $600,000 to assist African Americans who wished to settle abroad. Lincoln, who had been a longtime advocate of voluntary colonization, applauded both compensation to owners and appropriations for colonization. He approved at least two plans for colonizing African Americans in Central America, although only one of these, the settlement of a privately held island near Haiti, went forward. The experiment, involving about 400 free African Americans, failed within a year and the survivors returned to the United States.

Lincoln was enthusiastic for compensation and colonization for a number of reasons. For one, he had always been personally in favor of this gradualist approach to emancipation. He had been a member of a colonization society in Illinois, and he had advocated colonization in many of his political speeches of the 1850s. Also, as a lawyer experienced in property disputes, he regarded the uncompensated taking of innocent people's property by the government unacceptable, even in wartime.

1862
17 July

Second Confiscation Act: This US legislation declared free the slaves of any rebel in those areas of the Confederacy where the Union was not then in control (including parts of Virginia, Tennessee, Louisiana, and Mississippi). This Act also gave the president the authority to use contrabands as soldiers. It demonstrated the increasing shift toward emancipation among northerners

The Civil War had given Lincoln further reason to support the gradualist approach to emancipation. He came to the White House with a clear design for restoring the Union – a design that did not include emancipation – and he remained loyal to this strategy throughout the first year of the war. Political pressures from conservative Republicans, pro-Union Democrats, and border-state leaders stayed Lincoln's hand on slavery. In August 1861, when General John C. Frémont declared martial law in Missouri and proclaimed freedom throughout the state for all slaves owned by rebels, the president asked him to modify the order so that it conformed to the recently adopted First Confiscation Act. When Frémont refused to comply, Lincoln revoked the proclamation and soon removed the general from the volatile border area. In May 1862, when General David Hunter declared that all slaves in Florida, Georgia, and South Carolina would be freed and armed, Lincoln rescinded the order and precluded further such orders by proclaiming that only he, as commander-in-chief, had the power "to declare the Slaves of any state or states, free."[7] Antislavery optimists read the message as a signal that the president intended to use that power.

Underlying Lincoln's strategy toward emancipation was his belief that the Confederacy was fragile, controlled by a few southern hotheads, and that the rebellion would quickly disintegrate once the southern unionist majority rejected the rebel leaders. To convince southerners of the folly of secession, Lincoln hoped to score a single, humiliating military victory over the Confederacy. Meanwhile, he promoted gradual, compensated, state-initiated emancipation in the border states, hoping that if the border states abolished slavery, they would demoralize southern whites who expected those states to join the Confederacy. The president, who had been born in Kentucky, understood the resistance to abolition he would face in the border states, but he thought he could overcome most objections by adhering to the conservative system of emancipation that he had always preferred.

By the summer of 1862, neither of the president's strategies for weakening southern morale had succeeded. Instead of scoring a stunning military victory, the Union armies had suffered a number of embarrassing defeats or stalemates. The effort to encourage border-state emancipation had fared as poorly. In late 1861, Lincoln targeted Delaware, a state with only 1,800 slaves, as a test area for his compensated emancipation scheme. When congressmen from the small state, in cooperation with the president, promoted the gradual emancipation plan at home, opponents denounced the effort "to place the negro on a footing of equality with the white man."[8] Similar results awaited Lincoln's proposed resolution to Congress of March 1862, which pledged Federal funds to any state freeing its slaves. Although Congress approved the resolution, border-state congressmen received the measure coldly, and no actual scheme of subsidized emancipation was ever adopted. In a meeting with border-state congressmen just before Congress adjourned in July 1862, Lincoln pleaded his case again, but this time his request for gradual emancipation came with a warning: "if the war continue long, as it must,... the institution [of slavery] in your states will be extinguished by mere friction and abrasion – by the mere incidents of the war."[9] That poorly cloaked threat suggested that the president was ready to experiment with a new approach to slavery, and to the war. Ten days later, on July 22, 1862, he presented the first draft of the Emancipation Proclamation to the Cabinet.

The Proclamation signaled an important shift in Lincoln's conception of the war. Having failed to provoke a quick, internal collapse of the rebellion, the president was forced to resort to more aggressive methods of conquest. He did not yet relinquish his border-state strategy, however. Even the first draft of the Proclamation included a promise to recommend again his plan of gradual, compensated emancipation to Congress, a promise he never kept. Then, at the end of the document, almost as an afterthought, Lincoln added that, as commander-in-chief, he was ordering a "military measure" freeing slaves in rebellious areas as of January 1, 1863. Both of these policies, the Proclamation explained, were conservative means to restore "the constitutional relation between the general government, and each, and all of the states."[10]

Members of the Cabinet were concerned. Montgomery Blair, the postmaster-general, argued that the new measure:

> purports only to manumit the slaves in rebellious states yet in operation will
> in fact be universal, for no one will suppose that slavery can exist in the
> border states when it is abolished further south.[11]

The Proclamation went too far even for Salmon P. Chase, the most radical of Lincoln's secretaries. Fearing that a general order "would lead to universal emancipation," the treasury secretary recommended instead that each district commander issue a separate emancipation order while Lincoln "quietly... [allowed] Generals to organize and arm the slaves."[12] After the Cabinet meeting, Lincoln decided to postpone issuing the Proclamation, not because of the objections of Blair and Chase, but because of the point raised by secretary of state William Henry Seward, that the order might seem an act of desperation, a "last *shriek*, on the retreat."[13] It was better to await a military victory, agreed the president, so he put the document aside, tinkering with it now and then, and watched for positive news from his armies.

As the president prepared to take a new tack against slaveowners, he began to think more seriously about the fate of the slaves. In the first year of the war, Lincoln had generally avoided the question of how African Americans would make the transition from slavery to freedom. When he addressed the issue, he usually recommended colonization, though increasingly he had suggested temporary apprenticeships. The president did not abandon these two options once he decided to issue the

First Reading of the Emancipation Proclamation of President Lincoln, *an 1864 painting by Francis B. Carpenter, who spent six months in the White House at work on the portrait. (GLC 02598 The Gilder Lehrman Collection, courtesy of the Gilder Lehrman Institute of American History, New York)*

Proclamation, but he did open his mind to a third alternative: military enlistment for African Americans. Federal officials and commanders already had made significant strides toward arming free and enslaved African Americans. In 1862, Congress authorized military service for African Americans in the Second Confiscation Act and Militia Act, and Union officers like David Hunter in South Carolina and James Lane in Kansas unofficially began to raise African American regiments. Lincoln's secretaries were divided on the issue. Chase and secretary of war Edwin M. Stanton urged the President to arm the slaves, while Montgomery Blair voiced the common racist assumption that African Americans were too docile to fight.

Despite his own uncertainty about African American capabilities, Lincoln could not turn his back on the reservoir of manpower represented in the country's black population. A month after reading his Proclamation to the Cabinet, he authorized military officers in rebellious areas to recruit free and enslaved African American males as non-combat soldiers. Lincoln submitted to northern racial prejudice by limiting African American soldiers to drudge work, and he tried to soften the policy's effect on the border region by exempting from the order not only the Union slave states but North Carolina and Tennessee as well. This halting step gave way to active recruiting efforts in all of the slave states and intensified lobbying by abolitionists and military commanders for African American troops. Finally, with Lincoln's approval, the War Department created the Bureau of Colored Troops in the spring of 1863.

The previous July, however, when the president had read the first draft of his Emancipation Proclamation to the Cabinet, he had still been unsure about the ideal plan for the freed people or even the wisdom of emancipation. A month after the Cabinet meeting, the president responded to an editorial by Horace Greeley, the editor of the *New York Tribune*, which demanded a presidential decree of freedom, by declaring that his "paramount object in this struggle *is* to save the Union, and is *not* either to save or to destroy slavery."[14] Lincoln anticipated that many white northerners would denounce the Proclamation, and that Democrats would use the document against his party in the fall congressional elections. But he held fast to his promise to the Cabinet to issue the Proclamation as soon as the Union army had a victory. When the victory finally came in mid-September 1862 at Antietam, the president, on September 22, 1862, issued the preliminary Emancipation Proclamation.

This is a reproduction of a photograph of 27 soldiers from Company E, 4th US Colored Infantry, at Fort Lincoln, Washington. By 1865, when this photograph was taken, more than 180,000 African Americans were serving in Union uniform. (Library of Congress)

Lincoln's enemies were furious. Confederate leaders, who had long argued that Lincoln meant to free all the slaves, pointed to the hypocrisy of the man who had promised not to interfere with slavery where it existed. Southern newspapers depicted him as the devil incarnate, or at the very least the next John Brown. At the prospect of armed African Americans, southern whites reacted with horror. Eventually Jefferson Davis proclaimed that any captured African American Union soldiers would be treated as armed slaves in insurrection. They would be executed.

Meanwhile, in the North, Democrats charged that the Proclamation was an unconstitutional use of the war power and a dangerous threat to the country's racial order. One Democratic candidate for Congress warned that "our people are in great danger of being overrun with negroes set free by our army or by the President's proclamation."[15] By playing on the growing sentiment that the current administration would throw the country into constitutional and racial chaos, the Democrats scored major victories in the fall elections. As a result of the vote, the opposition gained three seats in the Senate and 34 in the House of Representatives, leaving Republicans still well in control of the upper house but only slightly dominant in the lower. The Democrats elected governors in two northern states, New York and New Jersey, and obtained majorities in three state legislatures, New Jersey, Indiana, and Illinois.

1862

22 September

Preliminary Emancipation Proclamation: This decree declared free slaves of all masters in parts of the South still in rebellion on January 1, 1863. By giving white southerners a window of opportunity to return to the Union with slavery intact, Lincoln was continuing to pursue a rapidly disappearing moderate course with regard to emancipation.

Although radical Republicans cheered the Proclamation, more moderate party members struggled to meet the opposition's objections to emancipation. Many denied that ex-slaves would migrate north or would achieve legal equality. To assuage racial fears, conservatives promoted colonization or invoked the popular notion that the darker race would naturally stay in the warmer southern climate. One Republican paper, which declared "America for white men," promised that thousands of white Europeans would flock to the United States in the wake of emancipation, while those of African descent would slowly expire: "as the Indians were crowded westward, and out of our bounds, by the irresistible advance of the white man, so will the blacks be."[16]

Republicans also countered the opposition's constitutional objections to emancipation. At the heart of the constitutional defense of emancipation was the assertion that the Proclamation was only a temporary measure. "Although every slave in the South be emancipated," argued a pro-administration paper in Ohio, "the 'institution' in its legal sense would not be destroyed. The Slaves, if they remained in the States, could all be reenslaved as soon as the army that liberated them was removed."[17] Some Republicans objected to such a prediction because it ignored the Proclamation's promise that emancipated slaves were "forever free" and ran counter to centuries of legal precedent that prohibited free people from being enslaved.

But did the Proclamation in fact make people free? As Lincoln would often observe, an unfriendly Congress or Supreme Court could strike down wartime emancipation once the war was over, thus revoking the promise of freedom. Most party members at the very least conceded that the surrender of the Confederacy would deny freedom to those slaves not yet liberated by Union armies.

To make emancipation permanent, Lincoln proposed three antislavery amendments to the US Constitution in his annual message to Congress of December 1, 1862. The first offered federal compensation to any state that abolished slavery by 1900. The second promised compensation to any slaveowner whose slave had been freed during the war. The final amendment authorized Congress to appropriate money for colonizing free blacks, "with their own consent," outside the United States.[18] The measures disappointed long-time abolitionists, who worried that Lincoln was softening the Emancipation Proclamation or perhaps even considering not issuing the final version of it. To be sure, the measures did contain elements of the president's old gradualist border-state strategy. Lincoln continued to believe that loyal slaveholders should be treated more benignly than disloyal ones, and he still hoped that the border states would take emancipation in their own hands. Yet, he understood that in making emancipation an explicit war aim, he was fundamentally changing the meaning of the conflict. In the same address to Congress in which he proposed his antislavery amendments, he declared, "in giving freedom to the slave, we assure freedom to the free... The world will forever applaud, and God must forever bless."[19]

Despite political criticism from anti-emancipationists and skepticism from abolitionists about the firmness of his convictions, Lincoln never retreated from the Emancipation Proclamation. He signed the final Proclamation on January 1, 1863, as promised. The main difference between this document and the preliminary version was that it included a long list of areas where the order did not apply. Exempted were the border states and almost every Confederate region then under Union occupation. Also excluded were Virginia's westernmost counties, which, the day before, Lincoln had agreed to admit to the Union as the new state of West Virginia. Official admission of the state would come six months later; by then, West Virginia had voted to abolish slavery gradually. Faced with the rejection of his gradual emancipation program by the existing Union slave states, the president had seen the wisdom of creating a new, more amenable border state (even John Brown, who had envisioned this region as the epicenter of emancipation, might have approved). To conservatives, the president soft-pedaled the Proclamation. One of his generals received his assurance that "the States not included in it... can have their rights in the Union as of old. Even the people of the states included, if they choose, need not to be hurt by it."[20] But the president knew that the Proclamation was in fact momentous, and for this reason he labored over the final wording. Unlike the preliminary order, this version contained no mention of colonization or compensation and did include the announcement that freed people would be accepted into the armed services. Also, in response to northern anxieties that

A lithograph by Currier and Ives from 1865 depicting Lincoln giving freedom to the slaves. The president has broken the slave's chains and now points to the heavens and quotes from the Bible, signaling that he is an instrument of God. African Americans are again shown as supplicants rather than as agents who played a crucial role in securing their own freedom. After Lincoln's assassination and martyrdom in 1865, he increasingly became known as the "Great Emancipator," though he had been slower than some to make emancipation a Union war aim. (Library of Congress)

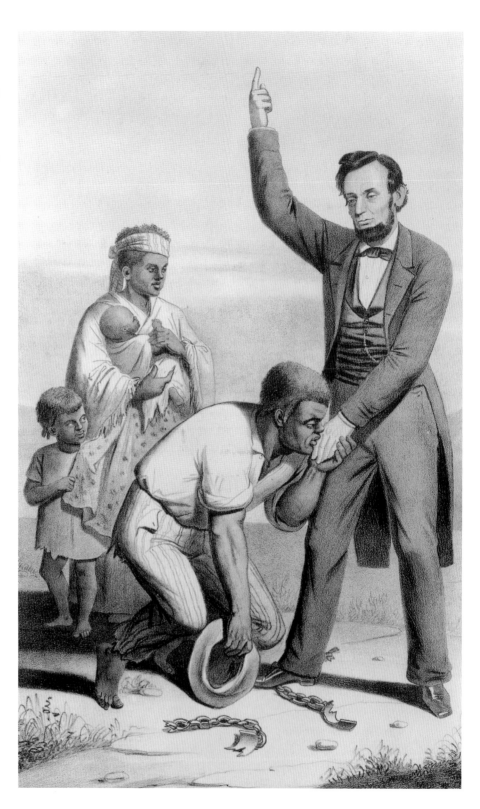

emancipation would lead to a servile insurrection, Lincoln inserted into the final Proclamation a request that ex-slaves "abstain from all violence, unless in necessary self-defence," and that "they labor faithfully for reasonable wages."[21] The president's addition of this clause had as much to do with foreign policy as domestic racial prejudice. European leaders had suspected Lincoln of trying to incite a slave rebellion when he issued the preliminary Proclamation, which restrained military officers from hindering "any efforts" the freed people made for "their actual freedom."[22] The new provision in the final Proclamation attempted to ease such anxieties. Moreover, as the president and his secretary of state intended, the Proclamation thwarted the movement in England and France to intervene on the side of the Confederates. Because both countries condemned slavery and had abolished it throughout their empires, they would resist waging war against a power ostensibly fighting for emancipation. As he had said in his 1862 address to Congress, he expected that "the world will forever applaud" the transformation of a war for union into a war for union *and* emancipation.

EMANCIPATION AND THE END OF THE CIVIL WAR

Despite Lincoln's signing of the final Emancipation Proclamation, African American freedom remained precarious. The Proclamation was a wartime declaration only: it would only have an actual effect if Lincoln held firm in his commitment to it, if he was able to win reelection against someone without such a commitment, and if he was able to defeat the Confederacy. From the moment that the president signed the Proclamation, he was under pressure to revoke it. The order prolonged the war, said his detractors, many of whom believed the misinformation spread by Confederate sympathizers in the North who suggested that the Confederacy was ready to surrender as soon as Lincoln backed off from emancipation. In fact, Confederate leaders required nothing less than recognition of Confederate independence before they would surrender. However, they were happy to let the rumor spread that emancipation was the only real obstacle to peace if it would injure Lincoln's reputation and improve the odds of his losing a reelection bid to someone willing to give up the war or at least negotiate a ceasefire. False notions in the North that emancipation alone prolonged the war did indeed damage Union morale. After the Union victories in mid-1863 in Vicksburg and Gettysburg produced no end to the war, northerners were quick to blame the emancipation cause. As a result, African Americans were the primary targets of mob violence in the draft riots of that year, the most famous and destructive of which seized New York City for a week in July.

1865

18 February

Charleston captured by US troops: Charleston was regarded as the birthplace of secession and its capture foreshadowed, for many, the end of the war. The first US soldiers to enter the city were a US Colored Troops regiment recruited from among local escaped slaves.

Lincoln refused to bow to pressures to rescind the Proclamation, however, and eventually northern whites came to accept the wisdom of emancipation. Public opinion pivoted mainly on the news of African Americans' success as soldiers. From Port Hudson in Louisiana to Fort Wagner in South Carolina, black soldiers and sailors proved their heroism and exposed the foolishness of leaving this reservoir of military manpower untapped. If some whites remained dubious of blacks' potential as soldiers, they were still likely to support blacks taking whites' places in the draft pool. Eventually, close to 200,000 African Americans served in Union armies and navies. That service, coupled with Confederate defeat, sealed the fate of the enslaved. As Lincoln wrote to one anti-emancipationist, if African Americans "stake their lives for us they must be prompted by the strongest motive – even the promise of freedom. And the promise being made, must be kept."[23]

Yet just what sort of freedom had been promised? Initially, African American soldiers received $3 less per month than white soldiers. Yet they risked far more. The Confederacy adopted a policy to treat captured African American soldiers not as prisoners of war but as rebellious slaves: they would be returned to slavery or executed. The injustice riled Hannah Johnson, a free African American from Buffalo, New York, who wrote to Lincoln that her son, who had been captured in the battle at Fort Wagner, deserved better. "I know that a colored man ought to run no greater risques than a white, his pay is no greater his obligation to fight is the same. So why should not our enemies be compelled to treat him the same, Made to do it."[24] Lincoln responded quickly to the Confederate policy. Just before Hannah Johnson wrote her letter, Lincoln had issued an order demanding equal treatment for black and white prisoners of war. He promised to execute one Confederate prisoner for every Union prisoner, black or white, executed by the Confederacy.

Meanwhile, enslaved African Americans in the border states still wondered what the promise of freedom meant to them. Lincoln never extended the Emancipation Proclamation to the border states, leading one Maryland slave, Annie Davis, to write to Lincoln in August 1864, "you will please let me know if we are free. and what i can do." Maryland abolished slavery by state legislation two months later, but slavery remained legal in Missouri, Kentucky, and Delaware. The absence of emancipation legislation in these states was particularly rankling to the African American soldiers who had been recruited there. While their freedom was assured as a condition of their military service, their family members remained slaves whose treatment was likely to be worse because of retaliatory masters. By mid-1864, Congress had passed legislation declaring free the relatives of African American soldiers from the border states, but law alone did not force slaveowners to give up their slaves. In Missouri, for example, one white woman continued to treat as slaves

the daughters of her former slave who now fought for the Union. Even after the soldier, Spotswood Rice, offered to pay for one of his children, she refused. Rice wrote to his children with a mix of anger at their continued enslaved status and a determination to free them himself if he had to. "I want you to be contented with whatever may be your lots," he told them, but "be assured that I will have you if it cost me my life." In his letter to his children he promised to arrive soon with an army of liberation composed of 800 white and 800 African American troops. In a separate letter to the woman who owned his children, he wrote:

> my Children is my own and I expect to get them and when I get ready to come… I will have bout a powrer and authority… to execute vengencens on them that holds my Child.[25]

In January 1865, the Missouri government passed an act for immediate emancipation – it had passed an act only for gradual emancipation two years before

An artist's depiction of slaves' reaction to emancipation. In the center scene, an enslaved family reads the Emancipation Proclamation. At the left are scenes from the past of slavery, including the whipping post. At the right are scenes from the future of freedom, including a school for freed children. (Library of Congress)

– but because of the Union army's continued policy to tread more lightly on slavery in the border states than elsewhere, African Americans in the region remained especially vulnerable to racial violence.

Lincoln and Congress did their part to follow the Emancipation Proclamation with law assuring freedom to *all* slaves. In April 1864, the US Senate adopted a resolution for a constitutional amendment abolishing slavery. The House of Representatives failed to carry the measure in June, but Lincoln helped to make the amendment a campaign issue by making sure that it was included in his party's national platform of 1864. More than that, when his opponents in the North howled for peace negotiations, Lincoln declared that he would not negotiate without the preconditions of union *and* emancipation. The requirement of emancipation was politically unsound – it nearly lost him reelection – but morally consistent. When he won reelection, he helped steer the antislavery amendment through Congress. Lincoln was no John Brown, but he had fulfilled Brown's vision of creating an army of African American men fighting for the end of slavery.

Yet there was a twist to the course of emancipation that not even Brown could have imagined. In late 1864, southern whites began voicing their support for conscripting slaves into Confederate military service. Confederate commanders had privately discussed the arming of African Americans for at least a year, leading President Jefferson Davis to order the stifling of such talk. But after the Union's major victories in the second half of 1864, especially the taking of Atlanta and Mobile Bay, even Davis had to concede that the depletion of white manpower in what had become a war of attrition necessitated African American conscription. The Confederate Congress debated the proposal and would have carried it but for the provision, supported by General Robert E. Lee among others, that slaves be promised their freedom in exchange for military service. Most southern whites could not reconcile Confederate emancipation with their understanding of their nation's commitment to *white* freedom. The editor of the Charleston *Mercury* declared that "The soldiers of South Carolina will not fight beside a nigger," and "to talk of emancipation is to disband our army."[26] The Confederate Congress balked at guaranteed emancipation for every slave recruit, as did every state in the Confederacy except Virginia. There, white commanders organized a few hundred emancipated slaves into regiments. Before these men could see action, however, Richmond fell and Lee surrendered. White Virginians had reacted with horror at John Brown's effort to free and arm blacks in 1859. The war now forced them to take a similar course.

Yet in Virginia, as in much of the South, emancipation had not resulted from a moral crusade against slavery such as Brown had envisioned. Rather, it was the

1868
9 July
Fourteenth Amendment: The cornerstone of much modern American law, the Fourteenth Amendment invalidated the Dred Scott decision of 1857 by prohibiting states from abridging the "privileges and immunities" of all citizens without due process. Although the amendment would be weakened by Supreme Court decisions in the 1870s, it laid the groundwork for the Civil Rights Movement of the mid-20th century.

product of what Lincoln termed the "friction and abrasion" of the Civil War. Resistance to emancipation lingered on well beyond the end of the Civil War. Andrew Johnson, who became president after Lincoln's assassination, made the ratification of the antislavery amendment a requirement of readmission for seceded states. A few states in the Deep South refused to comply, and even three Union states rejected ratification: Kentucky, Delaware, and New Jersey. But the amendment was adopted nonetheless, in December 1865. The nation that John Brown had spurned had finally made emancipation, not slavery, its cornerstone.

> *"The United States, France, and England... though politically divided constitute only one great society or commonwealth."*

Secretary of State William Seward, 1861

One great society
Europe and the Civil War

Hugh Dubrulle

European policy exerted a decisive influence on the American Civil War. Had Britain intervened alone or at the head of several European powers, the South would probably have won its independence. In the event, however, European neutrality allowed Federal forces to destroy the Confederacy.

Yet Europe did not merely influence the outcome of the war – the war also influenced Europe in significant ways. Indeed, America's war became Europe's war. The conflict was perhaps brought home to Europe most dramatically by the battle between the USS *Kearsarge* and the CSS *Alabama*, which took place within plain view of Cherbourg, France. At the same time, Europe felt the impact of the war in more substantial ways. The fighting in North America disrupted and distorted the European economies. As both the North and the South called upon the Old World to redress the balance of the New, the war created collisions over international law and altered European diplomatic calculations. Perhaps most important, the issues associated with the conflict gave rise to substantive debates about social and political questions throughout Europe.

The June 1864 battle between the commerce raider CSS Alabama *and the USS* Kearsarge *just off the coast of Cherbourg, France, captured the imagination of many Europeans. Édouard Manet, the prominent Impressionist, painted this version of the duel. Manet later visited the* Kearsarge *in Boulogne where he painted several seascapes that included the vessel. (Courtesy of the Philadelphia Museum of Art)*

This chapter surveys Europe's Civil War experience, which was decisively shaped by the nature of the antebellum European–American relationship. The vital elements that constituted the lifeblood of the relationship – public opinion, international law, economic exchanges, and diplomacy – were all interrelated. While all of these factors figured in the diplomatic outlook of European governments during the war, considerations of *realpolitik* trumped all others in dictating European neutrality.

ONE GREAT COMMONWEALTH: ANTEBELLUM EUROPE AND AMERICA

In the years before the war, Europe's relationship with America was both intimate and ambivalent. In 1861, with perhaps some exaggeration, secretary of state William Seward asserted America, Britain, and France "constitute only one great society or commonwealth."[1] Although Seward wrote in the context of trade, one could extend the metaphor to include a myriad of links that encompassed much of Europe. Europeans themselves admitted the United States belonged to a group of "great nations" whose "influence principally determined the march of modern civilization."[2] At the same time, however, the diplomatic, economic, social, and cultural exchanges that bound this commonwealth together produced a great deal of friction, while many Europeans worried about where exactly America intended to lead the "march of modern civilization."

Seward was correct in emphasizing the extent to which the United States and much of Europe formed one economic community. Extensive infusions of European labor, goods, and capital all helped account for America's phenomenal growth in the 19th century. In the 15 years before the Civil War, 3.7 million Europeans emigrated to the United States, including 1.5 million Irish and 1.3 million Germans. These immigrants did not merely provide strong backs for heavy labor, they also possessed skills as merchants, bankers, professionals, and mechanics. Through letters, remittances, and return migration, they forged an important transatlantic link.

Perhaps just as important, Europe, primarily Britain, exported great amounts of capital to the United States. By 1860, Europeans had invested over $400 million in America. Foreign capitalists bought state and municipal securities or stocks in private companies. These funded the turnpikes, canals, and railways that provided vital infrastructure for American commercial development and supported a well-integrated Atlantic economy.[3]

Sustained foreign investment also allowed Americans to purchase large quantities of European goods and services. In 1860, Britain and America were each other's best customers. Britain conducted about one-fifth of its trade with the United States. At the same time, Britain purchased about 50 percent of American exports while accounting for about 40 percent of American imports. The cotton trade dominated this exchange, accounting for some three-quarters of total American exports. By 1860, America provided 80 percent of Britain's cotton imports. Although the volume of trade between the United States and other European states was not as extensive, other countries relied on American imports in certain areas. For instance, in 1860, France obtained 90 percent of its cotton and 75 percent of its tobacco from the United States.[4]

Not all of Europe was as well integrated into an economic community that centered on the Atlantic. For example, American economic links with Scandinavia, the Netherlands, the Habsburg empire, and Russia were minimal. Moreover, extensive trade did not always lead to good feelings. Several of the United States discomfited their European investors by repudiating their debts in the early 1840s, while massive European immigration sparked the rise of nativism in America. Throughout the period, Europe and America bickered interminably over tariffs and trade regulations.

Yet America did not merely figure in European diplomatic calculations for purely economic reasons; it also constituted an integral, albeit peripheral, part of the European diplomatic system by exerting a palpable influence on the power politics of the Great Powers. The relentless expansion of the United States across the North American continent created constant friction with Britain, which sought to defend its New World interests by containing this advance. Britain and America not only clashed over the boundaries of Maine and Oregon, but jockeyed for influence in Central America and the Caribbean.

This competition was a crowded one, involving other Caribbean powers such as Spain and France. France pursued an ambivalent policy toward the United States, hoping at once to halt American expansion while using the Americans as a counterweight against Britain in international affairs. This conception of America as a potential distraction for Britain also informed the policy of the Russian empire, which competed with Britain in the Near East as well as Central Asia.

Although economic and diplomatic ties bound the commonwealth of which Seward spoke, its spirit consisted of a shared culture underpinned by a sense of common endeavor. The United States and the Great Powers of Europe saw themselves as leaders in the march of progress. This march involved an impressive array of abolitionist, feminist, temperance, prison, utopian, working-class, peace, political, and religious reform movements whose organizations spanned the Atlantic. Despite the breadth of these movements, there was little agreement on where the march of progress ought to lead, and this disagreement became most evident in the debate about American democracy.

In the 30 years before the Civil War, numerous European works analyzed American institutions, but none proved so influential, so representative, or so central to the debate as Alexis de Tocqueville's *Democracy in America*. Like most Europeans, Tocqueville believed America served as a harbinger of a democratic

Although Europeans displayed mixed feelings toward the antebellum United States, their satirical magazines often focused on American shortcomings. In "The Land of Liberty" Punch depicts the stock character of Brother Jonathan dreamily lolling on a seat with a foot resting on a toppled bust of George Washington. Clutching a six-shooter in his belt and with a cocktail close at hand, Jonathan dreams about slavery, debt repudiation, dueling, lynch law, and the Mexican War. (Courtesy of TopFoto)

future, and he sought to understand how Europe ought to prepare for this future. Tocqueville's analysis appealed across the ideological spectrum because almost all his European readers could find in his text ideas with which to buttress their own positions. Tocqueville's America became Europe's America. Europe debated what democracy had done to the Americans, if democracy was even responsible for their peculiarities, whether these peculiarities were laudable or blameworthy, and if America's experience had any relevance for the Old World.[5]

Throughout the antebellum period, the United States had few uncritical admirers. Even those who self-consciously arrayed themselves on the side of progress had their doubts about America. On the eve of the secession crisis, elements of educated European opinion disliked the United States as an ideological threat and a diplomatic rival. Those who thought of America in this vein rejoiced at secession. The preponderance of European opinion, however, displayed complex and mixed feelings toward the American. If Europeans criticized the American practice of democracy while asserting that the sheer size of America and its diversity of interests doomed federalism to failure, they also saw something noble in the United States. William Howard Russell, the *Times* correspondent in America from 1861 to 1862, detected many flaws in American social and political institutions, yet he declared, "there was, and is, so much of what is good and wholesome in American Democracy that it must be a source of regret if it be broken into discordant States, however inevitable the process may be."[6] Despite their criticisms, few Europeans contemplated the disintegration of the United States with equanimity.

EUROPEAN PUBLIC OPINION AND THE CIVIL WAR

European opinion toward the war has long fascinated historians, yet it has proven difficult to assess. Many Europeans were ignorant of America, indifferent toward the

In 1863, hoping to elude Anglo-French naval units should war break out in Europe over Poland, elements of the Russian Navy visited San Francisco and New York. Northerners misconstrued these visits as a friendly gesture by the Russian government. Czar Alexander II saw the United States as a counterweight to Britain and refused to countenance European diplomacy that would break up the Union. In this photograph, the crew of the frigate Osliaba pose for a photograph in Alexandria, Virginia. (Library of Congress)

conflict, or too inarticulate to express a coherent position. Other Europeans could not express their opinions because they did not enjoy freedom of speech or association. Dramatic developments throughout Europe during this period also distracted attention from American events, including the Prussian constitutional crisis, the Danish War, the Risorgimento in Italy, Russia's Great Reforms, and sustained political unrest in Austria.

Overall, the British and French people seemed most engaged in the Civil War. In France, Napoleon III's authoritarian regime allowed the press to conduct a lively discussion on American affairs. Initially, French newspapers universally condemned secession as an assault on an established power vital to French interests, but by the middle of 1861 the press began to divide along ideological lines. Republican and Orleanist organs supported the northern cause, largely because they associated slavery with the South and liberal institutions with the North.[7] Some historians have suggested that these opposition papers praised the democratic North as an oblique means of criticizing Napoleon III's authoritarian regime, but this point remains unclear.[8] At the same time, Imperialist and many Legitimist journals concluded the Union was doomed, largely because of its faulty political institutions. Unlike their more progressive counterparts, they did not dismiss mediation in principle, although some wondered about the utility of diplomatic intervention. These ideological divisions persisted throughout the war, with opinion fluctuating only minimally in response to events like the Emancipation Proclamation.[9]

The French press, however, did not necessarily mirror the state of popular opinion. The *procureurs-généraux* (prosecuting attorneys') reports that Napoleon III used to gauge attitudes "in the street" suggest French workers felt most concerned about the economic consequences of the war. The cotton famine and trade depression caused partly by the conflict led many to support Napoleon III's mediation schemes.[10] In all likelihood, the war divided French workers. If some republicans sympathized with the North, other articulate sectors of the working class clearly did not. Pierre-Joseph Proudhon, the influential and humble-born anarchist, believed the Federal government had no right to subjugate the South by force. He claimed the war against the Confederacy only showed that in the future, Americans ought to erase "from their *platforms* the words political liberty, republic, democracy, confederation and even Union." If southerners were "shameless slavers," he asserted, the North consisted of "hypocritical exploiters."[11]

Britain's far more intimate and complicated relationship with the United States created a different environment for the expression of public opinion. Not surprisingly, considering Britain's ambivalent antebellum relationship with the United States, the British public contemplated the Civil War with mixed feelings. Opinion did not divide cleanly along ideological or class lines. A complex constellation of forces – the exigencies of domestic politics, economic needs, abolitionist sentiment, racism, religion, nationalism, and considerations of national self-interest – influenced opinions that fluctuated in response to American events. Conservatives and the aristocracy tended to support the South, while the Union generally found support among "advanced" opinion, the middle classes, and the labor aristocracy. Yet the multitude of considerations that brought them to these positions remains difficult to decipher. Most generalizations fail to do justice to the complexity of British opinion.[12]

At the start of the secession movement, British opinion showed little sympathy for the South, which had initiated the crisis. The Federal government's apparent indecision, dithering, and ineffectiveness during much of 1861 exasperated British opinion, which sought an end to uncertainty in American affairs. Several Federal steps only served to antagonize British feelings. The Federal suspension of various civil liberties led many to conclude the North teetered on the edge of despotism. The Morrill Tariff, which imposed higher duties on American imports, appeared a particularly unfriendly act. The blockade of the South deprived Britain of cotton, interrupted trade, and put British merchantmen in the humiliating position of submitting to searches by US naval vessels. The vituperative response of the northern people and their government to Britain's proclamation of neutrality also seemed unwarranted. These irritants sparked a reckless war of words between British and American newspapers that only served to heighten antagonism between the two countries. If this bad feeling helped make the *Trent* affair so dangerous, the affair only exacerbated that feeling by bringing the two countries to the brink of war. Convinced the war revealed the deficiencies of democracy, many Conservative and even some Liberal journals used the American situation to attack British radicalism, an assault that would continue throughout the conflict.

British hostility to the North, however, did not necessarily translate into widespread sympathy for the Confederacy. Although some prominent figures in politics and journalism championed the South, most Britons knew too little about that section to confer upon it a distinct identity.[13] Those few notables who supported the Confederacy often did so for ideological reasons, defending its cause as a matter of national self-determination or, for the sake of domestic politics, using the opportunity to praise the aristocratic social constitution the South supposedly possessed.

The Union also possessed a small band of British supporters, although many of them remained very critical of the Federal government's conduct. These adherents of the northern cause suffered from great difficulties until the end of 1862. For one thing, much of British opinion, including many of those who supported the North, thought the Federal government could not defeat the South, let alone reconstruct the Union along democratic lines. Although abolitionism still retained great force in Britain, so long as the Federal government refrained from making emancipation a war aim, many could plausibly argue that one side possessed no moral advantage over the other. Indeed, using a turn of phrase lifted from the *Times*, foreign secretary

Scene from the American Tempest. Caliban (Sambo) says: "You Beat Him 'Nough, Massa! Berry Little Time, I'll Beat Him Too." Shakespeare (Nigger Translation). *The Emancipation Proclamation inspired a very mixed response from the European press. Believing it was intended to stir up a slave insurrection, many Europeans saw the proclamation as a war measure cynically dressed up as altruism. Others saw it as the ultimate useless gesture of a morally bankrupt Federal war effort. Drafted when Federal victories seemed rare, this ironic* Punch *cartoon implied Caliban's boast – as well as the Proclamation itself – was idle and almost comic. (Courtesy of TopFoto)*

SCENE FROM THE AMERICAN "TEMPEST."

CALIBAN (SAMBO). "*YOU* BEAT HIM 'NOUGH, MASSA! BERRY LITTLE TIME, I'LL *BEAT HIM TOO.*"—SHAKSPEARE. (*Nigger Translation.*)

Lord John Russell asserted that while the North fought for "empire," the South fought for "independence."[14]

The second half of 1862 represented a significant period in Britain's response to the war. Confederate victories in the eastern theater persuaded many that the South constituted a genuine nation and the North could not win. In October 1862, chancellor of the exchequer William Gladstone delivered his infamous speech at Newcastle declaring:

> there is no doubt that Jefferson Davis and the leaders of the South have made an army; they are making, it appears, a navy; & they have made what is more than either – they have made a nation. We may anticipate with certainty the success of the Southern States so far as regards their separation from the North. I cannot but believe that that event is as certain as any event yet future and contingent can be.[15]

The Emancipation Proclamation, issued in September 1862, exercised a divisive influence on British opinion. For those convinced the North could not win, the Proclamation was a cynical war measure, the futile and unconstitutional act of a desperate government inciting a slave insurrection.[16] Although many abolitionists criticized the Proclamation's limited nature, the initiative appears to have mobilized and inspired them to defend the northern cause much more actively. Finally, working-class misery associated with the "cotton famine" grew worse throughout this period, reaching its climax in December 1862. The nature, extent, and depth of pro-southern sentiment in Lancashire and other industrial areas remains uncertain, but economic dislocation associated with the blockade inspired some working-class support for the Confederacy.[17]

Well-organized partisans in Britain (assisted by agents sent by the belligerents) sustained a vigorous propaganda battle in which supporters of the North appear to have obtained the upper hand, assisted in part by northern victories from 1863 onward. During this period, while fighting for the northern cause, parliamentary Radicals, reformers of different stripes, Dissenters, and trade unionists forged an alliance that would prove important for domestic politics after the war.[18]

INTERNATIONAL LAW AND THE CIVIL WAR

American reliance on European labor, capital, and goods meant that when war broke out, both sides turned to Europe for men, money, and weapons. At the same time, each belligerent sought to deny to the other access to Europe. Since Europe had declared neutrality, American attempts to mobilize European resources raised important questions of international law. These questions became central to the diplomacy of the period.[19]

The first issues concerning international law emerged when Abraham Lincoln imposed a blockade on the Confederate coast (April 19, 1861). By imposing a blockade, the Federal government itself implicitly recognized a war with the South; only a belligerent fighting a war with another could employ such a device. The blockade thus compelled Britain (May 14) and France (June 10) to recognize a state of war and issue proclamations of neutrality providing the South with certain belligerent rights, including the right to obtain loans, buy weapons, and commission vessels.

Among the European powers, the Declaration of Paris (1856) governed the law of blockade. As a defender of an expansive position on neutral rights, the United States had never submitted to the declaration, but Seward did so in April 1861, hoping to forestall European recognition of southern belligerence. This tactic failed, but conflicting interpretations of the agreement would become a major point of friction between the North and Britain. The declaration determined that with the exception of contraband of war, neutral ships carrying enemy goods and neutral goods in enemy ships were both immune from capture. At the same time, "blockades, in order to be binding, must be effective."

Britain contemplated the blockade with mixed feelings. While the government sought to protect its merchant fleet from harassment, the Foreign Office and the Admiralty did not wish to create precedents subverting future British blockades.

To break the Federal blockade, the Confederate government sought to build a fleet of heavily armed rams in Britain and France. The Confederates never completely realized their ambitions, but they did manage to obtain the CSS Stonewall, a French-built ram that passed through Danish hands. The vessel reached Cuba in May 1865, too late to influence the war. Its lack of seaworthiness and other deficiencies make it unlikely that such a vessel could have changed the course of the war. (US Naval Historical Center)

Lord John Russell (and Napoleon III) eventually adopted a loose construction of the Declaration of Paris, recognizing the Federal blockade as effective because it posed an "evident danger" to vessels attempting to enter or leave southern ports.[20] At the same time, the Foreign Office accepted the North's affirmation of the old British doctrine of "continuous voyage" that had fallen into abeyance: as soon as cargo intended for a blockaded port left its point of origin, it was subject to seizure, even if it was to be transferred at an intermediate, neutral port to another vessel that would actually run the blockade.[21]

Southerners and their European sympathizers challenged the blockade not only in prize courts and parliament, but also through force. Using British shipyards, the Confederacy intended to build cruisers that would prey upon northern merchantmen and divert the US Navy from blockading duty. It also attempted to build ironclad rams that would puncture the blockade. Realizing these ambitions created a host of legal problems, largely because the vague Foreign Enlistment Act (1819) responsible for regulating British neutrality proved inadequate, James Bulloch, who led the South's building program in Europe, did his best to obey the letter of the law while violating its spirit. For most of the war, northern consuls and southern agents played a game of cat and mouse as the former attempted to obtain evidence necessary to seize various vessels under the act. Due to their unfamiliarity with the British legal system, hostile juries, and bad luck, the northerners suffered a number of reverses, leading to the escape of the CSS *Sumter*, *Florida*, *Georgia*, and *Alabama*.[22] The extensive depredations of these vessels led the Federal government to pursue claims against the British, who eventually settled in 1872 for over $15 million.

The British government understood the Foreign Enlistment Act's shortcomings but could not change the law for fear of appearing to truckle to northern pressure. At the same time, Palmerston's administration feared the escape of more British-built raiders would jeopardize relations with the Federals and that Confederate abuse of British neutrality would set a precedent in international law contrary to British interests. Influenced by these considerations in 1863, the British government made its first prosecution under the Foreign Enlistment Act when it seized the *Alexandra*, a raider built for the Confederacy in Liverpool. During the famous trial that ensued, it became clear that contemporary interpretation of the law permitted a belligerent to build any warlike vessel so long as it did not receive armament in Britain. The jury found for the defendants, making it clear that further prosecutions under the act would be pointless. Nevertheless, starting with the *Alexandra*, Russell determined to halt the Confederacy's shipbuilding program by employing a policy of legal obstruction, tying up suspicious vessels in endless lawsuits and appeals. Although the Confederacy later managed to purchase the CSS *Shenandoah*, Russell's new attitude put an end to the southern construction program.

Having worn out their welcome in Britain, Bulloch and his agents turned to France, believing a sympathetic Napoleon III would bend the law in the South's favor. The emperor and several of his ministers knew of Confederate activities, but turned a blind eye so long as they could avoid political complications. Unfortunately for Bulloch, a French shipyard clerk with access to the South's plans revealed almost everything to William Dayton, the American ambassador to France, for 15,000 francs. French foreign minister Drouyn de Lhuys compelled the builders to find new buyers for their vessels, but by a sleight of hand, one of Bulloch's ironclad rams passed from France to the Danish Navy and back to the Confederates to become the CSS *Stonewall*.[23] This vessel, however, did not reach the Caribbean until the war ended.

A host of other difficulties associated with international law arose throughout the war. European consuls in the Confederacy found themselves in an awkward position; all but one had received their exequators (a formal document conferring upon them their authority) from the Federal government. To ask for exequators from the Confederacy would imply recognition of that state and antagonize the North, yet operating in the South without some form of official sanction from its *de facto* government proved exceedingly difficult. Resenting the attempts of these consuls to prevent the conscription of British nationals, and piqued by Britain's unwillingness to recognize the South, Confederate secretary of state Judah Benjamin began expelling them in 1863.[24] At about the same time, the British government began suspecting the Federal government of recruiting illegally in Ireland, something the Foreign Enlistment Act clearly prohibited. Nevertheless, neither of these issues created as much friction as the blockade and the building of Confederate vessels in European shipyards.

ECONOMIC RELATIONS AND THE CIVIL WAR

Although the war's economic impact varied across Europe, it generally distorted and dislocated the exchanges of labor, capital, and trade that sustained the transatlantic economic community. Not only did these developments loosen the ties that bound Seward's commonwealth, they also caused temporary hardship in Europe and foreshadowed more permanent changes.

European immigration had fallen since the mid-1850s, and the outbreak of war reduced it still further. Deterred by political instability and economic uncertainty, Europeans came to America in very small numbers until 1863. Eventually, some 700,000 Europeans arrived in America between 1861 and 1865, somewhat less than the previous five years. The end of the war, however, heralded a massive resurgence that persisted to the end of the century.

A more dramatic dislocation took place in capital markets as Europeans (mainly British) not only ceased investing in America but also unloaded about half of their American securities by 1862. Although European capitalists eventually added northern investments to their portfolios, no major London house would sponsor the sale of Federal bonds. The Federal government's fiscal policy explains this attitude, particularly the suspension of specie payments (December 1861), the introduction of greenbacks under the Legal Tender Act (February 1862), and the assumption of a massive debt, all of which led to European fears of inflation.[25]

The Confederacy fared little better in this regard, for British investors had never established a close relationship with the South and still remembered Jefferson Davis's spirited defense of Mississippi's debt repudiation in the 1840s.[26] In 1863, however, the Paris house of Erlanger & Company floated a Confederate bond issue (backed by cotton) with a face value of £3 million in the London market. Although Erlanger's conditions proved onerous, the Confederacy probably could not have obtained better terms, and the £1.8 million realized from the sale represents something of a success.[27] These funds, however, did not begin to satisfy the South's need for foreign exchange.

The Confederacy's desperate recourse to a cotton loan highlights the influence of the Federal blockade, which fundamentally disrupted transatlantic trade. Although the US Navy only managed to catch a small minority of vessels attempting to run the blockade, it created enormous problems for the cotton trade. It deterred sailing vessels that were the most efficient means of carrying on the trade and forced merchants to mobilize specialized blockade runners – a costly and time-consuming process. It created bottlenecks at major blockade-running entrepôts like Nassau and Bermuda. It also forced trade out of its natural channels into ports like Wilmington and Matamoros, which were far from the cotton belt – adding more costs and inconvenience to the transportation of cotton. The North's capture of New Orleans and its ability to shut down major cotton ports like Mobile and Savannah also contributed to these difficulties.[28] During the five years of the war, the Confederacy only managed to export about 450,000 bales of cotton – roughly one-eighth of what the South had exported in the last year of peace.[29] Although the Confederacy's brief 1861 embargo on the export of cotton exercised an influence, the blockade deserves most of the credit for reducing the supply and raising the price of southern cotton.

Economic historians have long disputed the exact origins and nature of the economic crisis that hit Britain's textile industry in 1862.[30] At any rate, by late 1862, a shortage of cotton and anxieties about its future availability led to high prices and widespread unemployment in Lancashire. Out of a total of 533,000 British factory operatives, the "cotton famine" at its height (December 1862) reduced 166,000 to part-time work and 247,000 to unemployment.[31] Although many workers experienced hardship and some called for breaking the blockade, the government never felt sufficient pressure to change its neutrality policy. The industry began to recover slowly in 1863 as India (with substantial government assistance) and Egypt began accelerating cotton production in response to high prices.[32] Despite the dearth of cotton and the dramatic fall in northern demand for British goods (by 1862, British exports to

OPPOSITE *Families of mill workers suffering the effects of the cotton famine in England exchange tickets issued by the Manchester and District Provident Society, for goods at a provisions depot in 1862. Illustrating how the situation in America did indeed have a direct impact on the lives of the ordinary British people. (© CORBIS)*

1863
25 February

National Banking Act: This restored a national banking system that had ended under Andrew Jackson's administration. By taxing state banknotes, the act forced all private banks to issue Federal notes. In the process, it created a more streamlined and efficient northern economy.

Although many vessels managed to evade the Federal blockade, it still made the export of southern cotton difficult and expensive. Over the course of the war, the Confederacy could only manage to export 450,000 bales of cotton, precipitating a major crisis in the European textile industry. This cartoon from Punch *captures the early anxiety felt in Europe concerning the impact of the blockade. (Courtesy of TopFoto)*

America had fallen to half of their 1860 level), Britain's diverse economy held up well during the war years.

France, on the other hand, suffered badly throughout this period. The cotton famine augmented trouble caused by a poor 1861 harvest and increased competition from British imports due to the Anglo–French Free Trade Treaty (1860). Just as significant, northern demand for French exports – luxury items such as hats, gloves, perfume, wine, silk, liqueurs, and china – plummeted (in part due to the Morrill Tariff) to one-sixth of its antebellum level. The war accelerated a trend that had started in the 1850s whereby the relative importance of France's trade with America diminished for both parties.[33]

INTEREST AND NOT SENTIMENTS: EUROPEAN *REALPOLITIK* AND THE CIVIL WAR

In the mid-19th century, diplomacy remained the purview of monarchs and cabinets who pursued the national interest through *realpolitik*. As Napoleon III told John Slidell, the Confederate commissioner to France, "the policy of nations is controlled by their interest and not by their sentiments."[34] That interest dictated neutrality since the alternatives appeared dangerous. The complexity, unfamiliarity, and inflammability of American affairs would have made mediation difficult. Recognition of the South would have accomplished little aside from possibly sparking a transatlantic war. Indeed, the North's attitude made it unlikely that the European powers could have imposed a settlement without armed intervention. The force of these considerations weighed heavily on Britain, whose diplomatic stance determined that of Europe. Through the Royal Navy's capacity to dominate American waters, only Britain could act alone, and no other state could act without it.

Although none of the European powers initially showed enthusiasm for intervening in the conflict, they quickly took advantage of it by more aggressively pursuing their interests in the Caribbean. At San Domingo's invitation, Spain re-annexed its old colony (March 1861) after obtaining British and French permission. In October 1861, Britain, France, and Spain organized a joint expedition to compel Mexico to resume interest payments on its foreign debt. By the spring of 1862, Spain and Britain had abandoned the enterprise, leaving Napoleon III alone to pursue dreams of a Mexican empire.

Seward wanted to use these violations of the Monroe Doctrine as an excuse to rally southerners around the old flag with a foreign war and thus reunite the Union. Lincoln promptly quashed this idea, but Seward's policy toward Britain and France (with the notable exception of Mexico) throughout the war retained a quality of brinkmanship that discouraged European meddling in American affairs.[35] For instance, shortly after news of Britain's neutrality proclamation reached him, Seward exclaimed to Charles Sumner (chairman of the Senate Committee on Foreign Relations) "God damn 'em, I'll give 'em hell!" Lord Lyons, the British minister in Washington, was convinced that "Seward … is not without hope that he may really overawe England and France by threatening language."[36]

At the same time, inept southern diplomacy did not present a compelling argument for diplomatic recognition, let alone intervention. Most of the Confederate commissioners sent overseas proved unsuited for their positions, and aside from a "King Cotton" policy that bordered on extortion, they could not explain why Confederate survival was crucial to Europe.[37]

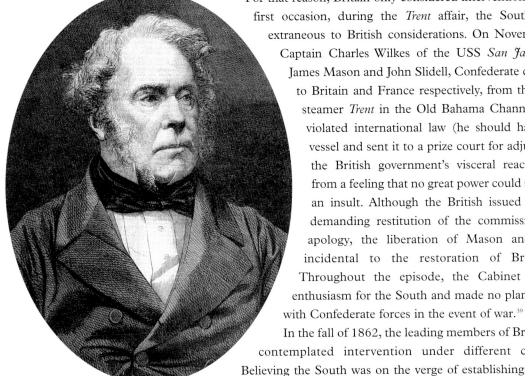

For that reason, Britain only considered intervention twice. On the first occasion, during the *Trent* affair, the South was almost extraneous to British considerations. On November 8, 1861, Captain Charles Wilkes of the USS *San Jacinto* removed James Mason and John Slidell, Confederate commissioners to Britain and France respectively, from the British mail steamer *Trent* in the Old Bahama Channel. Wilkes had violated international law (he should have seized the vessel and sent it to a prize court for adjudication), but the British government's visceral reaction stemmed from a feeling that no great power could submit to such an insult. Although the British issued an ultimatum demanding restitution of the commissioners and an apology, the liberation of Mason and Slidell was incidental to the restoration of British honor.[38] Throughout the episode, the Cabinet showed little enthusiasm for the South and made no plans to cooperate with Confederate forces in the event of war.[39]

In the fall of 1862, the leading members of Britain's Cabinet contemplated intervention under different circumstances. Believing the South was on the verge of establishing independence through military victory, Prime Minister Lord Palmerston prepared to extend recognition throughout the late summer. The stalemate at the battle of Antietam cooled his enthusiasm, however, leaving Russell and Gladstone to spearhead the movement for intervention. Russell felt a costly military stalemate, deepening political animosity, and the threat to order posed by the Emancipation Proclamation compelled mediation on humanitarian grounds. Gladstone claimed the existence of a southern nation made recognition a moral necessity. A French offer to Britain of joint mediation with Russia brought the issue to a head at a November 11 Cabinet meeting. Led by secretary of state for war Sir George Cornwall Lewis, the Cabinet deemed mediation too dangerous – Napoleon III was an untrustworthy partner, the Russians had no intention of participating in this venture, the South did not warrant recognition according to the precedents of international law, northern enmity could produce a catastrophic war, and European diplomats were not suited to mediate complex American problems.[40] Power politics compelled neutrality.

British neutrality stymied Napoleon III, who appeared more eager to intervene. Initially, the emperor had hoped the Union would survive as a counterweight to British power, but the cotton famine and sympathy for the principle of national self-determination pushed him toward intervention.[41] Napoleon III felt incapable of acting, however, without the British who could protect his diplomatic flank in

Europe and help him deal with the North. In 1862 and 1863, he repeatedly sounded out the British government on mediation and made a formal proposal in October 1862. Consistent rebuffs, however, made him increasingly reluctant to renew such offers. Nevertheless, in May 1863, when John Roebuck, a prominent Radical MP, introduced a motion in the Commons demanding recognition of the Confederacy, he sought to enhance his chances by asking Napoleon III to inform the British government that France still supported mediation – a request to which the emperor assented. A series of miscommunications, however, made it possible for Russell to deny during debate in the Commons that he had received an indication of French support for the initiative, and Roebuck withdrew the motion. Napoleon III felt wronged by his erstwhile ally. He must have felt even more aggrieved when Seward, who understood the true state of affairs, vented his wrath against the emperor – just when France's Mexican difficulties made Napoleon III more vulnerable to northern pressure.[42]

By 1863, the price of a Mexican empire appeared too great to Napoleon III. Increasingly, he hoped that by conveying Mexico to Archduke Maximilian he could obtain Habsburg support for his European projects, including the annexation of Venetia by Italy and the resurrection of Poland. Austrian unwillingness to cooperate with France, dogged Mexican resistance, and northern victories convinced Napoleon III to withdraw from Mexico under cover of Maximilian's enthronement.

Over the course of 1863, as the war turned decisively against the South and Europe witnessed crises in Poland and Germany, the likelihood of Great Power intervention in America evaporated. Even at the Confederacy's zenith in late 1862, Britain could not ignore the risks associated with interference in the conflict. Political and military considerations overrode all else. The diplomatic situation ensured that without Britain, France could not act. For Napoleon III, considerations of power politics trumped ideological sympathy and economic pressure. As Horace Greeley had wished, the "unprincipled egotism that is the soul of European diplomacy" had saved the Union.[43]

THE LEGACY OF THE CIVIL WAR IN EUROPE

Assessing the Civil War's lasting significance in Europe is difficult because the conflict's influence was broad, varied, and mixed. Undoubtedly, the survival of the United States had important European implications. Almost immediately, the United States resumed its traditional role in Caribbean and Central American diplomacy. In the long run, by preserving the Union, northern victory made it possible for the United States to become a 20th-century global power – with all that meant for both Europe and the rest of the world.

As the war dragged on, some Europeans came to see it as a pointless tragedy, costly in both blood and treasure. "The American Juggernaut," an 1864 cartoon from Punch, *captures the shocked awe of Europe as it received news of the heavy casualties incurred in the Federal offensives that year. (Courtesy of TopFoto)*

The war was also associated with lasting economic changes. Responding to the cotton famine, the trade that had once centered on Lancashire and the American South became global. India, Egypt, and Brazil began producing cotton while France and Russia embarked upon an imperial scramble to obtain cotton-growing areas.[44] This shift in the cotton trade symbolized a larger process by which the economic relationship between the United States and Europe (Britain in particular) became less exclusive. After 1865, the American economy became less complementary to Europe's and more competitive.

Historians have long emphasized the ideological impact of the war, asserting northern victory provided an impetus for the advance of liberalism and democracy in Europe. Making such a connection, however, proves difficult. Indeed, the war apparently convinced most Britons that their institutions were superior to those of the United States.[45] The alliance of radicalism, dissent, and labor that mobilized on behalf of the North during the war did indeed fight for extension of the franchise at home. This fight culminated in the Reform Act of 1867, which gave the vote to all borough householders in England, doubled the size of the electorate, and paved the way for modern popular politics. Yet the origins of the bill, along with its shape and passage, owed much to indigenous developments hostile to American principles of equality and republicanism.[46] Benjamin Disraeli, leader of the Conservative Party in the Commons and architect of the act (insofar as there was one), forcefully argued that "English" not "American" principles ought to guide reform: "I approve of American institutions, for they are adopted in the country in which they exist…. But I say none of the conditions exist in England which exist in America." On those grounds, "[Reform] ought to proceed from the principle that we are the House of Commons, not the House of the People."[47]

Similarly in France, the war may have mobilized liberals, but liberalization of Napoleon III's empire in the 1860s had little to do with American events.[48] Although the Prussian government had warmly supported the North during the war, American principles exerted little influence on German unification. Bismarck politely told Americans their federalism had inspired his political arrangements in Germany, but in a candid moment, he revealed that in making these arrangements he had used "a little of everything."[49] With a few exceptions, it appears Europeans increasingly felt the American example was irrelevant to their situation.

If the war saved one great society by reforging the United States, it also undermined another by corroding the ties that bound the transatlantic commonwealth. Toward the end of the antebellum era, the United States had just begun to grow less dependent on Europe both culturally and economically. The war hastened this independence by compelling the Federal government to assume a belligerent diplomacy toward Europe, embittering northern feeling against Britain and France, and reorienting trade in significant ways. At the same time, the war provided the United States with a new and important verse in a distinct epic that made Americans less inclined to look to Europe for guidance. As Disraeli and Bismarck's comments imply, European leaders also lost the sense of a common transatlantic endeavor with the United States. Concluding the American experience was exceptional rather than universal, they did not believe it offered solutions to European problems. When a transatlantic society reconstituted itself in the late 19th century, it would do so on a less intimate and less diverse basis.

"But this war was a fearful lesson, and should teach us the necessity of avoiding wars in the future..."

Ulysses S. Grant, *c.*1885

A fearful lesson
The Legacy of the American Civil War

Aaron Sheehan-Dean

In books of history, in popular television series, in the memorials and the very geography of the national capital, the Civil War is regarded as the event that made the modern United States of America. But the ease with which the war is invoked as a kind of all-purpose past obscures the actual consequences the war held for the inhabitants of mid-19th-century America. Further complicating the story is the contradictory nature of the changes the war wrought. In tandem with the two fundamental accomplishments of the war – emancipation and the repudiation of secession – the war increased racial and sectional animosities. As the preceding chapters have demonstrated, the war affected every area of American life. From the structure of the polity to the organization of the national economy, from the rapidly expanding West to the destitute South to the triumphant North, from the relationships between men and women, and between African Americans and whites, the consequences of the Civil War on American life were profound and far-reaching.

Live reenactments of Civil War battles provide spectators with their most tangible experience of the past. The scrupulousness with which most reenactors treat the physical aspects of the past contrasts with the often deliberate avoidance of any of the moral or political issues that sustained the war, a telling reminder of the continuing difficulty of discussing the war nearly 150 years after its conclusion. (Courtesy of TopFoto)

THE CONSEQUENCES OF VICTORY

Historians are nearly unanimous in agreeing that emancipation was the most significant change accomplished by the war. The liberation of 4 million African American slaves overturned two-and-a-half centuries of slaveholding in North America and forced the reshaping of political, economic, and social relations across the nation and within the South in particular. Henry Turner, a free African American minister in Washington, DC, remembered the day when Lincoln issued the Emancipation Proclamation as a transformative event: "It was indeed a time of times, and a half time," he wrote, "nothing like it will ever be seen again in this life."[1] Eight generations of Africans and then African Americans had lived in bondage in North America and eight generations of white Americans had owned them; the task of building a peaceful interracial society was daunting indeed.

Despite the hurdles presented by southern whites, African Americans eagerly embraced the opportunity to vote. They saw politics as a crucial tool with which to protect their new freedom. (Library of Congress)

African American southerners immediately seized control of the two things most expressly denied to them under slavery: their families and their livelihoods. The first instinct of most freedmen was to find and protect their loved ones. Retracing the sales and movements of slaves bonded to masters over the previous decades, spouses, children, and parents sought to reconstitute the families they knew before the war. In addition to reconstructing their families, ex-slaves built churches, schools, and benevolent associations to anchor their communities.

1865

31 January

Thirteenth Amendment: Confirming the policy that Lincoln initiated with the Emancipation Proclamation, the Thirteenth Amendment permanently ended racial bondage in the United States.

African Americans sought full autonomous citizenship, knowing that this meant not only a right to vote, but also the right to an education and the opportunity to move, work, and own land. They engaged in politics by voting, participating in Union League clubs, and joining the Republican Party. They relentlessly pursued literacy. They demanded fair wages for the work they performed, vigorously protected the enforcement of labor contracts, and sought their own land. White southern resistance and white northern apathy would eventually deny the promises of citizenship implicit in the Thirteenth, Fourteenth, and Fifteenth Amendments, but emancipation was not a failed "experiment." The success of African Americans' efforts to make emancipation real can be seen in the perpetuation of communities through the bleak decades around the turn of the century. The foundation laid by the postwar generation enabled the efforts of 20th-century activists to demand and claim full equality.

Reunion stood as the other northern war goal. Its significance today is often overlooked in the wake of the war's racial legacy, but participants and observers at the time understood the importance of the repudiation of secession. From the start of the conflict, Abraham Lincoln described the war as a contest over the viability of self-government, which he understood to be the core principle of democratic republics. By abandoning the political process in the wake of an unsatisfactory election, southerners were rejecting the guarantees of the rights of the minority granted under the Constitution. They were, in effect, denying the possibility of sustaining a large and diverse republic. In his First Inaugural Address, Lincoln argued that:

> perpetuity is implied, if not expressed in the fundamental law of all national governments. It is safe to assert that no government proper, ever had a provision in its organic law for its own termination.[2]

Victory in the war thus proved the northerners' contention that the Union was perpetual while at the same time demonstrating to the world that democracy could thrive even in places where the citizens possessed competing interests.

If the Civil War confirmed the resilience and strength of representative democracy as a form of government, it also had the effect, within the United States, of reifying

1870

3 February

Fifteenth Amendment: The last of the wartime amendments, this one prohibited discrimination of the right to vote by race or previous condition of servitude. It did not rule out literacy tests or understanding clauses (that is, non-racial prohibitions of the right to vote), thus not preventing the disfranchisement of most southern African Americans at the turn of the century.

the particular form that the American republic possessed at the time of the war. White male suffrage, the protection of the rights of political minorities, and self-determination became enshrined as the core elements of American democracy.

Other elements that today are viewed as essential, such as federal protection of the right to vote and the necessity of a full, accessible public education system, emerged only in later generations. Congress's failure to protect the rights of African American men to vote was the most glaring absence, something that would be remedied in the Fifteenth Amendment but not fully guaranteed until 100 years later with the passage of the Voting Rights Act of 1965.

Northern victory also sanctioned free-labor republicanism, the model of political economy espoused by the Republican Party. For northerners, the values of autonomy, self-reliance, and restraint that characterized northern working men and voters on the eve of the Civil War proved their worth by facilitating victory. A free-labor army had defeated a slave-labor army. The South's failure, by contrast, proved the weakness of slave labor and the corrosive influence it had on southern masculinity. The ideology of free labor developed along with the expanding national market economy in the 1830s, '40s, and '50s. Northerners regarded the productive decades in which they lived as the norm and they built a belief system that assumed the possibility of upward mobility and celebrated the virtue of labor. As Eric Foner has noted:

the mobility of the age of the independent producer, whose aspiration was economic self-sufficiency, was superseded by the mobility of industrial society, in which workers could look forward to a rising standard of living, but not self-employment.[3]

The difficulty lay in the uniformity and repetition of industrial labor and the consequent competition created for lower-skilled jobs. By validating the superiority of free labor, the Civil War bequeathed a new problem for a future generation of American workers – an ideology that glorified work contradicted by the reality of work that they had to perform.

Even with an emerging industrial economy, the system of free labor looked immensely attractive to ex-slaves. It promised them a fair return for labor performed – exactly what had been denied them under slavery. That prospect was exactly what angered southern landowners and they objected to northern efforts to incorporate former slaves into the new free-labor systems. White southerners predicted that slaves, with no native intelligence or acquisitive spirit, would drag the economy down. Freedmen quickly proved this fear false, eagerly entering into contracts with employers and demonstrating that they understood incentives and capitalism as well as whites. Jourdon Anderson, a former slave from Tennessee, responded to his ex-master's request to return to his old plantation and work for wages with a request that the ex-master should send the $11,680 to which Anderson and his wife were entitled based on their previous service to him as slaves. Anderson subtracted the cost of clothing and health care but asked that the former master include "interest." "Here I draw my wages every Saturday night, but in Tennessee there was never any pay day for negroes any more than for the horses and cows," he wrote.[4] Despite the ample evidence that African Americans were as eager to earn good wages through hard work as other Americans, white southerners obstructed the implementation of a true free-labor system, through revised penal codes that facilitated the construction of the convict lease system, their efforts to deny land ownership to blacks, and their refusal to modernize any part of the southern economy for fear of creating a tighter labor market. As a result, by the 1880s, the ideology of free labor proved as unsatisfactory to southern African Americans as it did to most northern whites.

In addition to demonstrating the superiority of the northern system, the war spurred the consolidation of political authority. Critics of Lincoln, both his contemporaries and later scholars, accused him of aggressively centralizing political authority in the Federal government, citing his suspension of habeas corpus and the

THE GETTYSBURG ADDRESS

DELIVERED BY ABRAHAM LINCOLN NOV. 19 1863

AT THE DEDICATION SERVICES ON THE BATTLE FIELD

Fourscore and seven years ago our fathers brought forth on this continent a new nation, conceived in liberty, and dedicated to the proposition that all men are created equal. * * * Now we are engaged in a great civil war, testing whether that nation, or any nation so conceived and so dedicated, can long endure. * * We are met on a great battle-field of that war. * We have come to dedicate a portion of that field as a final resting place for those who here gave their lives that that nation might live. * * It is altogether fitting and proper that we should do this. * * But in a larger sense we cannot dedicate, we cannot consecrate, we cannot hallow this ground. * The brave men, living and dead, who struggled here, have consecrated it far above our poor power to add or detract. The world will little note, nor long remember, what we say here, but it can never forget what they did here. * * It is for us, the living, rather to be dedicated here to the unfinished work which they who fought here have thus far so nobly advanced It is rather for us to be here dedicated to the great task remaining before us, that from these honored dead we take increased devotion to that cause for which they gave the last full measure of devotion; * that we here highly resolve that these dead shall not have died in vain; that this nation, under God, shall have a new birth of freedom, and that the government of the people, by the people, and for the people, shall not perish from the earth

detention of political prisoners. Both these actions, as serious as they were, did little to alter the dimensions of federal power after the war. Jefferson Davis, as president of the Confederacy, enacted the same measures, and neither southerners nor northerners imagined these practices would last beyond the war. Of more lasting consequence, in terms of the dimensions of federal authority, were the institutional changes that facilitated the war and proved, in the postwar years, to encourage economic growth. The Federal government seized a greater role in the organization and management of information, particularly economic information. It also acquired substantially more reliable knowledge about everything from train schedules to industrial production capabilities to the composition of the labor force.

Lincoln used the occasion of his speech commemorating the new national cemetery at Gettysburg, Pennsylvania, to argue for the benefits of northern victory. Rather than address the immediate war goals of reunion and emancipation, Lincoln cast the war as a struggle for popular democracy without reference to color. (Library of Congress)

In the postwar decades, most southern blacks worked in agriculture, either as sharecroppers or as farm laborers. The structural and racial restraints on their economic advancement undercut the Republican Party's philosophy of free labor, which rang increasingly hollow in a world where work brought little reward. The same sense of alienation developed among white northern workers who performed increasingly repetitive and unskilled labor in factories. (Library of Congress)

In the postwar years, this information proved invaluable as Congress and the White House set out to implement the industrialization of the nation. During the war, the Confederate States of America adopted much the same information-acquiring tactics as their northern peers, and exercised substantially greater control over the economy, thus providing another boost to this model of federal authority. In select industries, the integration of civil, corporate, and military administration proceeded beyond the process of information gathering. Railroads, munitions, and meatpacking all received a terrific boost from the war and all demonstrated the potential for future industrial growth in the United States.

The army, too, felt the effects of the war. At Appomattox and Durham Station, in the spring of 1865, the last Confederate armies were dismantled. The Federal army was rapidly demobilized as well, but by 1866 the regular Federal army stood at 54,000 soldiers, a three-fold increase over the size of the prewar army that greatly improved the effectiveness of the government against the Plains Indians in the devastating wars of the 1870s.[5] The size and institutional power of the new army ensured that it would play a larger role in postwar policy, something against which former Union general and former president Ulysses S. Grant cautioned in his memoir. "This war was a fearful lesson," he wrote, "and should teach us the necessity of avoiding wars in the future."[6] This recommendation came in vain; the military as an arm of the state played a larger role in the postwar era than it had before the war. In particular, the discipline and leadership generated during the Civil War facilitated the US effort to subdue the western tribes. The wars against the Plains Indians were led by the North's dominant Civil War generals, including William T. Sherman and Philip Sheridan. Sherman developed an absolutist dictum on the subject. "We must act with vindictive earnestness against the Sioux," he wrote in 1867, "even to their extermination, men, women, and children. Nothing less will reach the root of this case."[7] During the war, African American soldiers had proved themselves deserving of citizenship, but neither Sherman nor Sheridan considered whether Indians might warrant equal treatment.

SHAPING THE POSTWAR WORLD

Confining Plains Indians to reservations was a crucial part of the national economic strategy for the development of the western territories after the war. The white settlement and physical development of the territories had been stymied before the war by sectional politics. In particular, the war ended the stalemate over what many considered the key to expansion of the West: a transcontinental railroad. Prior to the war, both Stephen Douglas and Jefferson Davis championed the project, albeit with very different visions for where the track should be laid. With the resignation of most southern members of Congress in 1861, the major obstacles to a rail line evaporated and construction began during the war. The Homestead Act, passed in 1862, was another piece of this puzzle. Like the transcontinental railroad, passage of this bill had been mired in sectional politics, with southern members concerned about the rapid growth of new free states in the West. Although the war itself did not affect most of the West in the direct way it did the southeastern seaboard states, the political changes wrought by secession initiated a series of policies that transformed the whole region.

As northern investors began to organize themselves for the development of the American West, they were also confronted with the demands of an impoverished South. One of the indisputably radical effects of emancipation, and the war itself, was its economic impact. By bringing freedom to the slaves, emancipation nullified the capital value of these people under southern law. In effect, at least $3 billion in wealth held by southern white people vanished from their households.[8] By liberating enslaved African Americans, the North claimed that it was building a normal capitalist framework within which future growth would occur. Certainly, from the perspective of ex-slaves liberation brought economic advantages, for they now "owned" the profits of their own labor, but the structural effect on the South of eliminating the main source of southern capital hindered postwar business growth.

Combined with the repudiation of the Confederate debt, and the inability of southern states to make good on their wartime bonds, the war can be fairly said to have devastated the southern economy like no other event in American history. The depressions of the 1870s, 1890s, and 1920s all hit the South hard but none eradicated as much wealth or destroyed as much infrastructure in as short a space of time as the Civil War. Southern agriculture was especially hard hit, with widespread devastation of the land itself in the rich areas of central Virginia, central Tennessee, northern Alabama, and central Georgia. The implementation of hard war by the North ensured the destruction of millions of southern farm animals and the demolition of important parts of the southern transportation and communication network. The result was a massive decline in farmers' wealth holdings all across the South. Richard L. Ransom has calculated that the average total wealth of all southern farm operators in 1860 was $22,819. The war reduced this value by a factor of seven; in 1870, the average wealth of southern farm operators was $3,168.[9] It would be naïve to argue that the Civil War alone was responsible for all the South's late 19th-century economic problems, but just as surely it must be recognized that the war seriously retarded southern economic growth.

In contrast, the war promoted diversification and growth in the northern economy. Although the diversion of 2 million prime-age men to the armies hampered the economy in some respects, overall the war provided a boost to the northern economy and allowed northern corporations to build on the strengths they had been developing in the antebellum period. Those industries that produced war-related goods benefited most directly, but all across the North a tightened labor market and steady demand ensured good wages and low unemployment. Meatpackers in Chicago devised the first assembly-line techniques in their quest to supply northern soldiers with "fresh" meat. Armour and Swift both established dominance in the industry and created the foundation for postwar expansion as a result of government contracts. Textile manufacturers, shoemakers, shipbuilders, and weapons manufacturers likewise drew on war contracts to devise technological advances that facilitated postwar growth. In economic terms, the war widened the already significant breach between North and South in terms of levels of industrialization, commitment to technological development, and access to capital. This disparity would generate political and social strife for the better part of the next century.

THE CULTURAL IMPACT OF THE WAR

Hardest to assess yet perhaps most important because of their long-term nature were the cultural changes wrought by the war. Most prominent among these was the hardening of sectional animosities. The South of 1861 was a fragile and unlikely nation but the shared experience of suffering and loss welded the white South together by 1865. Fear and anger over the racial and economic uncertainty of the postwar world compelled many southerners to overlook the visible seams of their ad hoc wartime nation and, over time, most came to regard the South as a natural place of its own. The split in the historical experience between the North and South would only disappear with the US defeat in the Vietnam War over a century later. In the aftermath of the Civil War, southerners joined the majority of the world's population who had, at some point in their past, lost a war. This divergence only exacerbated the cultural alienation that each side now perceived. Northerners, having been the victors, could afford to be gracious about the vigor of southern resistance, but they did not celebrate the Confederate dead or offer pensions to Confederate veterans. In 1866, Herman Melville dedicated his collection of war poems called *Battle-Pieces* "to the memory of the three hundred thousand who in the war for the maintenance of the union fell devotedly under the flag of their fathers."[10] In only recognizing Union war dead as "devoted" soldiers, Melville's style of accounting did little to win southern readers.

Northerners took sanction from the sacrifice of their war dead. Victory in the war enshrined a nobleness about American action and purpose that had been present but unproven in prewar thought and discussion. With success on the battlefield, democracy confirmed, and the gracious gift of emancipation, northerners felt justified to consider new opportunities for sharing their institutions and values with the world. Watching the Grand Review of Union armies through Washington, DC, in May 1865, a *New York Herald* writer issued a tribute that forecast a bold and aggressive future for the young nation. Union veterans' "souls and those of their slain comrades will be marching on," he wrote, "till every nation is a republic, and every man a freeman. On – till the soldiers of Grant, Sherman, and Sheridan have saved the world as they have saved the Union."[11] With hindsight, the contradictions and problems with the writer's assessment fairly leap from the page. Many of the soldiers who stayed in uniform went not to make men free but to the western United States to fight Native Americans. Others would participate in the destruction of the Spanish empire and the creation of the American empire, through bloody conquests in Cuba, Puerto Rico, the Philippines, and Hawaii. The Civil War did not make American expansion inevitable, but it gave legitimacy and force to the visions of grandeur entertained by expansionists for many years before the war.

Although Richmond was consumed by fires started by departing Confederates after the fall of their capital in April 1865, its destruction aptly symbolized the cost paid by southerners for the war. Many cities, farms, railroads, and much of the southern industrial infrastructure lay in ruins at war's end, a legacy that inhibited southern economic recovery for many years. (Library of Congress)

Southerners, who returned home to devastated fields and fractured communities, harbored little good will toward their enemies. The hard war enacted by the North revealed the true barbarism of the Yankee character. The destruction of cities – Atlanta, Columbia, Richmond – proved their baseness and incivility. The looting that often accompanied the armies, as at Fredericksburg and through Georgia, revealed the avarice and greed that characterized most northerners. When Henry Grady, the postwar editor of the *Atlanta Journal and Constitution*, and tireless New South booster, spoke in New York in 1880 he referred to William T. Sherman as "kind of a careless man about fire." The joke masked a deep divide within the South, between those like Grady, who cheerfully confessed that southerners had "fallen in love with work," and those southerners who refused to reconcile themselves to the new order.[12] Even the mass of southern businessmen who rejected overt sectional antagonism in the interests of attracting capital felt a deep sense of alienation within the nation. The rise of organizations dedicated to celebrating the Confederacy and Confederate soldiers in the 1880s and 1890s drew on this sense of difference. The United Daughters of the Confederacy (UDC) and the United Confederate Veterans (UCV)

honored southern soldiers who fought against the North; the sentimentalism of their appeals may have muted the political content but few who participated in UDC or UCV rituals could have doubted that southerners held a unique identity.

The vigor of southern condemnations of northern character was, in part, a projection of the anxieties generated within the South by the conflict. The Civil War forced massive and unwanted changes on the South, particularly on southern men, and they responded by heaping scorn on others. The essence of antebellum southern masculinity had been the protection white men offered to their dependants in society, including women, children, and slaves. Confederate defeat in the war, the occupation of many parts of the South, and emancipation revealed the hollowness of that commitment. The war created a profound crisis in southern masculinity, one that spurred a recommitment to an earlier more hierarchical form of gender relations by both men and women in the wake of defeat. Southern women, left exposed at home to invading armies and escaping slaves, were forced to assume new responsibilities during the war, but defeat left them seeking stability in traditional gender relations just like men. The northern experience again was a stark contrast. Rather than a repudiation, the war confirmed the superiority of northern masculine values of order and control, as well as protection and authority.

If the war complicated southern gender relations, it quite nearly destroyed southern race relations. The efforts of enslaved people to aid the Union cause and seek their own freedom destroyed the old fantasy of the loyal slave. Southern whites, slaveowners and non, saw the actions of African American southerners as a betrayal and treated them after the war like enemies. Southern blacks, long familiar with the arbitrary and violent nature of masters, were perhaps not surprised by the reluctance of southern whites to accept them into society, but this did not slow their efforts to achieve a real and lasting freedom. The result was increasingly violent efforts by southern whites to control African Americans. These culminated in the legal system of Jim Crow, disfranchisement, and the rise of lynching. The economic hardships and political conflict of the postwar decades certainly played an important role in shaping race relations, but the Civil War itself, and its unanticipated outcome, created the conditions for suspicion, anger, and violence in the years after.

MEMORIES OF THE CIVIL WAR

The Civil War left another legacy, one less tangible but no less significant than its economic and political impact – the memory of the war. In officers' tents, around soldiers' campfires, in hungry and threadbare home front parlors, in the staterooms of Europe, and in the flight of the escaping slave, the experiences of the Civil War imprinted themselves on participants forever. Most of the people who lived through the war understood it as the central event in their lives. They maintained their own private memories of what the war meant and they passed these on through their families and their communities. Memories of the conflict differed dramatically by section and race. Northerners who saw the war as a noble affirmation of self-government and democracy took victory as a sanction for free-labor capitalism and republican government. Southerners who saw the war as a tragic repudiation of a benevolent and humane way of life took from defeat a darker lesson about the limits of change and the susceptibility of man to sin. African Americans struggled to retain slavery and emancipation as the crucial cause and outcome of the war even as whites, on both sides, reverted to the legalistic language of the Union and states' rights.

One of the most pervasive and pernicious influences on Americans' memory of the Civil War has been the Lost Cause, a particular set of beliefs about the causes and consequences of the war that emerged in the two decades after its conclusion. The Lost Cause consists of four core elements usually embedded in a patina of romantic memories about the courage and glories of individual officers or soldiers. The first element, which took shape through the postwar memoirs and writings of Confederate statesmen like Alexander Stephens and Jefferson Davis, argues that the South waged the Civil War as a fight over states' rights. Ignoring the mountains of evidence that demonstrated the centrality of slavery to the start of the war (much of it produced by politicians like Stephens and Davis themselves), these writers asserted that southerners pursued secession out of an abstract commitment to preserving the political practice of states' rights. By implication, the South's cause became a noble one in defense of an idea rather than a mean one in defense of material interests.

The Lost Cause took its name from an 1866 book by Richmond newspaper editor Edward Pollard that also established several of the other bedrock assumptions of the interpretation, including the second key element – the inevitability of Union victory due to its material and manpower superiority. Echoing Pollard, writers of the 1880s characterized northern victory as inevitable given the resource advantages it possessed. They drew strongly on hindsight to construct a narrative of the conflict that always yielded northern victory without making southern participation criminal. In this account, the futility of southern military efforts only intensified the tragedy and honor of their sacrifices. Third, the Confederacy was presented as the one true Christian society. Robert E. Lee, Stonewall Jackson, and white Confederate women, in particular, were held up as paragons of virtue and selflessness. In the wartime South, ministers had preached that defeats in individual battles came as God's judgment on a sinful people, but this interpretation was rarely applied to overall defeat, which was seen as a perverse triumph by the mammon-worshipping Yankees. At the end of the century, a profusion of historically minded organizations, including the UCV, the UDC, and the Southern Historical Society enshrined the Lost Cause as a kind of public religion, articulating its beliefs in rituals such as the dedication of monuments to Confederates, the publication of books and articles about the war, and the folk memory of the war.

Last, and most ominously, the Lost Cause presented antebellum slavery as essentially benevolent. Slavery was explained as the sincere efforts of southern whites to uplift an inferior race. Brought under the generous tutelage of southern masters, blacks "increased from a few unprofitable savages to millions of efficient Christian laborers," in Jefferson Davis's postwar phrasing.[13] Grounded in the hierarchical racial science of the late 19th and early 20th centuries, this argument pictured slaveholders as unfailingly generous and gentle toward their property and presented slaves as loyal and obedient. The prewar South was characterized as a time of near perfection, a utopia for white people and a blessing for African Americans. The peacefulness of this earlier era contrasted markedly with the frequently chaotic social life of the postwar South. In this way, the Lost Cause implicitly sanctioned the need for the more public and more violent racial hierarchy of the postwar era. The Ku Klux Klan, founded the year after the publication of Pollard's book, sought to eliminate the possibility of independent black political action and, indeed, any real space in public life for African Americans. The Lost Cause provided the justification for the implementation of organized violence against African Americans.

The solemn dignity of Robert E. Lee, perfectly captured the spirit that "Lost Cause" writers sought to evoke. Northerners and southerners alike embraced the memory of a "brothers' war" honorably fought as the sections moved toward reconciliation in the 1890s. (Library of Congress)

Although much of the Lost Cause seeks to absolve southerners of the blame for starting a war that cost so many lives, northerners actively participated in the construction of the interpretation from the 1880s until the present. Union veterans and other writers constructed the same images of the prewar South as Confederates did. For many northerners, imagining the antebellum South as a rural utopia allowed them to find an outlet for their fears and concerns about the rapid urbanization and industrialization of the country. As northerners struggled to absorb new immigrants from Central and Eastern Europe and to respond to labor unrest and the growth of monopolistic businesses, the plantation was lauded as an ideal form that fostered harmonious social relations between people of unequal status. The result of this conflation of interests was that the Lost Cause promoted sectional reconciliation – northerners and southerners could jointly agree that each side fought bravely and with honor for causes in which they believed. With the substance of those causes all but erased, reunion became much easier to manage.

The Lost Cause was vigorously contested at the time by African American folk memory and later in academic writing by African American scholars such as W.E.B. DuBois. DuBois's most direct attack on the intellectual tenets and historical foundation of the Lost Cause came in his 1935 *Black Reconstruction*.

Though not focused directly on the war, DuBois explained the racial, political, and class dynamics that emerged from the conflict. He repudiated the Lost Cause vision of a unified white society and sought to demonstrate the shared experiences and needs of poor southerners, white and black. DuBois lamented the failure of poor southern whites to overcome the racial barrier in search of a more equitable society, but he focused his anger on the historians who perpetuated false visions of racial supremacy as the basis for a reunified America. In the closing paragraph of the book, he denounced the injustices committed against people of color around the globe:

> Immediately in Africa, a black back runs red with the blood of the lash; in India, a brown girl is raped; in China, a coolie starves; in Alabama, seven darkies are more than lynched; while in London, the white limbs of a prostitute are hung with jewels and silk. Flames of jealous murder sweep the earth, while brains of little children smear the hills.

He closed by condemning the scholars who sanctioned the slaughter:

> This is education in the Nineteen Hundred and Thirty-Fifth Year of the Christ; this is modern and exact social science; this is the university course in 'History 12' set down by the Senatus Academicus…[14]

POPULAR MEMORIES OF THE CIVIL WAR

Despite the struggle by generations of African American and white historians to retain an accurate picture of the war's origins, course, and impact, the Lost Cause has retained a disturbingly vigorous hold on much of the popular imagination, particularly through its representation in film. D.W. Griffith's *The Birth of a Nation* (1915) and David O. Selznick's *Gone With the Wind* (1939), the two most influential Civil War films, both perpetuate many of the pernicious historical distortions upon which the Lost Cause rests. Each film emphasized different aspects of the myth but together they impressed the core aspects of the Lost Cause onto millions of viewers over the 20th century. *Birth of a Nation* is in many ways the founding story of the New South, one that features rapacious ignorant blacks, aggrieved and dignified southern whites, and gullible northern whites redeemed only when they respond to the better angels of their race. Based on Thomas Dixon's novel, *The Clansman*, the movie's malignant apotheosis comes with the rise of the Ku Klux Klan and the security they provide in the uncertain postwar world. *Gone With The Wind* extended many of the themes first addressed by Griffith. Slaves are presented as ignorant but loyal to whites who act with their interests in mind. Northerners, presented as

ruthless and predatory, come off worse than in their earlier screen portraits, perhaps a reflection of the cultural work done by southern historical organizations that had been demonizing northern soldiers for so many years.

More recent cinematic treatments of the war reflect the changed historical landscape following the Civil Rights movement of the 1950s and 1960s. Probably the most widely viewed film on the war in recent decades has been Edward Zwick's *Glory* (1989). *Glory* functions as a kind of antidote to the Confederate nostalgia in which *Birth of a Nation* and *Gone With The Wind* are saturated. It focuses on emancipation and the experience of the war for African Americans. The film does not shy away from depicting northern racism but the story it tells is ultimately a redemptive one; the viewer is compelled to identify with the struggle for freedom that the North waged. In the last several years, a host of strong films have chosen to present more personal stories of the war. Ang Lee's *Ride With the Devil* (1999) and Robby Henson's *Pharaoh's Army* (1995) complicate the traditional story of the war

In Birth of a Nation, *Gus, the depraved black Union soldier, chases a white girl to her death. The character captured all that southern whites imagined about blacks – their susceptibility to northern ideas of equality and their unquenchable lust for white women above all. Gus's story, including his lynching by the Ku Klux Klan, justified the violence that plagued the South for decades. (Courtesy of TopFoto)*

DAVID O. SELZNICK'S PRODUCTION OF MARGARET MITCHELL'S

"GONE WITH THE WIND"

In the splendour of 70mm wide screen and full stereophonic sound!

CLARK GABLE · VIVIEN LEIGH · LESLIE HOWARD · OLIVIA de HAVILLAND

A SELZNICK INTERNATIONAL PICTURE · VICTOR FLEMING · SCREEN PLAY BY SIDNEY HOWARD · METRO-GOLDWYN-MAYER · METROCOLOR

Gone With the Wind defined the war for generations of Americans. It immortalized the image of the idyllic plantation, complete with contented slaves and glamorous parties. The war, in contrast, brought death, destruction, and the greed of unrestricted capitalism that took root in the wake of the Yankees' invasion. (Courtesy of TopFoto)

by focusing on border areas, Missouri and Kentucky, respectively, and the complex moral quagmires that participants in the war created. In many of the recent movies, the sectional and racial antagonisms that played such a prominent role in earlier war films have given way to intimate moral struggles between individuals. This approach draws viewers in and humanizes the war while at the same time blurring the political causes and consequences of the conflict.

Offscreen, increasing numbers of people continue to engage in live-action representations of the Civil War. Reenactments in the North and South draw tens of thousands of participants and explain the Civil War for even larger numbers of spectators. Reenactors often maintain a scrupulous accuracy in terms of verisimilitude, crafting clothes, tools, and food in as authentic a way as can be done today. For visitors to reenactments, the result is a palpable, personal connection to the past, albeit one that, like many recent movies, divorces the conflict from its historical meaning. The Civil War as entertainment rarely offers a clear sense of the context within which the original conflict occurred and thus often confuses issues such as causation and motivation.

The challenge of humanizing the story while not losing sight of its historical significance has been taken up directly by the US National Park Service in recent years. Battlefield sites maintained by the Park Service have long functioned as the primary way that many Americans learn about and memorialize the Civil War. Over the last decade, and in the face of much protest, the Park Service has undertaken a significant revision of how its rangers and displays tell the story of the war.[15] Their effort has been to set the individual battles around which National Parks are built into the larger context of the causes and outcomes of the war. This requires a serious engagement with the issue of slavery, long neglected in most public representations of the conflict, and an honest appraisal of the near-sightedness and shortcomings of politicians and soldiers on both sides.

The diversity of perspectives among the personal, public, and academic narratives of the war indicates that the nation does not yet have, and may never have, a single explanation for what the war meant. The memory of the war will probably remain forever a contested and evolving space. Although historians will continue the discussion about the war's physical and political impact, hindsight makes some outcomes visible today that were obscure in years past. Emancipation was clearly a monumental achievement in human terms. Even the host of hurdles that African Americans faced in the postwar nation cannot conceal the significance of the event in our national story. Fulfilling Lincoln's prewar vision, the war established the perpetuity and strength of the American nation. At the same time, by giving focus and depth to the animosities of southerner against northerner the war exacerbated the divisions among Americans by region. If the problems of race, federalism, and sectionalism caused the Civil War, they were by no means clearly solved by it. That paradox explains part of our continuing fascination with the conflict; cause and consequence were fused together in the crucible of war and emerged with the qualities and deficiencies of the old materials and conditions recombined but not replaced.

ENDNOTES

Extremists at the gate

1. "Second Inaugural Address," in Roy P. Basler (ed.), *The Collected Works of Abraham Lincoln*, 9 vols (New Brunswick, Rutgers University Press, 1953–55) 8, pp.332–33.

2. "Declaration of the Immediate Causes Which Induce and Justify the Secession of South Carolina from the Federal Union," http://alpha.furman.edu/~benson/docs/decl-sc.htm, accessed July 21, 2005.

3. Otto Olsen, "Historians and the Extent of Slave Ownership in the Southern United States," in *Civil War History*, 50 (December 2004) pp.401–17.

4. Mark A. Noll, "The Bible and Slavery," in Randall M. Miller, Harry S. Stout and Charles Reagan Wilson (eds), *Religion and the American Civil War* (New York, Oxford University Press, 1998) pp.43–73.

5. John McCardell, *The Idea of a Southern Nation: Southern Nationalists and Southern Nationalism, 1830–1860* (New York, W.W. Norton, 1979) pp.199–200.

6. *Congressional Globe*, 34th Congress, 1st Session, Appendix, p.530.

7. Basler, *Collected Works*, 2, p.465.

8. "The Slavery Question," *The New York Times*, October 28, 1858 (emphasis in original).

I would not be master

1. Lincoln to Albert Hodges, April 4, 1864, in Roy P. Basler (ed.), *The Collected Works of Abraham Lincoln*, 9 vols (New Brunswick, Rutgers University Press, 1953–55) 7, p.282.

2. Lincoln to Orville H. Browning, September 22, 1861, in Basler, *Collected Works*, 4, p.532.

3. Lincoln to John C. Frémont, September 11, 1861, in Basler, *Collected Works*, 4, p.518.

4. J.G. Randall and Richard N. Current, *Lincoln the President*, 4 vols (New York, Dodd, Mead, 1945–54) 2, p.41.

5. William J. Cooper, Jr, *Jefferson Davis, American* (New York, Alfred A. Knopf, 2000) pp.352–53 (quotation), 355, 360, 393; Gary W. Gallagher, *The Confederate War* (Cambridge, MA, Harvard University Press, 1997) p.12.

6. Lincoln to Don C. Buell, January 13, 1862, and Lincoln to Joseph Hooker, June 10, 1863, in Basler, *Collected Works*, 5, p.98, and 6, p.257.

7. William O. Stoddard, *Inside the White House in War Times: Memoirs and Reports of Lincoln's Secretary*, ed. Michael Burlingame (Lincoln, University of Nebraska Press, 2000) p.101.

8. Cooper, *Jefferson Davis, American*, p.350.

9. Quoted in Mark E. Neely, "Abraham Lincoln vs. Jefferson Davis: Comparing Presidential Leadership in the Civil War," in James M. McPherson and William J. Cooper, Jr (eds), *Writing the Civil War: The Quest to Understand* (Columbia, University of South Carolina Press, 1998) p.99.

10. Douglas L. Wilson and Rodney O. Davis (eds), *Herndon's Informants: Letters, Interviews, and Statements about Abraham Lincoln* (Urbana and Chicago, University of Illinois Press, 1998) p.331.

11. Cooper, *Jefferson Davis, American*, p.355.

12. Ibid, pp.410–12.

13. Wilson and Davis, *Herndon's Informants*, p.168 [Leonard Swett].

14. Allen C. Guelzo, *Abraham Lincoln: Redeemer President* (Grand Rapids, William B. Eerdmans Publishing Co., 1999) p.363.

15. Lincoln to George G. Meade, July 14, 1863 ("never sent, or signed.") Basler, *Collected Works*, 6, pp.327–28.

16. Davis to Varina Howell Davis, May 16, 1862, in Lynda Lasswell Crist et al. (eds), *The Papers of Jefferson Davis* (Baton Rouge, Louisiana State University Press, 1995 [vol. 8], 1997 [vol. 9]) 8, p.179.

17. George C. Rable, *The Confederate Republic: A Revolution Against Politics* (Chapel Hill, University of North Carolina Press, 1994) passim.

18. *Chicago Tribune*, January 16, 1864.

19. Speech at Jackson, December 26, 1862; Speech at Richmond, January 5, 1863, in Crist, *Papers of Jefferson Davis*, 8, p.573; 9, pp.11, 14.

20. Quoted in Cooper, *Jefferson Davis, American*, p.495.

21. David M. Potter, "Jefferson Davis and the Political Factors in Confederate Defeat," in David Herbert Donald (ed.), *Why the North Won the Civil War* (Baton Rouge, Louisiana State University Press, 1960) pp.102, 112.

The power of the land

1. Nathaniel H. Harris in G.F.R. Henderson, *Stonewall Jackson and the American Civil War*, 2 vols (London, Longmans, Green & Co., 1898) 2, p.584.

2. Richard Harwell (ed.), *A Confederate Marine: A Sketch of Henry Lea Graves with Excerpts from the Graves Family Correspondence, 1861–1865* (Tuscaloosa, Confederate Publishing Company, Inc., 1963) p.47.

3. Trevor Royle, *A Dictionary of Military Quotations* (New York, Simon & Schuster, 1989) p.167.

4. Rear-Admiral John D. Hayes, in Robert D. Heinl (ed.), *Dictionary of Military and Naval Quotations* (Annapolis, United States Naval Institute, 1967) pp.53–54.

5. Scott letter to Secretary of War Floyd, May 8, 1857, in Heinl, *Dictionary*, p.173.

6. Scott to Davis, May 21, 1856, in Dunbar Rowland (ed.), *Jefferson Davis, Constitutionalist*, 10 vols (Jackson, Mississippi Department of Archives and History, 1923) 3, p.36.

7. Richard Taylor, *Destruction and Reconstruction* (Edinburgh and London, William Blackwood & Sons, 1879) p.38.

8. Harris in Henderson, *Stonewall Jackson*, 2, p.584.

9. R.A. Pierson letter, November 8, 1862, in T. Michael Parrish (ed.), *Brothers in Gray* (Baton Rouge, Louisiana State University Press, 1997) p.132.

10. Soldier's letter in the Raleigh *Standard*, August 5, 1863.

11. Lee conversation with William Allan, February 19, 1870, in Gary W. Gallagher (ed.), *Lee the Soldier* (Lincoln, University of Nebraska Press, 1996) p.18.

12. Holman S. Melcher letter in William B. Styple (ed.), *With a Flash of His Sword* (Kearney, Belle Grove, 1994) pp.297–301.

Our hearts were touched with fire

1. See Mark Pitcavage, *An Equitable Burden: The Decline of the State Militias, 1783–1858* (PhD diss. Ohio State University, 1995).

2. The population of the 11 states that would make up the Confederacy included 5,482,213 free and 3,521,150 enslaved people; the border states of Maryland, Missouri, Kentucky and Delaware counted 2,707,560 free and 429,401 enslaved; and the remaining Union states and territories (including the District of Columbia) held a population of 19,276,859. US Census Office, Eighth Census (1860), *Population*, Washington, DC, 1864.

3. James M. McPherson, *For Cause & Comrades* (New York, Oxford University Press, 1997) summarizes the motivations of soldiers on both sides for enlisting and fighting.

4. For an example of this process in the creation of a Union field army, see Gerald J. Prokopowicz, *All For The Regiment: The Army of the Ohio, 1861–62* (Chapel Hill, University of North Carolina Press, 2001) chapter 1.

5. James L. Morrison, Jr, *"The Best School in the World": West Point, the Pre-Civil War Years, 1833–1866* (Kent, Kent State University Press, 1986) app. 8. Graduates from the Class of 1832 and earlier are not included in this count.

6. G. Ward Hubbs (ed.), *Voices from Company D: Diaries by the Greensboro Guards, Fifth Alabama Infantry Regiment, Army of Northern Virginia* (Athens, University of Georgia Press, 2003) p.35, quoting from the diary of John Henry Cowin.

7. John W. Haley, *The Rebel Yell & the Yankee Hurrah: The Civil War Journal of a Maine Volunteer*, ed. Ruth L. Silliker (Camden, Down East Books, 1985) p.28.

8. A modern study of Civil War tactics that relies heavily on contemporary drill manuals is Brent Nosworthy, *The Bloody Crucible of Courage: Fighting Methods and Combat Experience of the Civil War* (New York, Carroll & Graf, 2003).

9. George R. Stewart, *Pickett's Charge: A Microhistory of the final attack at Gettysburg, July 3, 1863* (Boston, Houghton Mifflin, 1959) p.253. A song that entered the folk tradition in the South late in the 19th century titled "Oh I'm a Good Old Rebel" includes the lines, "At a little creek called Bull Run/We took their starry rag/To wipe our horses down with/and I ain't here to brag."

10. William F. Fox, *Regimental Losses in the American Civil War 1861–1865* (Albany, Rainbow Printing, 1889) p.73.

11. Compare Davis's proclamation of April 5, 1865, with Lee's farewell order to his men, April 10, 1865.

12. Wilbur F. Hinman, *Corporal Si Klegg and his "Pard": How They Lived and Talked, and What They Did and Suffered, while Fighting for the Flag* (Cleveland, N.G. Hamilton, 1889). The character Si Klegg originally appeared in stories in the *National Tribune*, a Union veterans' periodical. *Tribune* editor John McElroy later claimed that he and not Hinman had conceived of Klegg, and published his own series of "Si Klegg" novels.

13. Massachusetts veteran John D. Billings named his classic memoir *Hardtack and Coffee, or the Unwritten Story of Army Life* (Boston, G.M. Smith, 1887); information and commentary on food can be found in almost every first-hand account of Civil War soldier life.

14. Thomas Livermore, *Numbers & Losses in the Civil War in America, 1861–1865* (repr. Bloomington, Indiana University Press, 1957) remains a good starting point for Civil War statistics, all of which should be viewed with caution. Livermore estimates 204,000 deaths from battle and 414,000 non-combat deaths.

15. Edward Hagerman, *The American Civil War and the Origins of Modern Warfare: Ideas, Organization, and Field Command* (Bloomington, Indiana University Press, 1988) analyzes the evolution of transportation standards through the war.

16. John W. De Forest, *A Volunteer's Adventures: A Union Captain's Record of the Civil War*, ed. James H. Croushore (repr. Baton Rouge, Louisiana State University Press, 1996) p.92.

17. Alexander Campbell to Jane Campbell, July 28, 1861, in Terry A. Johnston, Jr, *"Him on the One Side and Me on the Other": The Civil War Letters of Alexander Campbell, 79th New York Infantry Regiment, and James Campbell, 1st South Carolina Battalion* (Columbia, University of South Carolina Press, 1999) p.33.

18. Of hundreds (perhaps thousands) of examples in the official records, see, for example, Report of Colonel Robert McMillan, 24th Georgia, commanding Cobb's brigade against Union charges across open ground at Fredericksburg: "As the column approached, I directed the small-arms to cease until the enemy should get nearer. So soon as he got within certain range, our fire mowed down his ranks until they faltered and the survivors retreated." US War Department, *The War of the Rebellion: A Compilation of the Official Records of the Union and Confederate Armies*, 128 vols (Washington, DC, GPO, 1880–1901) series 1: 21, p.608.

19. Ambrose Bierce, "What I Saw of Shiloh," in William McCann (ed.), *Ambrose Bierce's Civil War* (Washington, DC, Regnery Gateway, 1956) p.24.

20. The debate about the importance of the rifled musket was triggered (so to speak) by Paddy Griffith in *Battle Tactics of the American Civil War* (New Haven, Yale University Press, 1989), originally published as *Rally Once Again* (1987), and has been taken up by Brent Nosworthy and others in the pages of *North & South* magazine.

21. See Fox, *Regimental Losses*, pp.36–37, for a list of 63 Union regiments that lost 50 percent or more in a single engagement.

22. See, for example, George Squier to Ellen Squier, Chattanooga, October 13, 1864, in Julie A. Doyle, John David Smith, and Richard M. McMurry (eds), *This Wilderness of War: the Civil War Letters of George W. Squier, Hoosier Volunteer* (Knoxville, University of Tennessee Press, 1998) pp.92-96.

23. Abraham Lincoln, Second Inaugural Address, March 4, 1865. For the role of evangelical Christianity in the soldiers' experience, see Steven E. Woodworth, *While God Is Marching On: The Religious World of Civil War Soldiers* (Lawrence, University Press of Kansas, 2001).

24. Joshua Chamberlain, *The Passing of the Armies: an account of the final campaign of the Army of the Potomac, based upon personal reminiscences of the Fifth Army Corps* (1915; repr. Lincoln, University of Nebraska Press, 1998) p.20.

25. See S.L.A. Marshall, *Men Under Fire: The Problem of Battle Command in Future War* (New York, William Morrow, 1947).

26. Oliver Wendell Holmes, Jr, Memorial Day Address, May 30, 1884.

27. See Eric T. Dean, Jr, *Shook Over Hell: Post-Traumatic Stress, Vietnam, and the Civil War* (Cambridge, Harvard University Press, 1997).

28. Abraham Lincoln, Second Inaugural Address, March 4, 1865.

29. See Phillip S. Paludan, *Victims: A True Story of the Civil War* (Knoxville, University of Tennessee Press, 1981).

30. Mark Grimsley, *The Hard Hand of War: Union Military Policy Toward Southern Civilians, 1861–1865* (New York, Cambridge University Press, 1995) traces the growing severity of Federal soldiers through the war. Lonnie R. Speer, *War of Vengeance: Acts of Retaliation Against Civil War POWs* (Mechanicsburg, Stackpole, 2002) exposes a long-hidden aspect of the war.

31. Carlton McCarthy, *Detailed Minutiae Of Soldier Life In The Army Of Northern Virginia* (1882, repr. Lincoln, University of Nebraska Press, 1993) p.37.

32. Quoted in James M. McPherson, *Battle Cry of Freedom: The Civil War Era* (New York, Oxford University Press, 1988) p.835.

33. Frederick Douglass, "Should the Negro Enlist in the Union Army?" (July 6, 1863), in Philip Foner (ed.), *Frederick Douglass: Selected Speeches and Writings* (New York, International, 1945) p.72.

34. See David W. Blight, *Race and Reunion: The Civil War in American Memory* (Cambridge, Harvard University Press, 2001).

Remorseless, revolutionary struggle

1. Quoted in Brian Holden Reid, *The American Civil War and the Wars of the Industrial Revolution* (London, Cassell, 1999) p.195.

2. Ibid.

3. Quoted in Niall Ferguson, *The Pity of War* (New York, Basic Books, 1999) p.8.

4. Annual Message to Congress, December 3, 1861, in Roy P. Basler (ed.), *The Collected Works of Abraham Lincoln*, 9 vols (New Brunswick, Rutgers University Press, 1953–55) 5, pp.48–49.

5. "Extract from proceedings of the U. S. House of Representatives July 18, 1861," in US War Department, *War of the Rebellion: A Compilation of the Official Records of the Union and Confederate Armies*, 128 vols (Washington, DC, Government Printing Office, 1880–1901) series 2: 2, p.792.

6. McClellan to Simon Cameron, October 31, 1861, Stephen W. Sears (ed.) *The Civil War Papers of George B. McClellan: Selected Correspondence, 1860–1865* (New York, Ticknor & Fields, 1989) p.118.

7. Quoted in John A. Lynn, *The Bayonets of the Republic: Motivation and Tactics in the Army of Revolutionary France, 1791–94* (Urbana, University of Illinois Press, 1984) p.188.

8. Quoted in Michael Howard, *The Franco-Prussian War: The German Invasion of France, 1870–1871* (New York, MacMillan, 1961) p.299.

9. Bruce Catton, *Glory Road: The Bloody Route from Fredericksburg to Gettysburg* (Garden City, Doubleday, 1952) p.29.

10. "Why Did So Many Soldiers Die?", in James L. Roark et al., *The American Promise: A History of the United States* (Boston, Bedford Books, 1997) p.594.

11. Hancock's report, undated [1863], *Official Records* 27, pt.1, p.373.

12. Quoted in Douglas Southall Freeman, *R. E. Lee: A Biography*, 4 vols (New York, Charles Scribner's Sons, 1935) 3, p.389.

13. William T. Sherman, *Memoirs*, 2 vols in 1 (1875; Bloomington, Indiana University Press, 1957) 2, p.395.

14. Ibid., 2, p.396.

15. Lyman to his parents, May 18, 1864, George R. Aggasiz (ed.), *Meade's Headquarters, 1863–1865* (Boston, Atlantic Monthly Press, 1922) pp.99–100.

16. McClellan to Don Carlos Buell, November 7, 12, 1861, *Official Records*, 4, pp.342, 355–56.

17. Quoted in Mark Grimsley, *The Hard Hand of War: Union Military Policy Toward Southern Civilians, 1861–1865* (New York, Cambridge University Press, 1995) p.103.

18. Ibid., p.105.

19. Brian Bond, *The Pursuit of Victory: From Napoleon to Saddam Hussein* (New York, Oxford University Press, 1996) p.68.

Uncle Sam's web-feet

1. Winfield Scott to George McClellan, May 3, 1861, McClellan Papers, Library of Congress.

2. "Proclamation of a Blockade," April 19, 1861, in Roy S. Basler (ed.), *The Collected Works of Abraham Lincoln*, 9 vols (New Brunswick, Rutgers University Press, 1953–55) 4, pp.338–39.

3. William R. Roberts, *Now For the Contest: Coastal & Oceanic Naval Operations in the Civil War* (Lincoln, University of Nebraska Press, 2004) p.18.

4. Ibid., p.19.

5. Michael J. Bennett, *Union Jacks: Yankee Sailors in the Civil War* (Chapel Hill, University of North Carolina Press, 2004) pp.12, 28, 42, 155–81.

6. Robert E. Lee to Roswell Ripley, February 19, 1862, in Clifford Dowdey (ed.), *The Wartime Papers of Robert E. Lee* (New York, Da Capo Press, 1961) p.116.

7. Critics of the blockade include Frank Owsley, *King Cotton Diplomacy: Foreign Relations of the Confederate States of America* (Chicago, University of Chicago Press, 1931); and William N. Still, Jr in a number of works. The statistics are from Stephen R. Wise, *Lifeline of the Confederacy: Blockade Running During the Civil War* (Columbia, University of South Carolina Press, 1988) p.226.

8. David G. Surdam, *Northern Naval Superiority and the Economics of the American Civil War* (Columbia, University of South Carolina Press, 2001).

9. Abraham Lincoln to James Conkling, August 26, 1863, in Basler, *Collected Works*, 6, p.409.

10. Stephen Mallory to his wife, August 31, 1862, Stephen Mallory Papers, P.K. Yonge Library, University of Florida.

11. The *Albemarle* was subsequently destroyed in a daring night time raid by navy lieutenant William B. Cushing. For the story of Confederate ironclads, see William N. Still, Jr *Iron Afloat: The Story of the Confederate Armorclads* (Columbia, University of South Carolina Press, 1971).

12. Nearly a century and a half later, both the CSS *Hunley* and the iconic turret of the USS *Monitor* were recovered from the bottom of the sea and both are now on view to the public: the *Hunley* in Charleston, South Carolina, and the *Monitor*'s turret at the Mariners' Museum in Newport News, Virginia.

13. The United States protested British complicity in the construction of the rebel raiders and after the war an international tribunal ruled that the British had to pay the United States an indemnity of $15.5 million.

14. George W. Dalzell, *The Flight From the Flag: The Continuing Effect of the Civil War upon the American Carrying Trade* (Chapel Hill, University of North Carolina Press, 1940).

They came to butcher our people

1. Richard Taylor, *Destruction and Reconstruction: Personal Experiences of the Civil War* (New York, D. Appleton, 1879; repr. New York, Da Capo, 1995) p.13.

2. US War Department, *The War of the Rebellion: A Compilation of the Official Records of the Union and Confederate Armies*, 128 vols (Washington, DC, Government Printing Office, 1880–1911) series 3: 1, p.83 (Cited hereinafter as *OR*. All citations are series 1 unless stated otherwise.)

3. Thomas L. Snead, "The First Year of the War in Missouri," in *Battles and Leaders of the Civil War*, Robert Johnson and Clarence Buel (eds), 4 vols (New York, 1956) 1, pp.265–67.

4. Thomas Goodrich, *Black Flag: Guerilla Warfare on the Western Border, 1861–1865* (Bloomington, Indiana University Press, 1995) pp.18, 26; Michael Fellman, *Inside War: The Guerilla Conflict in Missouri During the American Civil War* (New York, Oxford University Press, 1989) p.151. Some 35,000 Missourians enlisted in Confederate armies while Union service drew 80,000.

5. Wiley Britton, *The Civil War on the Border: Volume II 1863–1865* (New York, 1899; repr. Ottawa, KN, 1994) p.379; Walter Williams, "Battle at Centralia, Mo.," in *Confederate Veteran*, 17, p.31.

6. *OR*, 4, p.73.

7. Jerry Thompson, *Henry Hopkins Sibley: Confederate General of the West*. (Natchitoches, Northern State University Press, 1987) pp.269, 273.

8. Jerry Thompson (ed.), *Civil War in the Southwest: Recollections of the Sibley Brigade* (College Station, Texas A&M Press, 2001) p.93.

9. *OR*, 8, p.749; William L. Shea, and Earl J. Hess, *Pea Ridge: Civil War Campaign in the West* (Chapel Hill, University of North Carolina Press, 1992) p.22.

10. *OR*, 8, pp.195, 790. Sharpshooters also killed McCulloch's second-in-command James McIntosh.

11. Robert L. Kerby, *Kirby Smith's Confederacy: The Trans-Mississippi South, 1863–1865.* (New York, Columbia University Press, 1972) p.236.

12. Norman D. Brown (ed.), *Journey to Pleasant Hill: The Civil War Letters of Captain Elijah P. Petty* (San Antonio, University of Texas Institute of Texas Cultures, 1982) p.150.

13. John Newman Edwards, *Shelby and His Men* (Cincinnati, Miami Printing and Publishing Company, 1867; repr. Waverly, General Joseph Shelby Memorial Fund, 1993) p.125.

14. Prairie Grove Staff Ride with Arkansas State Parks historian Don Montgomery, December 1997.

15. R.W. Johnson, Charles B. Mitchel, et al. to Jefferson Davis, February 2, 1863, Jefferson Davis Papers, Duke University, Perkins Library Special Collections.

16. James R. Seddon replaced Randolph in November 1862.

17. *OR*, series 2: 5, p.791; 6, pp.21–22, 115.

18. Taylor, *Destruction and Reconstruction*, pp.126, 153.

19. *OR*, 26, pp.1, 305.

20. Mamie Yeary (ed.), *Reminiscences of the Boys in Gray* (McGregor, 1912; repr. Dayton, Morningside, 1986) p.627; Cynthia Dehaven Pitcock and Bill J. Gurley (eds), *I Acted From Principle: The Civil War Diary of William McPheeters Confederate Surgeon in the Trans-Mississippi* (Fayetteville, University of Arkansas Press, 2002) p.141.

21. Gary Dillard Joiner, *One Damn Blunder From Beginning to End: The Red River Campaign of 1864* (Wilmington, Scholarly Resources, 2003) p.116; David D. Porter, *Incidents and Anecdotes of the Civil War* (New York, Appleton, 1885) pp.235–36.

22. United States Congress, *Report of the Joint Committee on The Conduct Of The War at the Second Session Thirty-Eighth Congress: Red River Expedition, Fort Fisher Expedition, Heavy Ordnance* (Washington, DC, Government Printing Office, 1865) p.8; John G. Walker, "The War of Secession West of the Mississippi River During the Years 1863–4 & 5," typescript, p.71, Myron Gwinner Collection, United States Military History Institute, Carlisle, Pennsylvania.

23. *OR*, 34, pt.1, pp.547, 597; Taylor, *Destruction and Reconstruction*, p.188.

24. *OR*, 48, pt.1, pp.1319–20; Edmund Kirby Smith to Soldiers, May 30, 1865, Kirby Smith Papers, Southern Historical Collection, University of North Carolina.

25. *OR*, 1, pp.683–84

26. Round Mountain is near present-day Yale and Chustenahlah is near present-day Tulsa.

27. Alvin M. Josephy Jr, *Civil War in the American West* (New York, Random House, 1991) pp.332–33.

28. Wilfred Knight, *Red Fox: Stand Watie's Civil War Years in Indian Territory* (Glendale, Arthur H. Clark Company, 1988) p.272. On July 14, Winchester Colbert's band of Chickasaws became the last Confederate ground troops to surrender.

29. "The Ninety-third Anniversary of the Birth of Pres. Jefferson Davis," in *Southern Historical Society Papers*, 29, p.5.

30. Samuel Curtis to William T. Sherman, July 28, 1862, Samuel Ryan Curtis Papers, Illinois State Historical Library, Springfield, IL.

That great essential of success

1. US War Department, *The War of the Rebellion: A Compilation of the Official Records of the Union and Confederate Armies*, 128 vols (Washington, DC, Government Printing Office, 1880–1911), series 1: 46, pt.1, p.481. (Cited hereafter as *OR*).

2. *Cincinnati Gazette*, July 13, 1863.

3. Edwin C. Fishel, "The Mythology of Civil War Intelligence," *Civil War History*, 10 (December 1964) pp.344–67.

4. Warren F. Spencer, *The Confederate Navy in Europe* (Tuscaloosa, University of Alabama Press, 1983) passim.

5. David E. Long, *The Jewel of Liberty: Abraham Lincoln's Re-election and the End of Slavery* (Mechanicsburg, Stackpole, 1994) pp.91–114. See also Larry E. Nelson, *Bullets, Ballots, and Rhetoric: Confederate Policy for the United States Presidential Contest in 1864* (Tuscaloosa, University of Alabama Press, 1980) and Oscar A. Kinchen, *Confederate Operations in Canada and the North* (North Quincy, Christopher Publishing House, 1970).

6. *OR*, series 4: 3, pp.172, 176, 177.

7. *OR*, series 4: 3, pp.202–03. See also D.H. Rule, "*Sultana*: A Case for Sabotage," *North & South*, 5 (December 2001) pp.76–87.

8. David Winfred Gaddy, "William Norris and the Confederate Signal and Secret Service," *Maryland Historical Magazine*, 70 (Summer 1975) pp.167–88.

9. Michael W. Kaufmann, *American Brutus: John Wilkes Booth and the Lincoln Conspiracies* (New York, Random House, 2004) pp.154–98, 387–90. See also William A. Tidwell, James O. Hall, and David Winfred Gaddy, *Come Retribution: The Confederate Secret Service and the Assassination of Abraham Lincoln* (Jackson, University Press of Mississippi, 1988) passim, and Elizabeth D. Leonard, *Lincoln's Avengers: Justice, Revenge, and Reunion after the Civil War* (New York, W.W. Norton, 2004) pp.33–135, 229–63.

10. Edwin C. Fishel, *The Secret War for the Union: The Untold Story of Military Intelligence in the Civil War* (New York, Houghton Mifflin, 1996) pp.24–28, 54–66, 284–86. Quoted in Kaufmann, *American Brutus*, p.381. See also Lafayette C. Baker, *A History of the United States Secret Service* (Philadelphia, L.C. Baker, 1867).

11. Fishel, *Secret War*, pp.53–101. See also Allan Pinkerton, *The Spy of the Rebellion* (repr. of 1888 ed.; Lincoln, University of Nebraska Press, 1989).

12. See Harriet Owlsey, "Henry Shelton Sanford and Federal Surveillance Abroad, 1861–1865," *Mississippi Valley Historical Review*, 48 (1961) pp.211–28 and David Hepburn Milton, *Lincoln's Spymaster: Thomas Haines Dudley and the Liverpool Network* (Mechanicsburg, Stackpole, 2003).

13. Michael I. Handel, *War, Strategy, and Intelligence* (London, Frank Cass, 1989) p.70.

14. William B. Feis, *Grant's Secret Service: The Intelligence War from Belmont to Appomattox* (Lincoln, University of Nebraska Press, 2002) pp.128–29.

15. Pension File of Charles De Arnaud, National Archives and Records Administration, Washington, DC. See also William B. Feis, "Charles S. Bell, Union Scout," *North & South*, 4 (September 2001) p.34.

16. James D. Hensal to Grenville M. Dodge, 1907, Grenville M. Dodge Papers, State Historical Society of Iowa, Des Moines, Iowa.

17. William Callender, *Thrilling Adventures of William Callender, Union Spy* (Des Moines, Mills & Company, 1881) p.17.

18. Statement of Levi Cecil, October 20, 1909, Benjamin Wilson Smith Papers, Indiana State Library, Indianapolis.

19. Peter Maslowski, "Military Intelligence Sources During the Civil War: A Case Study," in Lieutenant-Colonel Walter T. Hitchcock (ed.), *The Intelligence Revolution: A Historical Perspective* (Washington, DC, Government Printing Office, 1991), pp.39–47, 49–53; Fishel, *Secret War*, pp.1–7, 340–59.

20. Maslowski, "Military Intelligence," pp.53–56.

21. Ibid., pp.47–49; William B. Feis, "The Deception of Braxton Bragg: The Tullahoma Campaign, June 23–July 4, 1863," *Blue & Gray*, 10 (October 1992) p.20.

22. Fishel, *Secret War*, pp.102–64.

23. Ibid., pp.211–40.

24. Ibid., pp.275–97; Feis, *Grant's Secret Service*, pp.196–201, 259.

25. Meriwether Stuart, "Samuel Ruth and General R.E. Lee: Disloyalty and the Line of Supply to Fredericksburg," *Virginia Magazine of History and Biography*, 71 (January 1963) pp.35–109; Elizabeth R. Varon, *Southern Lady, Yankee Spy: The True Story of Elizabeth Van Lew, A Union Agent in the Heart of the Confederacy* (New York, Oxford University Press, 2003) pp.187–88; Feis, *Grant's Secret Service*, pp.240–41.

26. Feis, *Grant's Secret Service*, pp.237–41.

27. Varon, *Southern Lady*, pp.165–68.

28. David D. Ryan (ed.), *A Yankee Spy in Richmond: The Civil War Diary of "Crazy Bet" Van Lew* (Mechanicsburg, Stackpole Books, 1996) p.83.

29. Varon, *Southern Lady*, pp.135–52, 185–256. See also Meriwether Stuart, "Colonel Ulric Dahlgren and Richmond's Union Underground," *Virginia Magazine of History and Biography*, 72 (April 1964) pp.152–204; Quoted in Feis, *Grant's Secret Service*, p.240.

30. Fishel, *Secret War*, pp.454–83.

31. Maslowski, 49–50; Quoted in Feis, *Grant's Secret Service*, p.198.

32. Fishel, *Secret War*, pp.519–37.

33. Feis, *Grant's Secret Service*, pp.241–49.

34. Ibid., 126–74; Stanley P. Hirshson, *Grenville M. Dodge: Soldier, Politician, Railroad Pioneer* (Bloomington, Indiana University Press, 1967) pp.73–74.

35. William B. Feis, "'There is a Bad Enemy in This City': Colonel William Truesdail's Army Police and the Occupation of Nashville, 1862–1863," *North & South*, 8 (March 2005) pp.35–45; Feis, "The Deception of Braxton Bragg," pp.10–21, 46–53.

36. Robert Scott Davis, Jr, "The Curious Civil War Career of James George Brown, Spy," *Prologue*, 26 (Spring 1994) pp.17–31; Thomas G. Dyer, *Secret Yankees: The Union Circle in Confederate Atlanta* (Baltimore, The Johns Hopkins University Press, 1999) pp.115–54.

37. Feis, "Charles S. Bell," pp.26–37.

38. William Gilmore Beymer, *On Hazardous Service: Scouts and Spies of the North and South* (New York, Harper & Brothers, 1912) p.206.

39. Ann Blackman, *Wild Rose: Rose O'Neale Greenhow, Civil War Spy* (New York, Random House, 2005) pp.36–56, 305–07; For a critique of Greenhow's contributions, see Fishel, *Secret War*, pp.58–76.

40. Ruth Scarborough, *Belle Boyd, Siren of the South* (Macon, Mercer University Press, 1983) passim.

41. Feis, "Truesdail's Army Police," p.37.

42. Fishel, *Secret War*, 5–6; James O. Hall, "The Spy Harrison: A Modern Hunt for a Fabled Agent," *Civil War Times Illustrated*, 24 (February 1986) pp.18–25; James Dudley Peavey, *Confederate Scout: Virginia's Frank Stringfellow* (Onancock, Eastern Shore Publishing, 1956); Howard Canan, "Confederate Military Intelligence," *Maryland Historical Magazine*, 59 (March 1964) pp.36–38.

43. James M. McPherson, *Battle Cry of Freedom: The Civil War Era* (New York, Oxford University Press, 1988) pp.462–67; Fishel, *Secret War*, p.157.

44. Emory M. Thomas, *Robert E. Lee: A Biography* (New York, W.W. Norton & Co., 1995) pp.293–98.

45. Fishel, *Secret War*, p.571.

46. Howard Carter, *The Tomb of Tutankhamen: The Burial Chamber* (repr. of 1927 edition; London, Duckworth, 2001) p.20.

We never yielded in the struggle

1. Mauriel Phillips Joslyn (ed.), *Charlotte's Boys: Civil War Letters of the Branch Family of Savannah* (Berryville, Rockbridge Publishing Co., 1996) pp.310–11.

2. Diary of Samuel A. Agnew, September 27, 1863–June 30, 1864, Electronic Edition, *Documenting the American South*, Manuscripts Collection, Southern Historical Collection, University of North Carolina, Chapel Hill.

3. Mollie Houser to James Houser, March 21, 1864, May 23, 1864; Kit Hanger to Julia Houser, April 28, 1864, Augusta County Letters and Diaries, Civil War Letters, *Valley of the Shadow Project*, Electronic Text Center, University of Virginia. (Hereinafter cited as VSW Project.)

4. Rachel Cormany Diary, June 22, 1863, Chambersburg, Penn. Letters and Diaries, Civil War Letters, VSW Project.

5. Sue Carter to Mary A. Heirs, September 15, 1861, Augusta County Letters and Diaries, Civil War Letters, VSW Project.

6. Quoted in Jeanie Attie, *Patriotic Toil: Northern Women and the American Civil War* (Ithaca, Cornell University Press, 1998) p.53.

7. Quoted in Katherine M. Jones, *Heroines of Dixie: Confederate Women Tell Their Story of the War* (New York, Bobbs-Merrill Co., Inc., 1955) p.33.

8. Quoted in E.F. Conklin, *Women at Gettysburg, 1863* (Gettysburg, Thomas Publishing, 1993) p.7.

9. Quoted in Conklin, *Women of Gettysburg*, pp.15–16.

10. Rachel Cormany Diary, June 15, 1863, June 16, 1863, VSW Project.

11. Henrietta S. Jaquette (ed.), *Letters of Cornelia Hancock From the Army of the Potomac, 1863–1865* (Lincoln, University of Nebraska Press, 1998 [E-Book edition]) p.31.

12. Jaquette, *Letters of Cornelia Hancock*, p.58.

13. Quoted in Conklin, *Women of Gettysburg*, pp.228–33.

14. Quoted in Conklin, *Women of Gettysburg*, pp.237–39.

15. Speech of J.W.C. Pennington, August 14, 1863, quoted in William E. Gienapp (ed.), *The Civil War and Reconstruction: a Documentary Collection* (New York, W.W. Norton & Co., 2001) p.186.

16. The true identity of "Agnes" was kept secret by her friend Sara. Quoted in Sara Rice Pryor, *Reminiscences of Peace and War* (New York, Macmillan Company, 1904) pp.237–39.

17. John A. Beaman to Governor Zebulon Vance, undated, Governors Papers, Vance, North Carolina Department of Archives and History, Raleigh, NC. (Hereinafter referred to as NCDAH.)

18. Samuel L. Holt to Governor Zebulon Vance, May 24, 1863. Governors Papers, Vance, NCDAH.

19. Quoted in Pryor, *Reminiscences of Peace and War*, pp.292–94.

20. Martha A. Sheets to Aaron Sanders, January 27, 1865, Criminal Action Papers, Montgomery County, NCDAH.

21. Mollie Houser to James Houser, September 5, 1864, VSW Project.

22. Quoted in Victoria Bynum, *Unruly Women: The Politics of Social and Sexual Control in the Old South* (Chapel Hill, University of North Carolina Press, 1992) p.134.

23. Quoted in Conklin, *Women of Gettysburg*, p.404.

The world will forever applaud

1. James M. McPherson, *Battle Cry of Freedom: The Civil War Era* (New York, Oxford University Press, 1988) p.203.

2. Roy P. Basler (ed.) *The Collected Works of Abraham Lincoln*, 9 vols (New Brunswick, Rutgers University Press, 1953–55) 8, p.333.

3. William H. Lee to Jefferson Davis, May 4, 1861, in Ira Berlin, et al., *Free at Last: A Documentary History of Slavery, Freedom, and the Civil War* (New York, New Press, 1992) p.4.

4. *Douglass' Monthly*, May 1861, in Philip S. Foner (ed.), *The Life and Writings of Frederick Douglass* (New York, International Publishers, 1952) 3, pp.90–91.

5. A.J. Slemmer to Lorenzo Thomas, March 18, 1861, in US War Department, *The War of the Rebellion: A Compilation of the Official Records of the Union and Confederate Armies* (Washington, DC, *OR*, series 2: 1 p.750.

6. John Boston to Elizabeth Boston, January 12, 1862, in Berlin, *Free at Last*, pp.29–30.

7. Basler, *Collected Works*, 5, p.222.

8. H. Clay Reed, "Lincoln's Compensated Emancipation Plan and its Relation to Delaware," in *Delaware Notes*, 7th series (1931) p.51.

9. Basler, *Collected Works*, 5, pp.317–18.

10. Ibid., 5, pp.336–37.

11. Montgomery Blair to Lincoln, July 23, 1862, Blair family papers, Manuscripts Division, Library of Congress, Washington, DC.

12. John Niven (ed.), *The Salmon P. Chase Papers* (Kent, Kent State University Press, 1993) 1, p.351.

13. F.B. Carpenter, *Six Months at the White House with Abraham Lincoln* (New York, Hurd and Houghton, 1866) p.22.

14. Basler, *Collected Works*, 5, p.388.

15. James C. Allen in Quincy (Ill.) *Herald*, cited in Bruce Tap, "Race, Rhetoric, and Emancipation: The Election of 1862 in Illinois," in *Civil War History*, 39 (June 1993) p.116.

16. *New York Evening Post*, November 13, 1862, p.2.

17. *Toledo Blade*, reprinted in *Cincinnati Gazette*, October 17, 1862, p.2.

18. Basler, *Collected Works*, 5, p.530.

19. Ibid., 5, p.537.

20. Lincoln to John A. McClernand, January 8, 1863, Basler, *Collected Works*, 6, p.49.

21. Ibid., 6, p.30.

22. Ibid., 5, p.434.

23. Lincoln to James C. Conklin, August 26, 1863, Basler, *Collected Works*, 6, p.409.

24. Hannah Johnson to Abraham Lincoln, July 31, 1863, in Berlin, *Free at Last*, p.450.

25. Spotswood Rice to "My Children," September 3, 1864, in Berlin, *Free at Last*, pp.480–82.

26. Charleston *Mercury*, January 13, 1865, in Robert F. Durden (ed.), *The Gray and the Black: The Confederate Debate on Emancipation* (Baton Rouge, Louisiana State University Press, 1972) p.233.

One great society

1. D.P. Crook, *The North, The South, and the Powers* (New York, John Wiley & Sons, 1974) p.96.

2. Sir George Cornewall Lewis, "Election of President Lincoln and its Consequences," *Edinburgh Review*, 113 (April, 1861) p.555; Anthony Trollope, *North America* (New York, Da Capo Press, 1951) p.232.

3. Jay Sexton, "Transatlantic Financiers and the Civil War," *American Nineteenth Century History*, 2 (Autumn 2001) p.30.

4. Henry Blumenthal, *A Reappraisal of Franco-American Relations 1830–1871* (Chapel Hill, University of North Carolina Press, 1959) pp.103–05; Lynn M. Case and Warren F. Spencer, *The United States and France: Civil War Diplomacy* (Philadelphia, University of Pennsylvania Press, 1970) p.127; David Pinkney, "France and the Civil War," in Harold Hyman (ed.), *Heard the World: The Impact Abroad of the Civil War* (New York, Alfred A. Knopf, 1969) pp.120–21; Crook, *The North*, pp.16–17.

5. D.P. Crook, *American Democracy in English Politics 1815–1850* (Oxford, Clarendon Press, 1965) pp.166–95.

6. *The Times*, October 22, 1861, p.6.

7. George M. Blackburn, *French Newspaper Opinion on the American Civil War* (Westport, Greenwood Press, 1997) pp.23–40.

8. See Serge Gavronsky, *The French Liberal Opposition and the American Civil War* (New York, Humanities Press, 1968); Pinkney, pp.112, 119.

9. Blackburn, *French Newspaper*, pp.57–69.

10. See Lynn M. Case, *French Opinion on the United States and Mexico, 1860–1867: Extracts from the Reports of the Procureurs-Généraux* (New York, D. Appleton-Century Company, 1936); Pinkney, pp.100–02.

11. Thomas A. Sancton, "The Myth of French Worker Support for the North in the American Civil War," *French Historical Studies*, 11 (Spring 1979) pp.70–71.

12. R.J.M. Blackett, *Divided Hearts: Britain and the American Civil War* (Baton Rouge, Louisiana State University Press, 2001) pp.17, 35, 87, 120.

13. Marcus Wood, "The American South and English Print Satire, 1760–1865" from Joseph Ward (ed.), *Britain and the American South: From Colonialism to Rock and Roll* (Jackson, University Press of Mississippi, 2003) pp.123–40; Martin Crawford, *The Anglo-American Crisis of the Mid-Nineteenth Century: The Times and America, 1850–1862* (Athens, University of Georgia Press, 1987) pp.13–14.

14. *The Times*, October 16, 1861, p.8.

15. *The Times*, October 9, 1862, pp.7–8.

16. Howard Jones, *Union in Peril: The Crisis over British Intervention in the Civil War* (Chapel Hill, University of North Carolina Press, 1992) pp.138–39, 175–77.

17. See Mary Ellison, *Support for Secession: Lancashire and the American Civil War* (Chicago, University of Chicago Press, 1972); Blackett, *Divided Hearts*, p.119.

18. Eugenio Biagini, *Liberty, Retrenchment and Reform: Popular Liberalism in the Age of Gladstone, 1860–1880* (New York, Cambridge University Press, 1992) p.72; Blackett, pp.120, 123–212, 241.

19. Case and Spencer, p.126.

20. Crook, *The North, the South, and the Powers*, p.177; Case and Spencer, pp.147–48.

21. Stuart L. Bernath, *Squall across the Atlantic: American Civil War Prize Cases and Diplomacy* (Los Angeles, University of California Press, 1970) pp.63–98.

22. Frank Merli, *Great Britain and the Confederate Navy 1861–1865* (Bloomington, Indiana University Press, 1970) pp.167–71.

23. Case and Spencer, pp.427–79.

24. Eugene Berwanger, *The British Foreign Service and the American Civil War* (Lexington, University Press of Kentucky, 1994) pp.108–19.

25. Sexton, pp.31–32.

26. Ibid., pp.32–33.

27. Judith Fenner Gentry, "A Confederate Success in Europe: The Erlanger Loan," *Journal of Southern History*, 36 (May 1970) p.182.

28. Neil Ashcroft, "British Trade with the Confederacy and the Effectiveness of Union Maritime Strategy during the Civil War," *International Journal of Maritime History* 10 (December 1998) pp.155–76.

29. Stanley Lebergott, "Through the Blockade: The Profitability and Extent of Cotton Smuggling, 1861–1865," *Journal of Economic History* 41 (December 1981) p.881.

30. Eugene Brady, "A Reconsideration of the Lancashire Cotton Famine," *Agricultural History* 37 (July 1963): pp.156-62; David Surdam, "King Cotton: Monarchy or Pretender? The State of the Market for Raw Cotton on the Eve of the American Civil War," *Economic History Review* 51 (February 1998) pp.113–32.

31. Frank Owsley, *King Cotton Diplomacy: Foreign Relations of the Confederate States of America* (Chicago, University of Chicago Press, 1959) pp.141–47.

32. Frenise Logan, "India – Britain's Substitute for American Cotton, 1861–1865," *Journal of Southern History* 24 (November 1958) pp.472–80; Peter Harnetty, "The Imperialism of Free Trade: Lancashire, India, and the Cotton Supply Question, 1861–1865," *Journal of British Studies* 6 (November 1966) pp.70–96; Sven Beckert, "Emancipation and Empire: Reconstructing the Worldwide Web of Cotton Production in the Age of the American Civil War," *American Historical Review* 109 (December 2004) pp.1405–38.

33. Claude Fohlen, "La Guerre de Secession et le Commerce Franco-Américain," *Revue d'Histoire Moderne et Contemporaine* 8 (1961) pp.264–70; Pinkney, pp.120–37; Case and Spencer, pp.158–64, 374–79; Blumenthal, p.108.

34. Case and Spencer, p.304.

35. Glyndon Van Deusen, *William Henry Seward* (New York, Oxford University Press, 1967) p.301; Crook, *The North, the South, and the Powers*, p.63.

36. Deusen, pp.298–99.

37. Henry Blumenthal, "Confederate Diplomacy: Popular Notions and International Realities," *Journal of Southern History* 32 (May 1966) p.170; Charles Hubbard, *The Burden of Confederate Diplomacy* (Knoxville, University Press of Tennessee, 1998) pp.30–39, 177–81; Owsley, pp.15–42.

38. Norman Ferris, *The Trent Affair: A Diplomatic Crisis* (Knoxville, University of Tennessee Press, 1977) pp.45–48.

39. Kenneth Bourne, *Britain and the Balance of Power in North America 1815–1908* (Berkeley, University of California Press, 1967) p.243.

40. Jones, pp.181–220.

41. Case and Spencer, pp.23–32, 258, 289–91, 300–01.

42. Crook, *The North, the South, and the Powers*, pp.309–15.

43. Ibid., p.372.

44. Beckert, pp.1437–38.

45. Blackett, p.145.

46. Crook, *The North, the South, and the Powers*, pp.379–80; F.B. Smith, *The Making of the Second Reform Bill* (Cambridge, Cambridge University Press, 1966) p.231; Maurice Cowling, *1867: Disraeli, Gladstone and Revolution: The Passing of the Second Reform Bill* (Cambridge, Cambridge University Press, 1967) pp.1–7, 24, 47, 310.

47. *Hansard Parliamentary Debates* (Commons), series 3: 183 (1866) col. 110.

48. Pinkney, p.117.

49. John Hawgood, "The Civil War and Central Europe," in Harold Hyman (ed.), *Heard Round the World: The Impact Abroad of the Civil War* (New York, Alfred A. Knopf, 1969) p.174; Gordon Craig, *Germany 1866–1945* (New York, Oxford University Press, 1978) p.38.

A fearful lesson

1. Henry M. Turner, as quoted in James M. McPherson, *The Negro's Civil War: How American Blacks Felt and Acted During the War for the Union* (1965; New York, Ballantine Books, 1991) p.50.

2. Abraham Lincoln, "First Inaugural Address," March 4, 1861, in Roy P. Basler (ed.) *The Collected Works of Abraham Lincoln*, 9 vols (New Brunswick, Rutgers University Press, 1953–55) 4, p.252

3. Eric Foner, *Free Soil, Free Labor, Free Men: The Ideology of the Republican Party Before the Civil War* (New York, Oxford, 1970) p.33.

4. Jourdan Anderson, August 7, 1865, as quoted in Leon Litwack, *Been in the Storm So Long: The Aftermath of Slavery* (New York, Vintage, 1979) p.333.

5. John Hope Franklin, *Reconstruction after the Civil War* (Chicago, University of Chicago Press, 1961) p.35.

6. Ulysses S. Grant, *Personal Memoirs of U.S. Grant* (New York, Charles Webster, 1885; New York, Dover, 1995) p.459.

7. William T. Sherman, *Senate Executive Documents*, 40th Congress, First Session, No. 13 (1867).

8. Roger Ransom and Richard Sutch estimate the market value of the 2 million slaves held in the five Lower South states at $1.6 billion in 1860. Another 2 million slaves were held in Upper South states. Roger L. Ransom and Richard Sutch, *One Kind of Freedom: The Economic Consequences of Emancipation* (Cambridge, Cambridge University Press, 1977) p.52.

9. Richard L. Ransom, *Conflict and Compromise: The Political Economy of Slavery, Emancipation, and the American Civil War* (Cambridge, Cambridge University Press, 1989) p.227.

10. Herman Melville, *Battle-Pieces and Aspects of the War: Civil War Poems*, reprint (1866; repr. New York, DaCapo, 1995).

11. *New York Herald*, May 24, 1865, as quoted in Charles Roster, *The Destructive War: William Tecumseh Sherman, Stonewall Jackson, and the Americans* (New York, Vintage, 1991) p.417.

12. Henry Grady, *The New South: Writings and Speeches of Henry Grady* (Savannah, Beehive Press, 1971) pp.7, 8.

13. Jefferson Davis, as quoted in David Blight, *Race and Reunion: The Civil War in American Memory* (Cambridge, Harvard University Press, 2001) pp.259–60.

14. W.E.B. DuBois, *Black Reconstruction in America* (New York, Harcourt Brace, 1935) p.728.

15. For discussions of the controversies surrounding this policy shift, see "Park Service's Civil War reinterpretation delves into controversy behind battle," in *Seattle Times*, January 4, 2004; "Civil War Tour Guides To Address Slavery; Battlefields Seek More Black Visitors," in *Washington Post*, April 30, 2000; "New Battlefield; Cause of conflict, issue of slavery fuel debate over teaching at Civil War sites," in *Houston Chronicle*, May 14, 2000; and "New Reality for Civil War Sites," in *Boston Globe*, May 9, 2000.

FURTHER READING

Extremists at the gate

Basler, Roy P. (ed.), *The Collected Works of Abraham Lincoln*, 9 vols (New Brunswick, Rutgers University Press, 1953–55)

Cairnes, John Elliot, *The Slave Power: Its Character, Career, and Probable Designs; Being an Attempt to Explain the Real Issues Involved in the American Contest* (1863; repr. Columbia, University of South Carolina Press, 2003)

Davis, David Bryon, *The Slave Power Conspiracy and the Paranoid Style* (Baton Rouge, Louisiana State University Press, 1969)

Dew, Charles B., *Apostles of Disunion: Southern Secession Commissioners and the Causes of the Civil War* (Charlottesville, University Press of Virginia, 2001)

Fox-Genovese, Elizabeth and Eugene D. Genovese, "Yeoman Farmers in a Slaveholders' Democracy," in *Fruits of Merchant Capital: Slavery and Bourgeois Property in the Rise and Expansion of Capitalism* (New York, Oxford University Press, 1983)

McCardell, John, *The Idea of a Southern Nation: Southern Nationalists and Southern Nationalism, 1830–1860* (New York, W.W. Norton, 1979)

McPherson, James M., *Battle Cry of Freedom: The Civil War Era* (New York, Oxford University Press, 1988)

Noll, Mark A., "The Bible and Slavery," in Randall M. Miller, Harry S. Stout and Charles Reagan Wilson (eds), *Religion and the American Civil War* (New York, Oxford University Press, 1998) pp.43–73

Olsen, Otto, "Historians and the Extent of Slave Ownership in the Southern United States," in *Civil War History*, 50 (December 2004) pp.401–17

Potter, David. *The Impending Crisis, 1848–1861* (New York, Harper & Row, 1976)

Richards, Leonard L., *The Slave Power: The Free North and Southern Domination, 1790–1860* (Baton Rouge, Louisiana State University Press, 2000)

Wilson, Henry, *History of the Rise and Fall of the Slave Power in the United States* (1872; repr. New York, Negro Universities Press, 1969)

I would not be master

Carwardine, Richard, *Lincoln: A Life of Purpose and Power* (New York, Alfred A. Knopf, 2006)

Cooper, William J. Jr, *Jefferson Davis, American* (New York, Alfred A. Knopf, 2000)

Donald, David Herbert, *Lincoln* (New York, Simon and Schuster, 1995)

Escott, Paul D., *After Secession: Jefferson Davis and the Failure of Confederate Nationalism* (Baton Rouge, Louisiana State University Press, 1978)

Guelzo, Allen C., *Abraham Lincoln: Redeemer President* (Grand Rapids, William B. Eerdmans Publishing Co., 1999)

Hattaway, Herman and Richard E. Beringer, *Jefferson Davis, Confederate President* (Lawrence, University Press of Kansas, 2002)

Neely, Mark E., "Abraham Lincoln vs. Jefferson Davis: Comparing Presidential Leadership in the Civil War," in James M. McPherson and William J. Cooper, Jr (eds), *Writing the Civil War: The Quest to Understand* (Columbia, University of South Carolina Press, 1998)

Potter, David M., "Jefferson Davis and the Political Factors in Confederate Defeat," in David Herbert Donald (ed.), *Why the North Won the Civil War* (Baton Rouge, Louisiana State University Press, 1960)

Rable, George C., *The Confederate Republic: A Revolution Against Politics* (Chapel Hill, University of North Carolina Press, 1994)

Shaw Paludan, Phillip, *The Presidency of Abraham Lincoln* (Lawrence, University Press of Kansas, 1994)

Thomas, Emory M., *The Confederate Nation: 1861–1865* (New York, Harper & Row, 1979)

Williams, T. Harry, *Lincoln and His Generals* (New York, Alfred A. Knopf, 1952)

Woodworth, Stephen E., *Jefferson Davis and His Generals: The Failure of Confederate Command in the West* (Lawrence, University Press of Kansas, 1990)

The power of the land

Davis, William C. (ed.), *The Confederate General*, 6 vols (Harrisburg, National Historical Society, c.1991)

Glatthaar, Joseph T., *Partners in Command: The Relationships between Leaders in the Civil War* (New York, Free Press, 1994)

Goss, Thomas J., *The War Within the Union High Command: Politics and Generalship during the Civil War* (Lawrence, University Press of Kansas, 2003)

Krick, Robert K., *Stonewall Jackson at Cedar Mountain* (Chapel Hill, University of North Carolina Press, 1990)

McMurry, Richard M., *Two Great Rebel Armies* (Chapel Hill, University of North Carolina Press, 1989)

Military Analysis of the Civil War: An Anthology by the Editors of Military Affairs (New York, KTO Press, 1977)

Warner, Ezra J., *Generals in Blue, Lives of the Union Commanders* (Baton Rouge, Louisiana State University Press, 1964)

Our hearts were touched with fire

Griffith, Paddy, *Battle Tactics of the Civil War* (New Haven, Yale University Press, 1989)

Higginson, Thomas Wentworth, *Army Life in a Black Regiment* (1869; repr. New York, Penguin, 1997)

Hinman, Wilbur F., *Corporal Si Klegg and his "Pard": How They Lived and Talked, and What They Did and Suffered, while Fighting for the Flag* (1889; repr. Ashburn, 1997)

Linderman, Gerald, *Embattled Courage: The Experience of Combat in the American Civil War* (New York, Free Press, 1987)

McPherson, James M., *For Cause & Comrades: Why Men Fought in the Civil War* (New York, Oxford University Press, 1997)

Mitchell, Reid, *Civil War Soldiers: Their Expectations and Their Experiences* (New York, Simon and Schuster, 1988)

Stern, Philip Van Doren, *Soldier Life in the Union and Confederate Armies* (New York, 1961)

Wiley, Bell I. *The Life of Johnny Reb: The Common Soldier of the Confederacy* and *The Life of Billy Yank: The Common Soldier of the Union* (Baton Rouge, 1943 and 1952)

Remorseless, revolutionary struggle

Förster, Stig, and Jörg Nagler (eds), *On the Road to Total War: The American Civil War and the German Wars of Unification, 1861–1871* (Washington, German Historical Institute; New York, Cambridge University Press, 1997)

Griffith, Paddy, *Battle Tactics of the Civil War* (New Haven, Yale University Press, 1989)

Grimsley, Mark, *The Hard Hand of War: Union Military Policy Toward Southern Civilians, 1861–1865* (New York, Cambridge University Press, 1995)

Hagerman, Edward, *The American Civil War and the Origins of Modern Warfare: Ideas, Organization, and Field Command* (Bloomington, Indiana University Press, 1988)

Hess, Earl J., *Field Armies and Fortifications in the Civil War: The Eastern Campaigns, 1861–1864* (Chapel Hill, University of North Carolina Press, 2005)

McWhiney, Grady, and Perry D. Jamieson, *Attack and Die: Civil War Military Tactics and the Southern Heritage* (Tuscaloosa, University of Alabama Press, 1982)

Nosworthy, Brent, *The Bloody Crucible of Courage: Fighting Methods and Combat Experience of the Civil War* (New York, Carroll and Graf, 2003)

Reid, Brian Holden, *The American Civil War and the Wars of the Industrial Revolution* (London, Cassell, 1999)

Royster, Charles, *The Destructive War: William Tecumseh Sherman, Stonewall Jackson, and the Americans* (New York, Alfred A. Knopf, 1991)

Uncle Sam's web-feet

Anderson, Bern, *By Sea and By River: The Naval History of the Civil War* (New York, Alfred A. Knopf, 1962)

Cooling, B. Franklin, *Forts Henry and Donelson: The Key to the Confederate Heartland* (Knoxville, University of Tennessee Press, 1987)

Davis, William C., *Duel between the First Ironclads* (Baton Rouge, Louisiana State University Press, 1975)

Luraghi, Raimondo, *A History of the Confederate Navy* (Annapolis, Naval Institute Press, 1996)

Musicant, Ivan, *Divided Waters: The Naval History of the Civil War* (New York, HarperCollins, 1995)

Roberts, William H., *Now for the Contest: Coastal and Oceanic Naval Operations in the Civil War* (Lincoln, University of Nebraska Press, 2004)

Scharf, J. Thomas, *The Confederate States Navy* (New York, Rogers & Sherwood, 1887)

Slagle, Jay, *Ironclad Captain: Seth Ledyard Philips and the U.S. Navy, 1841–1864* (Kent, Ohio, Kent State University Press, 1996)

Still, William N., Jr, *Iron Afloat: The Story of the Confederate Ironclads* (Nashville, Vanderbilt University Press, 1971)

Wise, Stephen R., *Lifeline of the Confederacy: Blockade Running during the Civil War* (Columbia, University of South Carolina Press, 1988)

They came to butcher our people

Christ, Mark K. (ed.), *Rugged and Sublime: The Civil War in Arkansas* (Fayetteville, University of Arkansas Press, 1994)

Fellman, Michael, *Inside War: The Guerilla Conflict in Missouri During the American Civil War* (New York, Oxford University Press, 1989)

Frazier, Donald S., *Blood and Treasure: Confederate Empire in the Southwest* (College Station, Texas A&M Press, 1995)

Goodrich, Thomas, *Black Flag: Guerilla Warfare on the Western Border, 1861–1865* (Bloomington, Indiana University Press, 1995)

Hauptman, Laurence M., *Between Two Fires: American Indians in the Civil War* (New York, Free Press, 1995)

Johnson, Ludwell H., *Red River Campaign: Politics and Cotton in the Civil War* (Baltimore, Johns Hopkins University Press, 1958; repr. Kent: Kent State University Press, 1993)

Josephy, Alvin M., Jr, *The Civil War in the American West* (New York, Random House, 1991)

Kerby, Robert L., *Kirby Smith's Confederacy: The Trans-Mississippi South, 1863–1865* (New York, Columbia University Press, 1972)

Knight, Wilfred, *Red Fox: Stand Watie's Civil War Years in Indian Territory* (Glendale, Arthur H. Clark Company, 1988)

Parrish, William E., *A History of Missouri: 1860–1875* (Columbia, University of Missouri, 1973)

Piston, William Garrett and Richard W. Hatcher III, *Wilson's Creek: The Second Battle of the Civil War and the Men Who Fought It* (Chapel Hill: University of North Carolina, 2000)

Prushankin, Jeffery S., *A Crisis in Confederate Command: Edmund Kirby Smith, Richard Taylor, and the Army of the Trans-Mississippi* (Baton Rouge, Louisiana State University Press, 2005)

Shea, William L. and Earl J. Hess, *Pea Ridge: Civil War Campaign in the West* (Chapel Hill, University of North Carolina Press, 1992)

Winters, John D., *The Civil War in Louisiana* (Baton Rouge, Louisiana State University Press, 1963)

Wooster, Ralph, *Texas and Texans in the Civil War* (Austin, Eakins Press, 1995)

That great essential of success

Blackman, Ann, *Wild Rose: Rose O'Neale Greenhow, Civil War Spy* (New York, Random House, 2005)

Canan, Howard, "Confederate Military Intelligence," in *Maryland Historical Magazine*, 59 (March 1964) pp.36–38

Dyer, Thomas G., *Secret Yankees: The Union Circle in Confederate Atlanta* (Baltimore, The Johns Hopkins University Press, 1999)

Feis, William B., *Grant's Secret Service: The Intelligence War from Belmont to Appomattox* (Lincoln, University of Nebraska Press, 2002)

Fishel, Edwin C., *The Secret War for the Union: The Untold Story of Military Intelligence in the Civil War* (New York, Houghton Mifflin, 1996)

Gaddy, David Winfred, "William Norris and the Confederate Signal and Secret Service," in *Maryland Historical Magazine*, 70 (Summer 1975) pp.167–88

Maslowski, Peter, "Military Intelligence Sources During the Civil War: A Case Study," in Lieutenant-Colonel Walter T. Hitchcock (ed.), *The Intelligence Revolution: A Historical Perspective* (Washington, DC, Government Printing Office, 1991)

Nelson, Larry E., *Bullets, Ballots, and Rhetoric: Confederate Policy for the United States Presidential Contest in 1864* (Tuscaloosa, University of Alabama Press, 1980)

O'Toole, G.J.A., *Honorable Treachery: A History of U.S. Intelligence, Espionage, and Covert Action from the American Revolution to the CIA* (New York, Atlantic Monthly Press, 1991)

Tidwell, William A., James O. Hall, and David Winfred Gaddy, *Come Retribution: The Confederate Secret Service and the Assassination of Abraham Lincoln* (Jackson, University Press of Mississippi, 1988)

Varon, Elizabeth R., *Southern Lady, Yankee Spy: The True Story of Elizabeth Van Lew, A Union Agent in the Heart of the Confederacy* (New York, Oxford University Press, 2003)

We never yielded in the struggle

Attie, Jeanie, *Patriotic Toil: Northern Women and the American Civil War* (London, Cornell University Press, 1998)

Bernstein, Iver, *The New York City Draft Riots: Their Significance for American Society and Politics in the Age of the Civil War* (New York, Oxford University Press, 1990)

Blair, William, *Virginia's Private War: Feeding Body and Soul in the Confederacy, 1861–1865* (New York, Oxford University Press, 1998)

Bynum, Victoria, *Unruly Women: The Politics of Social and Sexual Control in the Old South* (Chapel Hill, University of North Carolina, 1992)

Bynum, Victoria, *The Free State of Jones: Mississippi's Longest Civil War* (Chapel Hill, University of North Carolina, 2001)

Faust, Drew Gilpin, *Mothers of Invention: Women of the Slaveholding South in the American Civil War* (Chapel Hill, University of North Carolina Press, 1996)

Inscoe, John C., and Robert C. Kenzer, *Enemies of the Country: New Perspectives on Unionists In the Civil War South* (Athens, University of Georgia Press, 2001)

Paludan, Phillip Shaw, *"A People's Contest": The Union and Civil War, 1861–1865* (New York, Harper & Row, 1988)

Rable, George C., *Civil Wars: Women and the Crisis of Southern Nationalism* (Chicago, University of Illinois Press, 1989)

Whites, LeeAnn, *Gender Matters: Civil War, Reconstruction, and the Making of the New South* (New York: Palgrave Macmillan, 2005)

The world will forever applaud

Berlin, Ira, Barbara Jeanne Fields, Steven F. Miller, Joseph P. Reidy, and Leslie S. Rowland, *Free at Last: A Documentary History of Slavery, Freedom, and the Civil War* (New York, New Press, 1992)

Berlin, Ira et al., *Freedom: A Documentary History of Emancipation*, 4 vols to date, (Cambridge, Cambridge University Press, 1982–ongoing)

Cornish, Dudley Taylor, *The Sable Arm: Black Troops in the Union Army, 1861–1865*, rev. ed. (Lawrence, University Press of Kansas, 1987)

Cox, LaWanda, *Lincoln and Black Freedom: A Study in Presidential Leadership*, rev. ed. (Columbia, University of South Carolina Press, 1981)

Durden, Robert F. *The Gray and the Black: The Confederate Debate on Emancipation* (Baton Rouge, Louisiana State University Press, 1972)

Franklin, John Hope, *The Emancipation Proclamation*, rev. ed. (Wheeling, Harland Davidson, 1995)

Guelzo, Allen C., *Lincoln's Emancipation Proclamation: The End of Slavery in America* (New York, Simon and Schuster, 2004)

McPherson, James M. (ed.), *The Negro's Civil War: How American Negroes Felt and Acted during the War for the Union*, rev. ed. (Urbana, University of Illinois Press, 1982)

Robinson, Armstead L., *Bitter Fruits of Bondage: The Demise of Slavery and the Collapse of the Confederacy, 1861–1865* (Charlottesville, University of Virginia Press, 2005)

Vorenberg, Michael, *Final Freedom: The Civil War, the Abolition of Slavery, and the Thirteenth Amendment* (Cambridge, Cambridge University Press, 2001)

One great society

Blackburn, G., *French Newspaper Opinion on the American Civil War* (Westport, Greenwood Press, 1997)

Blackett, R.J.M., *Divided Hearts: Britain and the American Civil War* (Baton Rouge, Louisiana State University Press, 2001)

Case, L. and Spencer, W. *The United States and France: Civil War Diplomacy* (Philadelphia, University of Pennsylvania Press, 1970)

Crook, D.P., *The North, the South, and the Powers* (New York, John Wiley & Sons, 1974)

Ellison, M., *Support for Secession: Lancashire and the American Civil War* (Chicago, University of Chicago Press, 1972)

Ferris, N., *The Trent Affair: A Diplomatic Crisis* (Knoxville, University Press of Tennessee, 1977)

Hubbard, C., *The Burden of Confederate Diplomacy* (Knoxville, University Press of Tennessee, 1998)

Hyman, H. (ed.), *Heard Round the World: The Impact Abroad of the Civil War* (New York, Alfred A. Knopf, 1969)

Jenkins, B., *Britain and the War for the Union*, 2 vols (Montreal, McGill-Queens University Press, 1974, 1980)

Jones, H., *Union in Peril: The Crisis over British Intervention in the Civil War* (Chapel Hill, University of North Carolina Press, 1992)

Merli, F., *Great Britain and the Confederate Navy 1861–1865* (Bloomington, Indiana University Press, 1970)

Owsley, F., *King Cotton Diplomacy: Foreign Relations of the Confederate States of America* (Chicago, University of Chicago Press, 1959)

A fearful lesson

Blair, William, *Cities of the Dead: Contesting the Memory of the Civil War in the South, 1865–1914* (Chapel Hill, University of North Carolina Press, 2004)

Blight, David, *Race and Reunion: The Civil War in American Memory* (Cambridge, Harvard University Press, 2001)

Foster, Gaines, *Ghosts of the Confederacy: Defeat, the Lost Cause, and the Emergence of the New South, 1865–1913* (New York, Oxford University Press, 1988)

Goldfield, David, *Still Fighting the Civil War: The American South and Southern History* (Baton Rouge, Louisiana State University Press, 2002)

Grant, Susan-Mary and Peter J. Parish (eds), *Legacy of Disunion: The Enduring Significance of the American Civil War* (Baton Rouge: Louisiana State University Press, 2003)

Pollard, Edward A., *The Lost Cause* (1866; New York: Gramercy Books, 1994)

Reagan, Charles Wilson, *Baptized in Blood: The Religion of the Lost Cause, 1865–1920* (Athens: University of Georgia Press, 1983)

Silber, Nina, *The Romance of Reunion: Northerners and the South, 1865–1900* (Chapel Hill, University of North Carolina Press, 1993)

Warren, Arthur Penn, *The Legacy of the Civil War: Mediations on the Centennial* (New York, Random House, 1961)

INDEX

Figures in **Bold** in refer to illustrations

A

Adams, Charles Francis 52, 130
Adams, John Quincy 199
aerial reconnaissance 160, 161
African Americans
    attitude to the war 176–7
    in battle 16
    in Confederate armies 19, 95, 200, 214
    Confederate treatment of African
    American prisoners 144, 183–4, 208,
    212
    Fort Pillow Massacre (1864) 17
    and labor 240–1, **242**
    and New York City conscription riots
    (1863) 16, 186–7, **187**, 211
    postwar race relations 247, 249–50, 251
    soldiers' attitude to 94–5
    in Trans-Mississippi 134
    in Union armies 92, 94, 144, **198**,
    200–1, 206–7, **207**
    in US Navy 117
    and voting **238**, 239, 240
    see also emancipation; slaves and slavery
Agnew, Samuel Andrew 177
agriculture
    and African Americans **242**
    postwar 244
    Tax-in-Kind Law (1863) 16, 190
    wartime 185, 189
Alabama, CSS **112**, 130, 154, **216**, 226
Albemarle, CSS 127–8
Alden, Captain James 129
Alexander, Edward P. 161
Alexander, Edward Porter 73
Alexandra, CSS 227
Alexandria, Louisiana 143, 146, 147
Allatoona, Confederate attempt on (1864)
    18
American Civil War (1861–65)
    analogies with other conflicts 98–100
    causes and origins 10–11, 14, 21–39
    chronology 14–19
    European public opinion 221–5
    influence on later wars 111
    legacies 12–13, 99, 233–53
    northern expectations of early win 204
    peace negotiations 19
    reasons for North's win 11–12, 131
American Revolution (1775–83) 98, 197
Amnesty and Reconstruction,
    Proclamation of (1863) 17, 144
Anaconda Plan 14, 72, 114, **116**
Anderson, Jourdon 241
Anderson, William ("Bloody Bill") 18, 138

Antietam, battle of (1862) 15, **53**, 75, 86,
    164
Appomattox Court House: Confederate
    surrender (1865) 19, 130
Arizona 138
Arkansas 45, 135, 140–3
Armistead, Lewis A. **66**
artillery
    at Fredericksburg (1862) **74**
    impact on the war 104
    naval 118
    Union advantage 73
Atlanta
    battle of (1864) 18
    campaign (1864) 17–18, 168–9
    fall of (1864) 18, 56, **108**
atrocities *see* brutality and atrocities
Averasborough, battle of (1865) 19

B

Babcock, John C. **164**, 165
Bailey, Colonel Joseph 146–7
Baker, Lafayette C. 156–7
balloons, reconnaissance **160**, 161
banking 16, 229
Banks, Nathaniel P. 16, 17, 145–7, **145**
Barlow, General Francis Channing **73**
Barnard, George N.: photos by **106**
Battery Wagner, Union assault on (1863)
    94–5
battle style, sights, and sounds 87–91, **88**,
    89
battlefield maintenance 253
Baylor, John 138
Beaman, John 178, 189, 191
Beaman, Malinda Cranford 178, 191
Beauregard, General P.G.T. 170
Beecher, Henry Ward 38
Beefsteak Raid (1864) 18
Bell, Charles S. 169
Bellows, Henry Whitney 180–1
benevolent work 180–4
Benjamin, Judah P. 51, 227
Bennett, Michael 117
Bentonville, battle of (1865) 19
Bermuda Hundred signal tower **159**
Bierce, Ambrose 89–90
Big Bethel: earthworks at 105
Big Black River, battle of (1863) 16
Billings, John D. 255
Bird Creek, battle of (1861) 148
The Birth of a Nation (film) 250, **251**
Bismarck, Otto von 235
Blackwell, Dr. Elizabeth 180
Blair, Francis 135
Blair, Montgomery 205, 206

Blunt, James G. 142, 149, 150, **150**
BMI *see* Bureau of Military Intelligence
Bond, Brian 111
Booth, John Wilkes 155–6, 157
Boston, John and Elizabeth 200
Bourlier, Émile 169
Bowser, Mary Elizabeth 165
Boyd, Belle 154, 157, 170
Boydton Plank Road, fighting at (1864) 18
Bragg, Braxton 17, 71, 86–7, 163
Branch, Charlotte 175, 193
Brandy Station, battle of (1863) 16
Bristoe Station, battle of (1863) 17
Brooklyn, USS 129
Brown, James G. 168
Brown, John 195–6, **197**
    and Harpers Ferry (1859) 14, 22, 23,
    38, 195, 197
    and Pottawatomie Creek (1856) 33,
    134, 197
Brown, Joseph E. 52
Brownsville, Union capture of (1863) 144
brutality and atrocities 91–5, 137–8, 144,
    150
Buchanan, Flag Officer Franklin 126, 129
Buchanan, James 34–6, **34**
Buckner, General Simon Bolivar, Jr. 77
Buell, Don Carlos 15, 71, 93
Buena Vista, battle of (1847) 64
Buffalo Bill *see* Cody, William
Bull Run, battles of (1861 and 1862) *see*
    Manassas, first battle of; Manassas,
    second battle of
Bulloch, James D. 130, 154, 157, 226–7
Bureau of Military Intelligence (BMI)
    164–7, **164**, 172–3
Burgess' Mill, battle of (1864) 18
Burns, Anthony 35, 36, **37**
Burnside, Ambrose E. 15, 16–17, 69–71,
    87, 164–5
Bushwhackers 137
Butler, General Benjamin F. 19, 117, 201

C

Calhoun, John C. 14, 24
California 14, 138, 140
Callender, William 160–1
Camp Andersonville 92–3
Camp Jackson affair (1861) 14
camps, prison 92–3
Canada
    Confederate covert actions in 154–5
    spies in 169
Canby, Edward R.S. 19, 139, **139**, 148
Caribbean 231
Carleton, James 140

Carolinas campaign (1865) 19, 111
Carondelet, USS **122**, 123
Carpenter, Francis B.: paintings by **206**
Carter, Howard 173
Carter, Sue 179
casualties
    at Cold Harbor (1864) 90
    from disease 86
    at Gettysburg (1863) 90
    officers 66–7
    Red River campaign (1864) 146
    at Wilderness (1864) 87
Catton, Bruce 101
cavalry
    Cavalry of the West 145
    Confederate Iron Brigade 142
    and military intelligence 171–2
    popularity 62
    southern initial superiority 73
    Union cavalry weapons 104
Cedar Creek, battle of (1864) 18
Cedar Mountain, battle of (1862) 15
Centralia Massacre (1864) 18, 138
ceremonies
    flag presentation 81–2
    muster into national service 81
Chaffin's Bluff, fighting at (1864) 18
Chamberlain, Colonel Joshua Lawrence
    76–7, 91
Chambersburg
    burning of (1864) 93
    and Gettysburg (1863) 178
Champion's Hill, battle of (1863) 16
Chancellorsville, battle of (1863) 16
    battle style 111
    company strength 63
    Confederate reunion after **96**
    earthworks at 106
    Jackson at 87
    terrain 75
Chaplin Hills, battle of (1862) *see* Perryville,
    battle of
charging tactics 103
Charleston, Union capture of (1865) 19,
    212
Chase, Salmon P. 51, 205, 206
Chattanooga
    campaign (1863) 16–17
    siege of (1863) 17
Chew, R. Preston 73
Chickamauga, battle of (1863) 17, 61, 75,
    76, **76**, 87
China: Tai-ping Rebellion (1851–64) 98
Chivington, Major Thomas 140
Christian, Colonel Thomas Jonathan
    Jackson, Jr 77
ciphers 161–2
City Point supply depot 155

civilians
    soldiers' treatment of 93–4, 98, 107–11,
    108–10, 137, 182–3
    see also home front
class issues 176–7, 185–6, 189–90, 193
Clay, Clement C. 154
Cleburne, General Patrick 18, 95
clothing *see* uniforms and clothing
Cobb, Howell 95
codes 161–2
Cody, William ("Buffalo Bill") 138
coffee 84
Cold Harbor, battle of (1864) 17, 90
Cole, Henry 169
Coleman's Scouts 172
Colonel Lamb **120**
Colorado 138–40
Columbia, Union capture of (1865) 19
Columbus, Confederate occupation of
    (1861) 46
commerce raiding 113, 114, 130–1
Compromise of 1850 14, 31–2
Confederacy
    British consider recognition of 48, 232
    constitution 43
    covert actions 154–6
    Declaration of Secession 22
    European ambassadors to 227
    expansionist ambitions 13
    finances 47, 51, 229
    government evacuates Richmond 19
    government moves to Richmond 14
    government team 51–2
    organizations to celebrate 246–7
    president and vice-president elected 14,
    15
    spies 160–3
    spies in Confederate White House 165
    surrender 19, 130, 151
    see also South and Southerners
Confederate forces
    brigade organization 82
    command structure 52
    logistics 67
    mobilization 50
    navy
      operations 126–7, 128–31
      technological innovations 125–9
    officer selection 64–6
    size 49–50, 61–2, 100
Confederate forces: sub-units
    26th North Carolina 90
    Army of New Mexico 138–40
    Army of North Virginia 64, 105, 172
    Army of the Tennessee 88
    Army of the Trans-Mississippi 142
    Cavalry of the West 145
    Hill's Light Division 86

Stonewall Brigade 82
Confiscation Acts
    First (1861) 15, 201–2
    Second (1862) 15, 202–3
Congress, USS 126
Conklin, James C. 113
Conrad, Thomas Nelson 155
conscription 15, 16, 50, 64–5, 93–4, 100,
    185–6
    exemptions 184–6, 189–90
    riots against (1863) 16, 186–7, **187**, 211
Constitution: antislavery amendments 16,
    239, 240
Cooper, Douglas 148
Corinth
    battle of (1862) 15
    Confederate evacuation (1862) 15
Cormany, Rachel 177, 178, 183
Cormany, Samuel 178
Corporal Si Klegg and His "Pard" (Hinman)
    83, **84**
Corwin, Thomas 199
cotton growing **20**, 25, 28, **28**, 196–7
    blockade's effects 47–8, 219, 223, 225,
    228, 229–30, 234
    Trans-Mississippi Cotton Bureau 144,
    147
    Union attacks on 145–6
Courtenay, Thomas E. 155
covert actions 154–7
Crater, Battle of the (1864) 18
Crittenden, John J. 199–200
Crittenden-Johnson Resolutions (1861) 14
Cross Keys, battle of (1862) 15
cultural attitudes
    postwar 245–7
    prewar 12, 24–7, 43
Cumberland, USS 126
Currier and Ives lithographs **210**
Curtis, General Samuel 140–2, 151
Cushing, William B. 256
Cushman, Pauline 168
Custer, George Armstrong 76

D

Dahlgren, John 166
Dahlgren, Ulric 166
daily life: soldiers 83–7
Dallas, Georgia, fighting around (1864) 17
Darbytown Road, fighting at (1864) 18
Davidson, J.O.: paintings by **128**
Davis, Annie 212
Davis, Jefferson **43**, **44**, **48**, **58**
    and administration 51
    and African American conscription 214
    as communicator 56–9

elected president of South 11, 14, 15
inauguration **40**
and Lincoln's assassination 155–6
memoirs 248, 249
and Mexican-American War (1846–48) 64
personality 53–4
and prewar debt repudiation 229
and Scott 72
and transcontinental railroad 243
and Trans-Mississippi 134
Union capture of 19
as war leader 12, 41–59, 64
Davis, Sam 168, 170–1
Dayton, William 227
Declaration of Paris (1856) 225–6
Delaware 45, 204, 212, 215
democracy
European debate about US 219–21, 239–40
US's influence abroad 234–5
Democratic Party
beliefs and style 41
and Lincoln's conduct of war 54, 186
and Lincoln's second-term election 154–5, 207
power in South 22–3
and slavery 207, 208
deserters 191–2
diet *see* food
Dinwiddie Court House, fighting around (1865) 19
diplomatic relations *see* foreign relations
discipline 65
Disraeli, Benjamin 235
Dix, Dorothea 180
Dodge, Brigadier-General Grenville M. 168, 169, 170
Douglas, Stephen A. 10, 14, 32–3, 34–6, **34**, 243
Douglass, Frederick 197
Dowling, Lieutenant Dick 144
Dred Scott decision (1857) 14, 31, 33–4
Drewry Bluff **68**
Du Pont, Flag Officer Samuel F. 15, 118, 119
DuBois, W.E.B. 249–50
Dudley, Thomas Haines 157
Dunmore, Lord 197

E

Early, Jubal 18, 19, 167
earthworks *see* fieldworks
eastern theater **70**
operations 69–71

terrain 68–9
economics and economies
as cause of the war 24
commerce raiding 113, 114, 130–1
emancipation's effect 243–4
northern economic warfare on South 47–8, 107–11, 114–21, 225–6, 229–30
northern wartime economy 50, 185
prewar regional economies 24–7, 44
southern economy 47, 51
war's impact on Europe 228–30, 234
war's impact on USA 243–4, **246**
see also industry; trade
Elkhorn Tavern, battle of (1862) *see* Pea Ridge, battle of
emancipation 195–215, 238–9
abolition of Atlantic slave trade 196
abolition passes into law 19, 214, 239, 240
boost from enlistment of African Americans 94–5
compensation to slaveowners 203
in DC 203
economic effect 243–4
Emancipation Proclamations (1862 and 1863) 15, 16, **194**, 205, **206**, 207–11
European attitude 223–4
freedmen in South **202**
Frémont's proclamation 46, 137, 204
Lincoln's plans for freed slaves 203, 205–7
slaves' reaction **213**
see also African Americans; slaves and slavery
equipment 86
espionage *see* spies
Europe, and the war 217–35
diplomatic relations 46–8, 52, 225–7, 231–3
economic relations 228–30
public opinion 221–5
the war's legacy 233–5
see also France; Great Britain
Ewell, Richard S. 72
Ewing, Thomas 137
Ezra Church, attack at (1864) 18

F

Fair Oaks, battle of (1862) *see* Seven Pines, battle of
Farragut, David Glasgow 18, 125, 128–9
fieldworks 105–7, **105**, **106**
films 250–2
Fisher's Hill, battle of (1864) 18, 167
Five Forks, battle of (1865) 19
flags: significance 81–2

Florida: joins Union 14
Florida, CSS 226
Foner, Eric 240
food 83–4
Foote, Flag Officer Andrew Hull 123
Forbes, Edwin: paintings by **82**, **83**
Ford, John "Rip" 144, 148
foreign relations 46–8, 52, 217–35
formations, military 81
Forrest, General Nathan Bedford 15, 17, 73, 172
Forrest, General Nathan Bedford III 77
Fort Beauregard, Union capture of (1861) 118
Fort Craig, Confederate attempt on (1862) 138–9
Fort Donelson, battle of (1862) 15, 77, 91, 121, 123
Fort Fisher, fighting around (1864–65) 19
Fort Gibson, Union capture of (1863) 150
Fort Harrison, fighting at (1864) 18
Fort Henry, Union capture of (1862) 15, 121, 122–3
Fort Hindman, Union capture of (1863) 16
Fort McAllister, Union capture of (1864) 18
Fort Pillow Massacre (1864) 17
Fort Stedman, attack on (1865) 19
Fort Sumter, Confederate capture of (1861) 14, 45
Fort Wagner, Union attack on (1863) 16
Fort Walker, Union capture of (1861) 118, **119**
fortifications, field *see* fieldworks
France
and cotton 234
diplomatic relations with US 219
French Revolution (1789–99) 99–100
in Mexico 145, 231, 233
Paris Commune 98
trade with US 219
and the war 147, 211, 222, 225, 227, 232–3
economic impacts 230
the war's legacy 234, 235
Franco-Prussian War (1870–71) 111
Franklin, battle of (1864) 18, 87
Franklin, William 146
Frayser's Hill, battle of (1862) *see* Glendale, battle of
Fredericksburg, battle of (1862) 16, **74**
aftermath 106
Confederate memories of 255
Lincoln on 49–50
Marye's Heights assault 61, 87
Union use of false intelligence 161–2

and USCC **183**
Fredericksburg, Union raid on (1865) 165
Free Soil Party 14
Free State of Jones 191
Frémont, John C. 14, 46, 136–7, 204
French Revolution (1789–99) 99–100
Front Royal, battle of (1862) 15, 170

G

Gag Resolution (1836) 14, 31
Gaines's Mill, battle of (1862) 15
Garrison, William Lloyd 14, 36
gender, and the war *see* women
Georgia, CSS 226
German unification 111, 235
Gettysburg, battle of (1863) 16
    50th anniversary reunion **94**
    attack on wounded after 93
    casualties 90
    civilian experiences of 178, 182–3
    Culp's Hill 61
    earthworks at 106
    Jackson's absence 76
    Little Round Top 75, 91
    and military intelligence 167, 171, 172
    Pickett's Charge **66**, 81–2, 87, 103–4
Gettysburg Address 10, 17, **241**
Gettysburg campaign (1863) 166, 171, 172
Gladstone, William 224, 232
Glendale, battle of (1862) 15
Glorieta Pass, battle of (1862) 14, 139–40
Glory (film) 251
Goldsboro, Union occupation of (1865) 19
Gone With the Wind (film) 250–1, **252**
Gordon, General John B. 73
Gorgas, Josiah 67
Grady, Henry 246
Grant, General Ulysses S.
    and Confederate surrender 19
    and Fort Donelson (1862) 122–3
    and fortifications 107
    military appointments 17, 92
    and military intelligence 162, 163, 165, 168, 169
    and peace negotiations 19
    reputation 46
    and Vicksburg campaign (1863) 16, 71, 111, 125
    on the war's lessons 237, 243
    in western theater 168
Great Britain
    power conflicts with US 219
    Reform Act of 1867 234–5
    trade with US 218–19
    Union and Confederate ambassadors to 52

and the war 47–8, 130, 154, 211, 217, 222–7, 231–3
    economic impacts 228–30
Greeley, Horace 207, 233
Greenhow, Rose O'Neal 154 157, **169**, 170
Grierson, Benjamin 16
Griffith, D.W. 250
Griffith, Paddy 104

H

H.L. Hunley 129, **129**
Halleck, Henry W. 15, 71, 137
Hampton, General Wade 73
Hampton Roads, battle of (1862) 15, 126–7
Hancock, Cornelia 183–4, 193
Hancock, Winfield S. 104
Hardee, William J. 19
hardtack 84
Harpers Ferry
    raid (1859) 14, 22, 23, 38, 195, 197
    Union surrender of (1862) 91
Harrison, Henry T. 171, 172
Hartford, USS 129
Hatcher's Run, battle of (1865) 19
Hatteras, USS 130
Hay, John 51
Hays, Brigadier-General Alexander 81–2
Helena, fall of (1862) 141–2
Hensal, James A. **152**, 160
Henson, Robby 251
Herron, Francis 142
Hill, A.P. 86
Hindman, General Thomas C. 142–3, **142**
Hine, Sarah L. 175, 193
Hines, Thomas 154
Hinman, General Wilbur F. 83, 84
Hodges, Albert 44
Holly Springs raid (1862) 16
Holmes, Oliver Wendell, Jr 79, 91
Holmes, General Theophilus 142
Holt, Edwin M. 189
Holt, Joseph 156
Holt, Samuel L. 190
home front 175–93
    class distinctions 176–7, 185–6, 189–90, 193
    protest and dissent 16, 186–92
    war work 179–84, **179**, **181**, **183**
    women's role 175, 177–84, **179**, **181**, **183**
Homer, Winslow: paintings by **92**
Homestead Bill (1862) 15
Honey Spring, battle of (1863) 150
Hood, John Bell 18, 19, 71, 87
Hood, John H.G.: paintings by **152**

Hooker, Joseph
    campaigns 17, 69–71, 161
    and insignia 82
    military appointments 16
    and military intelligence 161, 164–5
Housatonic, USS 129
Houser, Mollie 177–8, 192
Houston, Sam 135
Hulin, Caroline 191
Hulin, Jesse 192
Hulin, John 192
Hulin, William 192
Hunley, CSS 256
Hunt, General Henry J. 73
Hunter, General David 204, 206
Hunter, Sherod 140
hygiene 85–6

I

immigration 218, 228
Indian Territory
    population 134
    war in 148–51
Indians, Native American
    in Confederate armies 141, 144, **147**, 148–51
    in Union armies 149, 150
    the war's legacy 243
industry 25, 101, 185
    shipbuilding 115–16, 125–6, 127–8, 130, 154, 157, 226–7
    the war's legacy 240, 242, 244
    see also cotton growing; trade
infantry, use of mounted 74–5
Ingalls, James 137
insignia 82
intelligence war 153–73
    covert actions 154–7
    military intelligence 157–73
international law, and the war 225–7
Intrepid **160**
Ireland, recruitment in 227
Island Number 10, Union capture of (1862) 121, 123, **124**
Iuka, battle of (1862) 15

J

J.R. Williams, USS 150
Jackson, Andrew 24, 31
Jackson, Claiborne 135, 136
Jackson, General Thomas Jonathan ("Stonewall")
    at Chancellorsville (1863) 87
    death 16, 75–6

descendants 77
and Shenandoah Valley campaign
(1862) 15, 170
Jackson, engagement at (1863) 16
James, Frank and Jesse 138
Jayhawkers 138
Jefferson, Thomas 28–9
Jefferson City, Union capture of (1861)
136
Jenkins Ferry, battle of (1864) 146
Jenkins Ferry Massacre (1864) 144
Jennison, Dr. Charles 137
Johnson, Andrew 57, 215
Johnson, Hannah 212
Johnston, Albert Sidney 14, 75, **77**, 140
Johnston, Joseph E.
and Carolinas campaign (1865) 19
Davis's confidence in 52
military appointments 16, 17, 18
and peace negotiations 19
strategy 65
and western theater 71
Jomini, Antoine Henri 61
Jonesboro, battle of (1864) 18
Jordan, Captain Thomas 170
Judd, Clara 170–1

K

Kansas
Lawrence riots (1856) **32**, 33, 134
"slavery" wars 33, 197
and the war 134–5, 136–8
Kansas–Nebraska Act (1854) 14, 32, 33
Kearny, General Phil 75
Kearsage, USS 130, **216**
Kearsey, Archibald 177
Kennesaw mountain, Union assault on
(1864) 18, **106**
Kentucky
Bragg's invasion (1862) 15
emancipation in 212, 215
guerrilla warfare 93, 108
neutrality period 14, 45
Polk's invasion (1861) 46
strategic importance 45
Kernstown, second battle of (1864) 18
Kidd, James 84
King, Carrie 168–9
Knight, Newt 191, **191**
Knight Company 191
Knoxville
battle of (1863) 17, 61
campaign (1863) 16–17
Ku Klux Klan 249, 250
Kunstler, Mort: paintings by **96**

L

labor: postwar model 240–1
Lake Erie 155
Lamon, Marshal **53**
Lane, James 137, 206
Lawrence
raid (1863) 16, 108, 137
riots (1856) **32**, 33, 134
leadership
military 11–12, 52, 61–77
presidential 12, 41–59
Lee, Ang 251
Lee, Fitzhugh 65
Lee, Robert E. **60, 249**
abilities 71
after Chancellorsville (1863) **96**
and Confederate surrender 19
and defense of Richmond 65
and defense of southern coastline
118–19
in eastern theater 69–71
experience 61
and Gettysburg (1863) 172
on Jackson 76
and Maryland campaign (1862) 164
military appointments 15, 19, 65
and military intelligence 161–2, 163,
164, 171, 172, 173
nickname 75
on Pelham 74
popularity 82
Scott on 72
and slavery 214
and strategy 49, 65
Leetown, battle of (1862) 140
Legal Tender Act (1862) 15, 229
letters
as intelligence source 162–3
women's 177–9, 187
Lewis, Sir George Cornwall 232
Lhuys, Drouyn de 227
The Liberator (newspaper) 14
lice 85
Lincoln, Abraham **48, 53, 55, 57, 58, 206,
210, 213, 224**
and administration 51
assassination 19, 95, 155–6
background 101
centralizing tendencies 241
as communicator 54–6
and Confederate attack on Washington
(1864) 18
on democracy 41
and Douglas 10, 14
First Annual Message 5
First Inaugural Address 21, 239

first-term election 10–11, 14, 38–9, 135
Gettysburg Address 10, 17
"house divided" speech 33–6
kidnap attempt 155
and Meade 76, 77
and Mexican-American War (1846–48)
31
and military intelligence 163
and naval war 113, 114–15, 125
and peace negotiations 19
personality 53–4
popularity 44–5
and reunion 239
Second Inaugural Address 19, 21, 90,
196
second-term election 17, 18, 53, 56,
154–5
and slavery 10, 11, 38, 195, 196, 197,
199–200, 203–14
and Trans-Mississippi 134
as war leader 12, 41–59
on war's conduct 97
Livermore, Mary 180
Logan, General John A. 73
Logan's Cross Roads, battle of (1862) *see*
Mill Springs, battle of
logistics 67, 101, 102, 111
Longstreet, General James 17, 171
Lookout Mountain, Union capture of
(1863) 17
Lost Cause 248–50
Louisiana 135, 143–4, 145–8
Louisville, Bragg's attempt on (1862) 86–7
Lowe, Thaddeus S.C. **160**, 161
Lowry, Colonel Robert 191
Lyman, Theodore 107
Lyon, Nathaniel 46, 135–6, **137**
Lyons, Lord 231

M

McClellan, General George B.
background 101
campaigns 69, 105, 164, 172
on Confederates 99
military appointments 15, 164
and military intelligence 157, 159, 163,
164
nominated for president 18, **58**
popularity 82–3
on power as a general 61
reputation 46
and strategy 49
and treatment of civilians 93, 107–8
McClernand, John 15

McCulloch, General Ben 140
McDowell, battle of (1862) 15
McElroy, John 255
McEntee, Captain John **164**, 165
McGuire, Judith Brockenbrough 177, 182
McIntosh, James 148
McMillan, Colonel Robert 255
McPheeters, William 133, 146
McPherson, James B. 17, 18
Magruder, John 144
Mahan, Dennis Hart 105–6
Mallory, Stephen 51, 125–6, **126**, 154
Manassas
  first battle of (1861) 14, 89, 157, 169, 170
  second battle of (1862) 15, 111, 171
  terrain 87
Manchester, England **228**
Manet, Édouard: paintings by **216**
Mann, Horace 26
Mansfield, battle of (1864) 146
manufacturing *see* industry
Marblehead, USS **117**
March to the Sea (1864) 18, 93
marching 86–7
marksmanship 81
marriage, war's effect on 177–8
Maryland 45–6, 164, 212
Mason, James 52, 232
Maximilian, Archduke 233
Meade, George Gordon **77**
  and Gettysburg (1863) 71, 76, 167
  and Lincoln 54
  military appointments 16
  reputation 76, 77
  skirmishing in South (1863) 17
Mechanicsville, battle of (1862) 15, 172
medicine
  nursing 179–84, **179**, **181**, **183**
  spread of disease 86
Melville, Herman 245
Memminger, Christopher 51
memoirs and memorials 95
Memphis, Confederate surrender of (1862) 15
Meridian campaign (1864) 17
Mexican-American War (1846–48) 14, 30, 31, 64, 72
Mexico 14, 145, 231, 233
military organization *see* organization, military
Mill Springs, battle of (1862) 15
Milledgville, Union capture of (1864) 18
Milliken's Bend, Confederate attack on (1863) 16, 144
Mine Run, battle of (1863) 17
mines *see* torpedoes

Missionary Ridge, storming of (1863) 17, 75, 76, **76**
Mississippi 191, 212–14, 229
Missouri
  guerrilla warfare 93, 108, 137–8
  strategic importance 45, 46
  and the war 134, 135–8, 140–1, 147
Missouri Compromise (1820) 14, 32
Mobile
  attack on (1865) 19, 139
  fall of (1865) 19
Mobile Bay, battle of (1864) 18, 128–9, **128**
mobilization and recruitment 49–51, 79–80
  exemptions from military service 184–6, 189–90
  Ireland 227
  see also conscription
Moltke, Helmuth von 97–8, **98**, 100, 102
money
  "greenbacks" 15, 229
  National Banking Act (1863) 16, 229
  southern inflation 47, 51
  war's effect on capital markets 228–9
  see also economics and economies
Monitor, USS 15, 126, **127**, 256
Monocacy, battle of (1864) 18
Moore, Thomas 135
Morgan, General John Hunt 170
Morrill Tariff 223, 230
Mosby, Colonel John S. 110, 172
motivation and morale: soldiers 90–1
Munfordville, battle of (1862) 15
Murfreesboro
  battle of (1862) 16, 75
  raid (1862) 15
Myer, Major Albert 161

N

Napoleon Bonaparte: influence 102
Napoleon III, Emperor 145, 222, 226, 227, 231, 232–3
Nashville
  battle of (1864) 88
  Buell's capture (1862) 15
  siege of (1864) 18
  Union occupation and spies 168, 171
National Detective Bureau 156–7
naval war 113–31
  commerce raiding 113, 114, 130–1
  control of waters 68–9
  Red River campaign (1864) 17, **69**, 145–7
  river war 121–5
  technological innovations 125–9
  Union blockade 47–8, 114–21, 225–6, 229–30

Nebraska: Kansas–Nebraska Act (1854) 14, 32, 33
New Jersey, and slavery 196, 215
New Market, battle of (1864) 17
New Market Heights, fighting at (1864) 18
New Mexico 138–40
New Orleans
  Confederate plans to relieve (1863) 143
  Union capture of (1862) 15, 125
New York City: conscription riots (1863) 16, 186–7, **187**, 211
newspapers: as intelligence source 162–3
Noll, Mark A. 29
Norris, Major William 155, 162
North and northerners
  attitude to the war 44–5, 186–7
  ethnic mix 44
  postwar economy 244
  prewar situation and economy 25–7, 44
  protest and dissent 186–7, 211
  shipbuilding 115–16
  wartime economy 50, 185
North Anna River, battle of the (1864) 17
North Carolina 45, 191–2
Northrop, Lucius B. 67
Northwest Conspiracy (1864) 154–5
nursing 179–84, **179**, **181**, **183**

O

Oak Hills, battle of (1861) *see* Wilson's Creek, battle of
officers 61–77
  abilities of individual 69–72
  average age 64
  casualties 66–7
  loyalty to 75–6, 82
  nicknames 75
  selection 64–6, 80
  training and experience 63–4, 72–3, 80
  US Navy 116–17
Oliver, Lieutenant Paul **164**
Olsen, Otto 27
Opothleyahola, Chief 148
Orchard Knob, Union capture of (1863) 17
organization, military 62–3, 80, 82
  Trans-Mississippi 134
Osliaba 221
Overland campaign (1864) 87, 107
Overton, Martin 191

P

Palmerston, Lord 232, **232**
Palmito Ranch, battle of (1865) 19, 148
Paris Commune 98

Partisan Rangers 110
Pea Ridge, battle of (1862) 15, **132**, 140–1
Peachtree Creek, battle of (1864) 18
Pegram, Willie 73
Pelham, Major John 73, **74**
Pemberton, John C. 16
Peninsula campaign (1862) 163–4
Perryville, battle of (1862) 15
Petersburg, battles around (1864) 18
Pharaoh's Army (film) 251–2
Phillips, William 150
Pickett, Major-General George 167
Pickett's Charge (Gettysburg, 1863) **66**,
    81–2, 87, 103–4
Piedmont, battle of (1864) 17
Pierce, Franklin 34–6, **34**
Pike, Albert 148
Pikes Peakers 139–40
Pillow, Gideon 14
Pine Mountain, battle of (1864) 18
Pinkerton, Allan **156**, 157, 163, 164, 165
Pittsburgh Landing, battle of (1862) *see*
    Shiloh, battle of
Plank, Elizabeth 182
Pleasant Hill, battle of (1864) 146
Plough, Annie 178
Plough, Jonathan 178
Poison Spring Massacre (1864) 144
Polignac, General Camille 147
politics
    19th-century election turnout 80
    democracy 219–21, 234–5, 239–40
    foreign relations 46–8, 52, 217–35
    war's political legacies 234–5, 241–2
    see also Democratic Party; Republican
    Party; Whig Party
Polk, James K. 30, 31
Polk, General Leonidas 18, 46
Pollard, Edward 248
Pook, Samuel 122
Pope, General John 69–71, 123, 171
population, prewar 25, 254
Port Gibson, battle of (1863) 16
Port Hudson, siege of (1863) 16, 125
Port Republic, battle of (1862) 15, 75
Port Royal Sound, Union capture of (1861)
    15, 118, **119**
Porter, Admiral David Dixon 16, 19, 69,
    123, 125, 145–7
Pottawatomie Creek 33, 134, 197
Potter, David 59
Prairie Grove, battle of (1862) 16, 142–3
press, Lincoln's use of 55
Price, Sterling 18, 135, 136, 140, 147–8
prisoners **166**
    Confederate treatment of African
    American 144, 183–4, 208, 212
    interrogation of 161, 166

treatment of 91–3
protest and dissent 186–92, 211
Proudhon, Pierre-Joseph 222
Prussian Army 97, 98, 111
Pryor, Sara Rice 187, 190-1

Q

Quantrill, William J. 16, 137-8
Queen, James Fuller: chromolithographs
    by **198**

R

railroads 101, **101**, 243
Raleigh, fall of (1865) 19
Randolph, George Wythe 143
Rankin, Oliver Smith 161
Ransom, Richard L. 244
Rappahannock Station, battle of (1863) 17
rations *see* food
Raymond, battle of (1863) 16
Reagan, John H. 51
Reagan, Ronald 27
Reams' Station, battle of (1864) 18
Reconstruction: Trans-Mississippi 151
recruitment *see* mobilization and
    recruitment
Red-Legs 137
Red River campaign (1864) 17, **69**, 145–7
reenactments **236**, 252–3
religion
    churches' attitude to slavery 29, 178
    Lincoln's use of churches 55–6
    as motivation for soldiers 90
Republican Party
    and labor 240
    origins 14
    and slavery 197, 208
    and USCC 180–1
    working-class resentment of 186
Resaca, battle of (1864) 17
Reynolds, General John F. 75
Rice, Spotswood 213
Rich Mountain: earthworks on 105
Richardson, Major John 172
Richmond, Kentucky, battle of (1862) 15,
    91
Richmond, Virginia
    bread riots (1863) 16, 187, **188**, 190
    fall of (1865) 19, **246**
    fighting around (1864) 18
    northern campaigns against 65, 165–6
    spies in 165–6
Ride With the Devil (film) 251–2
Rio Grande 144–5

rivers
    river war 121–5
    role 68–9, **69**
Roebuck, John 233
Rosecrans, Major-General William S. 15,
    16–17, 71, 168
Ross, John 148, 149
Round Mountain, battle of (1861) 148
Russell, Lord John 224, 226, 227, 232
Russell, William Howard 44, 221
Russia 219, **221**, 232, 234
Ruth, Samuel 165

S

Sabine Crossroads, battle of 17
Sabine Pass, battle of (1863) 17, 144
St Louis 135, 140, 147
Salomon, Frederick 149
San Domingo 231
San Jacinto, USS 15, 47, 232
Sanders, Sheriff Aaron H. 191, 192
Sanders, Romulus F. 191
Sanford, Henry 157
Santo Domingo 196
Savage Station, battle of (1862) 15
Savannah campaign (1864) 18, 111
Schofield, General John M. 18, 19, 142
Scott, Dred 14, 31, 33–4, **33**
Scott, General Winfield **43**, **72**
    and Anaconda Plan 14, 114
    background 72
    replaced as general-in-chief 15
    training manual 81
scouts **159**, 160–1, 167, 168, 169, 171–2,
    171
    see also intelligence war
Second Great Awakening 90
Sedgwick, John 75
Selznick, David O. 250
Semmes, Rear-Admiral Raphael 113, 130
Seneca Falls Convention (1848) 180
Seven Days battles (1862) 15, 161
Seven Pines, battle of (1862) 15
Seward, William Henry **38**
    and Emancipation Proclamation 205
    and Europe 46, 218, 231, 233
    and slavery 38
    and Union blockade 225
sharecroppers **242**
Sharpe, Colonel George H. **164**, 165, 167
Sharpsburg, battle of (1862) *see* Antietam,
    battle of
sharpshooters 73–4
Sheets, Martha Cranford 192
Shelby, Joseph 142
Shelton Laurel Massacre (1863) 93

Shenandoah, CSS 130, 227
Shenandoah Valley campaign (1862) 15, 170
Shenandoah Valley campaign (1864) 18, 72, 167
Sheridan, General Philip H. 71–2, 93, 98, 243
Sheridan's Scouts 153, 167
Sherman, General William Tecumseh
    abilities and achievements 71
    and Atlanta campaign (1864) 17–18, 56, 168–9
    on breech-loading arms 104
    and Carolinas campaign (1865) 19, 111
    at Chattanooga (1863) 17
    and Indian wars 243
    and logistics 111
    on Mahan 106
    March to the Sea (1864) 18, 93
    and Meridian campaign (1864) 17
    military appointments 17
    and military intelligence 168–9
    and Moltke 97, 98
    nickname 75
    and peace negotiations 19
    South's verdict on 246
    treatment of civilians 93
Shiloh, battle of (1862) 15, 75, 87, 89
ships
    90-day gunboats 116, **117**
    blockade runners **120**
    commerce raiders 130
    ironclads 12, **122**, 126–8, **127**
    monitors 127, **128**
    northern shipbuilding 115–16
    "Pook's turtles" 122, **122**
    southern shipbuilding 125–6, 127–8, 130, 154, 157, 226–7
Shreveport 145–6
Sibley, General Henry Hopkins 138–40
Signal and Secret Service Bureau 155, 162, 163, 171
signal towers **159**, 161
Silk Dress Balloon 161
Six Weeks' War (1866) 111
slaves and slavery **213**
    abolition movement
        agitation and militancy 36–8
        The Liberator founded 14
        in South 26, 29, 31
        Uncle Tom's Cabin published 14
    access to justice 31, 32, 33
    and American Revolution 197
    attitudes to 193
    as cause of the war 10–11, 14, 21–39
    churches' attitude to 29, 178
    Confederate treatment of liberated 144, 183–4, 208, 212

and cotton growing 20, 28, **28**
fugitive slaves 23, 31–2, **35**, 36–8, **37**, 183–4, 197, 199, 200
    "contrabands" 117, 183–4, 201, **201**
geographical extent of legality 14, 31–2, 33–4
Kansas–Missouri border disputes 134
legislation and court decisions
    Compromise of 1850 14, 31–2
    Confiscation Acts (1861 and 1862) 15, 201–3
    Crittenden-Johnson Resolutions (1861) 14
    Dred Scott decision (1857) 14, 31, 33–4
    Gag Resolution (1836) 14, 31
    Wilmot Proviso (1846) 14
Lincoln on 10, 11, 38
in the North 196
in the South 24–5, 27–30, 196–7
    postwar nostalgia 249–50
in Trans-Mississippi 134
Turner's rebellion (1831) 14, 199
see also African Americans; emancipation
Slidell, John 231, 232
Slough, John P. 139
Smith, A.J. 146
Smith, Edmund Kirby 19, 143–4, **143**, 146–8
soldiers 79–95
    attitude to draftees 93–4
    brutalization 91–5
    daily life 83–7
    memoirs and memorials 95
    motivation and morale 90–1
sounds, battlefield 87
South and southerners
    attitude to the war 176, 187
    institutions and ideology 12, 26–7, 43
    postwar nostalgia 245–6, 248–50, 252
    postwar economy 243–4, **246**
    postwar race relations 247, 249, 251
    prewar situation and economy 24–5
    protest and dissent 187–92
    shipbuilding 125–6, 127–8, 130, 154, 157, 226–7
    slavery in 24–5, 27–30, 196–7
    Union blockade 47–8, 114–21, **120**, 225–6, 229–30
    Union soldiers' treatment of 107–11, 190, 246, **246**
    war's legacy 13
    wartime shortages 189
    see also Confederacy
South Carolina Declaration of Secession 22
Spain, and the Caribbean 231
speculators 189
spies 158–60, 163–73

see also intelligence war
Spot Resolutions (1847) 31
Spotsylvania Court House, battle of (1864) 17
Spring Hill 18
Stager, Anson 162
Stanton, Edwin M. 51, 206
Stanton, Elizabeth Cady 180
Stanwix Station, firefight at (1862) 140
Steele, Frederick 146
Stephens, Alexander H. 14, 52, 195, 248
Stone, Lucy 180
Stone's River, battle of (1862) *see* Murfreesboro, battle of
Stonewall, CSS **226**, 227
Stowe, Harriet Beecher 14, 55
strategy 45–51
Stringfellow, Franklin 171
Stuart, General J.E.B. 17, 62, 65, 171, 172
submarines 114, 115, 129, **129**
suffrage 239–40
Sultana, USS 155
Summerlin, Mary 169
Sumner, Charles 33, 231
Sumner, Edwin 140
Sumter, CSS 226
Surdam, David 121
Surratt, John H. 155
Surratt, Mary 155

T

tactics 73–5, 102–4
Tai-ping Rebellion (1851–64) 98
Taney, Chief Justice Roger B. 31, 34–6, **34**
taxation
    1824 tariff increase 14, 24
    Morrill Tariff 223, 230
    Tax-in-Kind Law (1863) 16, 190
Taylor, James E.: drawings by **110**
Taylor, Richard 17, 135, 143–4, 146, 147
technological innovation 125–9, 162
Tecumseh, USS **128**, 129
telegraph 162, **162**
temperance 26
Tennessee: secession 45
Tennessee, CSS **128**, 129
terrain 67–9, 75
Terry, Alfred 19
Texas 14, 135, 144–8
Thomas, Major-General George H. 17, 18, 168–9
Thompson, Jacob 154
Thoreau, Henry David 38
tobacco **83**
Tocqueville, Alexis de 219–20
Tom's Brook, fighting at (1864) 18

Torpedo Bureau 155
torpedoes 128–9
Torres Vedras, lines at 105
trade
    America and Europe 218–19, 223,
    228–30, 234
    commerce raiding 113, 114, 130–1
    underground 177
    Union blockade of South 47–8, 114–21,
    120, 225–6, 229–30
    see also cotton growing; industry
training
    men 80–1
    officers 64, 80
Trans-Mississippi Cotton Bureau 144, 147
transport, military 86–7, 100–1
Trent 15, 47, 223, 232
Truesdail, Colonel William 168
Tullahoma campaign (1863) 168
Turner, Henry 238
Turner, Nat 14, 199

U

UCV *see* United Confederate Veterans
UDC *see* United Daughters of the
    Confederacy
Uncle Tom's Cabin (Stowe) 14
uniforms and clothing 84–5, **85**
Union
    covert actions 156–7
    finances 51
    government team 51–2
    spies 163–9
Union forces
    brigade organization 82
    command structure 52
    cooperation between army and navy
    122, 123, 125
    logistics 67
    mobilization 50
    size 49–50, 61–2, 100
    war's legacy on regular army 242–3
    see also US Navy
Union forces: sub-units
    II Corps 82
    III Corps 82
    1st Alabama Cavalry 168
    2nd Minnesota 90
    4th US Colored Infantry **207**
    7th New York **78**
    20th Maine 91
    25th Massachusetts 90
    54th Massachusetts (black) 94–5
    Army of the Frontier 142
    Army of the Gulf 145–7

Army of the Ohio 86–7
Army of the Potomac 73, 172
    intelligence sources **159**, 165, 167, **171**
    Indian Brigade 150
    Iron Brigade 82
United Confederate Veterans (UCV)
    246–7, 248
United Daughters of the Confederacy
    (UDC) 246–7, 248
United States
    1860 map **26**
    European views of 219–21, **220**
    postwar expansionism 245
urbanization, northern 25–6
US Military Telegraph (USMT) 162
US National Park Service 253
US Navy
    and blockade of South 47–8, 114–21,
    120, 225–6, 229–30
    and Confederate innovations 125–9
    cooperation with army 122, 123, 125
    fueling 117–18
    officers 116–17
    and river war 121–5
    size 117
US Sanitary Commission (USSC) 180–2,
    181, **183**

V

Valverde, battle of (1862) 139
Van Dorn, General Earl 16, 140–1, **141**
Van Lew, Elizabeth 165–6
Vance, Governor Zebulon 189, 190, 192–3
Vandivar, Frank E. 50
Vicksburg
    campaign (1863) 15, 16, 71, 111, 169
    siege of (1863) 16, 125
Virginia 45, 209, 214–15
Virginia, CSS 15, 126, **127**
visibility, battlefield 87, **89**
Vrancx, Sebastian: paintings by **109**

W

Waddell, Captain James I. 130
Wakarusa War 134
Walke, Commander Henry **121**, 123
Walker, David 197–9
war crimes trials 93
War of 1812 25
war work 179–84, **179**, **181**, **183**
Washington, Confederate attack on (1864)
    18
Washington, George 197

Watie, General Stand **147**, 148, 150–1
Waynesboro, battle of (1865) 19
WCRA *see* Women's Central Relief
    Association
weapons
    breech-loading rifles 104
    Dreyse "needle guns" 111
    naval 113
    rifled muskets 73–4, 88–90, 102–4
    see also artillery
Weer, William 149
Weldon Railroad
    battle for the (1864) 18
    battle of the (1864) 18
Welles, Gideon 51, 115, **115**, 127
West: postwar development 243
western theater **71**, 133–51, **136**
    military intelligence 168, 170–1
    operations 71
    river war 121–5
    terrain 68–9
Westport, battle of (1864) 18, 147
Wheeler, Joseph 172
Whig Party: end of 14
Whitman, Walt 95
Wilderness, battle of the (1864) 17, 87
Wilkes, Captain Charles 232
Wilmington, surrender of (1865) 19
Wilmot Proviso (1846) 14
Wilson, Henry D. 170
Wilson's Creek, battle of (1861) 14, 136,
    137, **149**
Winchester
    first battle of (1862) 15
    second battle of (1863) 16
    third battle of (1864) 18, 167
Wirz, Henry C. 93
women
    and Free State of Jones 191
    postwar southern 247
    protests 187, **188**
    rights 180
    and the war 175, 177–84, **179**, **181**, **183**
Women's Central Relief Association
    (WCRA) 180
Women's Rights Seneca Falls Convention
    (1848) 180
Wright, Rebecca 167

Yellow Bayou, battle of (1864) 17
Yellow Tavern, battle of (1864) 17
Young, Major Henry K. 167

Zouave companies 81
Zwick, Edward 251